KING OF CREATION

D1556888

By
Henry M. Morris, Ph.D.
Director
Institute for Creation Research

Foreword by
Josh McDowell

CLP **C·L·P PUBLISHERS**
SAN DIEGO, CALIFORNIA

King of Creation
Copyright © 1980

Henry M. Morris
San Diego, California

Library of Congress Catalog Card Number 80-80558
ISBN 0-89051-059-8

Cataloging in Publication Data

Morris, Henry Madison, 1918-
   King of creation.
   1. Creation. I. Title.
              213   80-80558
   ISBN 0-89051-059-8

Printed in the United States of America

Praise ye the Lord, the Almighty
The King of Creation!
O, my soul, praise Him, for He is
Thy health and salvation.
All ye who hear,
Now to His temple draw near,
Join me in glad adoration!

Neander

able of Contents

Foreword vii
Acknowledgments ix
About The Author xi
Introduction xiii
Chapter I.   THE KING OF CREATION 1
                    King of Kings   3
                    The Host of Heaven   6
                    Man on Earth   14
                    Creation and the Birth of Christ   17
                    The Miracle of God in Man   23
                    Creation and Redemption—A Tale of
                        Two Weeks   26
                    The Ages to Come   32

Chapter II. **CREATION AND THE KING'S WORD . 39**

Biblical Inerrancy and Special Creation   41

The Foundational Importance of Creationism 46

In Praise of Creation's Creator   49

The Living Word   52

Jesus the Creationist   53

Creation and the Seven-Day Week   55

Noah and the Faith that Saves   62

The Gospel of Creation   64

Chapter III. **THE WORLD AGAINST CREATION ..67**

The Anti-Gospel of Evolution   69

The Motivations of Evolutionary Humanism 75

Evolution and the Illogical Theologicals   83

Progressive Creationists and the Strategy
   of Compromise   86

Atheists and the Battle for Evolution   96

Revolutionary Evolutionism   99

Chapter IV. **ALLIANCE WITH TRUE SCIENCE... 109**

Creation and the Laws of Science   111

Thermodynamics and the Origin of Life   118

The Testimony of Complex Systems   127

Missing Links and Hopeful Monsters   137

Fossils and the Flood   147

Human Language and the Tower of Babel   169

Chapter V. **SOLDIERS OF THE KING............ 183**

Creation and True Evangelism   185

Creation and the Churches   190

The Affairs of this Life   194

The Spiritual Victories of Creationism   202

The Weapons of Our Warfare   209

Index of Subjects **221**

Index of Names............................ **230**

Index of Scriptures **233**

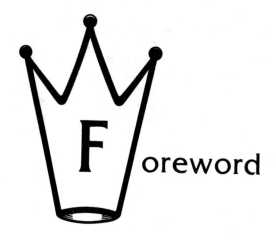

Foreword

Several years ago I began to hear rumors about debates on college campuses between certain creationists and university professors on the issue of creation versus evolution. Later I learned that the two creationists were Dr. Duane Gish and Dr. Henry Morris of the Institute for Creation Research. It wasn't long before the rumors turned out to be the main topic of conversation between many students and faculty at the universities.

My desire to hear these men was partially fulfilled at a national apologetics conference in Dayton, Ohio. There I had the opportunity to hear Dr. Henry Morris speak on creation versus evolution. I was fascinated! Soon my attention moved from my upcoming talk to taking notes on the material I was hearing. It was then that I prayed that this material would come out in book form containing all the documentation given that evening.

This is why I was so thrilled when I received the manuscript for *The King of Creation* and was asked to do the Foreword. However, I never dreamed that I would discover such a wealth of revelant, factual, and down-to-earth material. *The King of Creation* excites and encourages me for many reasons. First of all, it is scholarly. There is a wealth of documentation, sound reasoning, and extensive research that is made available to the reader. Dr. Morris shows how many evolutionists have had a radical change in their approach to the subject of the origin of man. Much of this new attitude is the result of finding that there are whole missing chains of evidence for evolution instead of only a few missing links.

Second, *The King of Creation* is relevant. It deals with such timely subjects as the nature of the universe, evolution and the origin of man, the Tower of Babel and human language, the flood, the second law of thermodynamics, the fossil record, and the age of man, all in the light of Biblical inerrancy and the authority of Scripture. We now have an authoritative volume in which one can find the answers to these penetrating questions.

Third, it is Scriptural. Dr. Morris does an excellent job in reconciling Genesis and modern science.

Fourth, it is honoring to Christ. Jesus Christ is finally given His rightful place in relationship to the universe and creation. One cannot help but begin to praise Christ and desire to make Him Lord of our lives.

Fifth, *The King of Creation* is practical. It doesn't leave you guessing about what to do but rather gives you practical suggestions on how to relate Jesus Christ, the King of Creation, to others.

Sixth, Dr. Morris is motivating. His enthusiasm for creationism and its scientific base is contagious. You find yourself wanting more, as he gives forth the creationist viewpoint in a provocative, poignant, and forthright manner. You may not agree with everything Dr. Morris says, but you will be challenged by the logic of the facts presented.

This could be one of the most significant books that you will ever read. *The King of Creation* will definitely be one of my main reference books, and I wholeheartedly recommend it to you.

Josh McDowell
March, 1980

Acknowledgments

I am especially grateful to Josh McDowell for reading the manuscript and writing the Foreword to *King of Creation*. Josh is probably the most popular speaker on Christian evidences of our generation, as well as the most effective campus evangelist, and it is a privilege to be associated with him in this way. I am also grateful to Dr. Duane Gish, Associate Director at I.C.R., for reviewing the manuscript, to my secretary, Mrs. Linda Rees, for typing it, to Annette Bradley, of Creation-Life Publishers, for her fine editorial work, and to I.C.R.'s artist, Marvin Ross, for the jacket design. Finally, all my colleagues at the Institute for Creation Research share with me the burden of the book—that all people everywhere may come to know and serve the Lord Jesus Christ as the great King of Creation.

Henry M. Morris
San Diego
February 1980

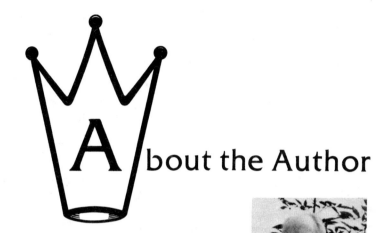bout the Author

Henry M. Morris, Ph.D.

Dr. Henry M. Morris has been actively working in the field of scientific Biblical creationism for over 35 years. Author of many well-known books on Christian evidences and the scientific accuracy of the Bible (including *The Genesis Flood, Scientific Creationism, Many Infallible Proofs, The Troubled Waters of Evolution, Education for the Real World,* and *The Genesis Record),* Dr. Morris is now Director of the Institute for Creation Research and President of Christian Heritage College, in San Diego. He has a B.S. from Rice University and a Ph.D. from the University of Minnesota. For 28 years he was on the faculties of major universities, including 13 years as Chairman of the Civil Engineering Department at the Virginia Polytechnic Institute and State University. Dr. Morris is a founder and former president of the Creation Research Society.

Introduction

The revival of a serious scientific study of creationism in the past decade has attracted widespread secular interest. Major articles on the creation movement have appeared in such leading national periodicals as *Scientific American, Wall Street Journal, Science, Newsweek, McClean's, Science-80,* and others, as well as most major metropolitan newspapers. Literally thousands of well-qualified scientists have repudiated their former faith in evolution and have become creationists.

Nevertheless, in spite of the increasing creationist interest in the educational and scientific worlds, large segments of the outwardly Christian world remain either opposed, unconvinced, or indifferent to creationism. In view of the fact that the Bible and Christianity itself are inescapably founded on creationism, this is an amazing and disturbing situation.

One has to assume that such a loose attitude by professed Christians toward the factual doctrine of creation results from lack of real understanding of the person and purposes of the Creator. Since the very minds and hearts with which we reason concerning life's problems were themselves created by Him, it follows directly that we must know and believe our Creator before we can have real hope of understanding or solving any of these problems or of meeting any of life's needs—especially that of personal salvation and guidance.

The hope of winning all who consider themselves Christians to a strong faith in Jesus Christ as both Creator and Savior, and then to enlist them as active soldiers in the great battle for the minds and hearts of people everywhere is the reason for writing this book. "For if the trumpet give an uncertain sound, who shall prepare himself to the battle?" (I Corinthians 14:8).

Before a Christian can be a really effective soldier in the great spiritual warfare in which every true believer must be engaged, the Christian must demonstrate a solid conviction concerning the absolute integrity and authority of the written Word of God, knowing absolutely that the whole creation thoroughly supports its testimony. Equivocation on the foundational doctrine of special creation will dilute and undermine his witness concerning personal salvation and all *other* Christian doctrines. Christ must be known as He *is*—not as "another Jesus" (II Corinthians 11:4)—and He is both Creator and Sustainer of all things (Colossians 1:16, 17), as well as individual Savior (Galatians 2:20).

Therefore, He is presented in this book first of all as the great King of Creation. As Creator of all, He must also be Judge of all, and, therefore, by His grace He is finally the Savior of all who come to Him in faith.

Since He is King and Sovereign over the whole creation, He is able to reveal Himself to His creatures, and—when He speaks—all who truly know and love Him will surely believe and obey His Word. Sadly, however, there is a great host of rebels against the King, both men and angels—rebels who are a part of the creation, but refuse to believe in creation and its Creator. The entire history of the world has thus far been occupied with this rebellion and its tragic effects throughout the universe.

Nevertheless, all the revelation of Scripture and the true understanding of the universe unite in asserting the fact of creation and the gracious omnipotence of its Creator. Consequently, it is foolish and dangerous for those who profess to know God to compromise with His enemies. Armies do not win battles by consorting with their opponents or accommodating their goals. Victory depends on strengthening their own positions and aggressively carrying out the battle plan.

These are the themes and burdens of this book. As soldiers in the spiritual army of the great King, we seek both to strengthen others already in our own ranks and to win many new battalions of recruits. There is mortal combat ahead . . . with eternal consequences, and we need to be prepared for the coming days.

The Institute for Creation Research, with its monthly newsletter, *Acts and Facts,* has already been heavily involved in the battle for creation for almost ten years. It is the writer's prayer, and that of many others, that *The King of Creation* as a book will bring honor to our great King in the heavens and many recruits to His cause.

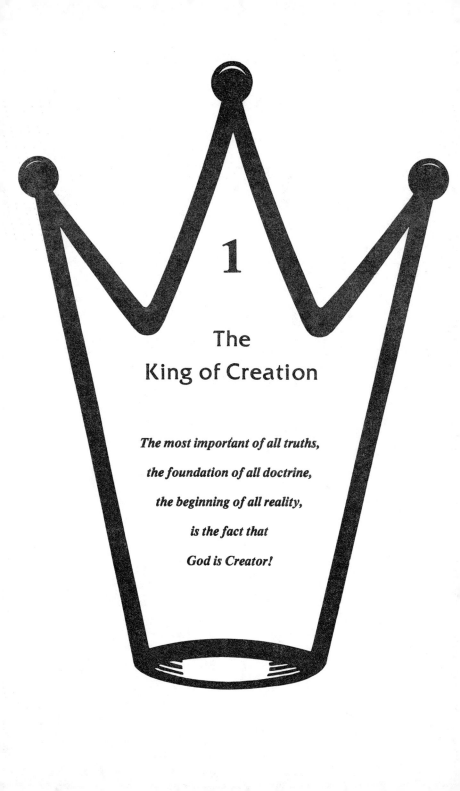

1

The
King of Creation

The most important of all truths,

the foundation of all doctrine,

the beginning of all reality,

is the fact that

God is Creator!

1 The King of Creation

KING OF KINGS

The most important of all truths, the foundation of all doctrine, the beginning of all reality, is the *fact* that God is Creator! There is no possibility of really knowing the fullness of *anything* until we first know that the origin and meaning of *everything* is God. What He *does* is *right,* and what He *says* is *true*—by definition!

"In the beginning God created the heaven and the earth." These opening words of the Bible constitute what is at once the most simple and the most profound statement ever made. This is the most widely-known sentence ever written, easily understood by the simplest child, yet inexhaustibly compatible with the most advanced scientific comprehension of the universe. The *eternal* God created Time in the beginning of time. The *infinite* God created the unbounded Space of the heavens. The *omnipotent* God created the elements of Matter comprising the earth and all other systems permeating the Space/Time cosmos. The *transcendent* God created, for He· was prior to created time and external to created space. The Creator is an eternal, infinite, omnipotent, transcendent Being.

Furthermore, God is both personal and omniscient, capable of creating spiritual intelligent beings who in turn can examine and comprehend the intelligible universe He created. And since He created both the universe and the creatures who must comprehend it, it is clearly necessary that acknowledgment of Him as Creator must precede any meaningful study of His creation.

When the primeval words of Genesis 1:1 were first spoken and recorded (most likely to and by Adam himself), there was no need to defend them, for there was no one who disbelieved them. But then sin came into the world. In heaven, at the very throne of the King of creation, one of God's created spirit beings, the anointed Cherub, Lucifer, rebelled against His Creator (despite the revealed fact that he had been "created" [Ezekiel 28:15]). Lucifer sought to "exalt his throne" and to be "as the most High" (Isaiah 14:13, 14), therefore, he was cast down to the earth (Ezekiel 28:17), the dominion of those whom God had created "in His own image" (Genesis 1:27) . . . and *for* whom Lucifer and all other angels had been created as "ministering spirits" (Hebrews 1:14). On earth, as "that old Serpent" (Revelation 12:9), he led the first man and woman to follow his own rebellious desire to be "as gods" (Genesis 3:5), and since that time all mankind has shared in Adam's primeval sin, "worshiping and serving the creation more than the Creator, who is blessed for ever" (Romans 1:25). In the minds and hearts of men, God is no longer King, and therefore they are "without God" (literally "a-theists" [Ephesians 2:12]). They may love "the things that be in this world" (I John 2:15), and "walk according to the course of this world" (Ephesians 2:2), serving "the god of this world" (II Corinthians 4:4), but there is no hope in this world (Ephesians 2:12).

Nevertheless, it is Lucifer (now become Satan, the Adversary) who has been dethroned, not God! God is still on His throne, the eternal King of creation.

It is important to note in Scripture just a few of the many references to God as King. He is "a great King" (Malachi 1:14), an "everlasting King" (Jeremiah 10:10), and is "the blessed and only Potentate" (I Timothy 6:15).

1. He is the **King of Time,** because He created Time: He is *"my King of old"* (Psalm 74:12) and "sitteth *King forever"* (Psalm 29:10).
2. He is the **King of Space,** because He created infinite Space. He is *"King of heaven"* (Daniel 4:37), the *"King invisible"* (I Timothy 1:17), who "hast made heaven, the heaven of heavens, with all their host" (Nehemiah 9:6), though even "heaven and the heaven of heavens cannot contain thee" (II Chronicles 6:18).
3. He is the **King of Matter,** because He made all "things" in Space and Time. He is *"king of all the earth"* (Psalm 47:7), and all "give glory and honour and thanks to Him that sat on the throne, . . . saying, Thou art worthy . . . for thou hast created all things . . . " (Revelation 4:9, 11).
4. He is the **King of Energy,** for He has energized and empowered an infinite and eternal universe. God is Light, "the *King of glory"* (Psalm 24:10), "dwelling in the light which no man can approach unto" (I Timothy 6:15).
5. He is the **King of Life,** since He is "the *King immortal"* (I Timothy 1:17), "who only hath immortality" (I Timothy

6:16), and is the one who "giveth to all life, and breath, and all things" (Acts 17:25).

6. He is the **King of all the Angels**, the host of heaven, "For by Him were all things created, that are in heaven . . . whether they be thrones or dominions or principalities, or powers . . . " (Colossians 1:16). He is "the *King, the Lord of hosts" (Zechariah 14:16).*

7. He is the **King of all Nations**, both "the *King of Israel"* (John 1:49) and *"King of Nations"* (Jeremiah 10:7, literally *"King of Gentiles")*.

8. He is the **King of all the Redeemed**, those who have been "translated into the kingdom of His dear Son" by "redemption through His blood, even the forgiveness of sins" Colossians 1:13, 14). Therefore, He has become also the *"King of saints"* (Revelation 15:3) and will one day be universally acclaimed as *"King of Kings,* and Lord of Lords" (I Timothy 6:15; Revelation 17:14; 19:16).

Since He created all things, He is indeed the *King of all creation,* the Potentate and Sovereign, Master and Ruler, Lord and Judge of all things. As His creatures, we can only acknowledge His authority, trust His wisdom, believe His Word, obey His commandments, receive His grace, accept His salvation, and praise His name!

But the odd thing is that there are multitudes of people who rebel against His authority, refuse His salvation, and even deny His true existence as a personal Creator God. "Professing themselves to be wise, they became fools, and changed the glory of the uncorruptible God into an image made like to corruptible man, and to birds, and fourfooted beasts, and creeping things" (Romans 1:22, 23).

In every age people have been unwilling to believe in God as Creator and to submit to His authority, so they have invented lesser gods to serve. They have given the created world itself the attributes of deity, believing that the universe is the ultimate reality. They have "changed the truth of God into a lie, and worshiped and served the creation more than the Creator" (Romans 1:25).

Of course, the only alternative to creation is evolution, whether it is the naive evolutionism of ancient polytheism (which deified the forces of nature as heavenly "birds and fourfooted beasts and creeping things") or the more modern evolutionism of the Darwinians (which invests such impersonal processes as mutation and natural selection with imaginary creative powers). No substitute for the Creator, of course, can really *create* anything, and the only explanation for the age-long compulsion of men to believe in such counterfeits is that "they did not like to retain God in their knowledge" (Romans 1:28). They have "imagined a vain thing" (Psalm 2:1).

But whether or not men believe in the great King of creation, He still *is* the Creator. "For what if some did not believe? shall their unbelief make the faith of God without effect? God forbid: yea, let God be true, but every man a liar" (Romans 3:3, 4).

The believer in evolution (whether the pantheistic polytheism of the ancients or the naturalistic humanism of the moderns) is described in the Bible as "without excuse" and "willingly ignorant" (Romans 1:20; II Peter 3:5). He must believe that *effects* can be greater than their *causes*, that *random* mindless particles can generate *complex* reasoning people, and that magic wands can transform frogs into princes.

When the Israelites turned from serving their Creator to worshiping idols, God rebuked them in these words:

> As the thief is ashamed when he is found, so is
> the house of Israel ashamed . . . saying to a stock,
> Thou art my father; and to a stone, Thou hast
> brought me forth . . . (Jeremiah 2:26, 27).

And if it is shameful foolishness for a man to believe that his origin was from a stone image which he himself had made, how much more foolish it is to believe that a living, thinking human being could emerge from the nonliving chemicals of a primeval soup!

Surely the readers of these words will not be guilty of such unreasoning credulity as that! "Know ye that the Lord He is God: it is He that hath made us, and not we ourselves; we are His people, and the sheep of His pasture" (Psalm 100:3). "For the Lord is a great God, and a great King above all gods (Psalm 95:3).

THE HOST OF HEAVEN

"The host of heaven cannot be numbered" (Jeremiah 33:22).

Man has always been intrigued and fascinated by the heavens. The scholars of antiquity, whether in Sumer, Egypt, China, Mexico, or any of the other early civilizations, were well versed in the locations and orbits of all the visible stars. They had

counted and cataloged and grouped them all and had pronounced the total number to be almost two thousand stars!

But the Holy Scriptures were far ahead of these ancient
scientists. According to the Bible, the stars were as great in
number as the sands of the seashore (Genesis 22:17) and simply
could not be numbered! The vast reaches of the heavenly
spaces were—and are—utterly incomprehensible to man. "For
as the heavens are higher than the earth, so are my ways
higher than your ways, and my thoughts than your thoughts"
(Isaiah 55:9).

The giant telescopes of the present day have only begun to
reveal the immense numbers and fantastic variety of the stars.
With literally billions of galaxies, and billions of stars in every
galaxy, the number of the stars seems to increase almost without limit. The variety is equally amazing—red giants, white
dwarfs, Cepheid variables, neutron stars, pulsars, and on and
on! As the Bible says in an incisive foregleam of modern
astronomy: "There is one glory of the sun, and another glory
of the moon, and another glory of the stars: for one star
differeth from another star in glory" (I Corinthians 15:41).

Origin and Purpose of the Universe

The origin and purpose of the stars was no more perplexing
to the ancient stargazers than to our modern astronomers. Of
course, there is no shortage of theories purporting to explain
the origin and evolution of the universe, and new theories
are developed rather frequently.

But, one after another, each new theory eventually seems to
encounter such problems and difficulties that it falls by the
wayside and is eventually abandoned. In an incisive review of
modern cosmology, a leading astronomer has said:

> Is it not possible, indeed probable, that our present
> cosmological ideas on the structure and evolution
> of the universe as a whole (whatever that may mean)
> will appear hopelessly premature and primitive to
> astronomers of the 21st century? Less than 50 years
> after the birth of what we are pleased to call "modern
> cosmology," when so few empirical facts are pass-
> ably well established, when so many different over-
> simplified models of the universe are still competing
> for attention, is it, we may ask, really credible to
> claim, or even reasonable to hope, that we are

presently close to a definitive solution of the cosmological problem? [1]

The author concludes his survey of cosmology by stating:
"It seems safe to conclude that a unique solution of the cosmological problem may still elude us for quite sometime."[2]

The two leading types of cosmological theories have been
the "steady state" and "big bang" theories. Both of these
are evolutionary theories and each includes the "expanding
universe" concept, according to which the galaxies are all
rapidly receding from one another. The "steady state" theory
has also been called the "continuous creation" theory, attempting to explain the decay and disappearance of matter and
energy by the continual evolution (not "creation") of new
matter out of nothing. The "big bang" theory is usually also
known as the "oscillating universe" theory supposing that the
universe continuously alternates between processes of expansion and contraction and that its present expansion began with
a superdense state following its most recent contraction about
twenty billion or so years ago.

Within the framework of either type of cosmology, numerous
subsidiary theories of galactic and stellar evolution have been
published, dealing with the supposed development of particular
types of stars or galaxies or clusters of galaxies from other
types. The very variety of stars and galaxies tends to encourage
such evolutionary speculation.

Stability of the Heavens

Nevertheless, it should be quite obvious that no such evolutionary processes can actually be observed. No astronomer has
ever observed a "red giant" evolving into a "white dwarf,"
or a "spiral nebula" into a "globular cluster," or any other
such change. Within the time of human observation, no such
evolutionary changes have ever been seen to occur at all.

This being the case, there is nothing whatever to prevent us
from proposing the theory that they *don't* take place. This is
by far the most reasonable theory, since it is supported by all
the actual astronomic measurements that have ever been col-
lected since man first began making such observations. If we
limit ourselves to real, observational *science,* rather than

---

1. G. de Vaucouleurs: "The Case for a Hierarchical Cosmology," *Science,*
   Vol. 167, February 27, 1970, p. 1203.

2. Ibid: p. 1212.

indulging in philosophical speculation, we would have to say that the stars and galaxies have always been just as they are now, since the time they were created.

Is the Universe Expanding?

Someone may object to such a suggestion by contending that the universe is expanding and therefore evolving. This deduction is not necessary, however. In the first place, whether or not the universe is actually expanding is still an unsettled question. The famous "Doppler effect"—the red shift in the light spectra from distant galaxies—is the only observational basis for such expansion, and this interpretation has been challenged by various cosmologists, especially in view of the anomalous red shifts recently noted in quasars.

> One of the astrophysical conundrums that will not go away concerns the objects that appear to be expanding or splitting faster than the speed of light . . . . There are now four such objects, three quasars and a galaxy. They include nearly half of the strong, compact very distant radio sources. That one is a galaxy precludes explaining away the apparent superluminal velocities as due to misinterpretation of the objects' distances.[1]

Assuming, however, that the universe really is expanding, in accordance with the standard interpretation of the red shifts, there is still no proof that this phenomenon is part of some evolutionary process. The expansion could just as well have been initiated by an act of creation at *any* arbitrary position of the various galactic components of the universe.

Fiat Creation

Not only is the concept of special complete creation most logical and consistent in accord with God's character and ability, but it is surely the concept most in accord with Biblical revelation on this subject. "For in six days, the Lord made heaven and earth, the sea, and all that in them is" (Exodus 20:11). On the fourth of these days, "He made the stars" (Genesis 1:16). "Thus the heavens and the earth were *finished,* and all the host of them" (Genesis 2:1). "By the word of the Lord were the heavens made; and all the host of

---

1. "Maybe They are Faster than Light," *Science News,* Vol. 112, September 1977, p. 120.

them by the breath of His mouth . . . . For He spake, and it was done; He commanded, and it stood fast" (Psalm 33:6,9).

The idea of a simple fiat creation of the entire universe in its present form may seem too naive to evolutionary astronomers and cosmologists. Nevertheless, it fits all the facts of observational astronomy more easily and directly than does any other theory. The objection that special creation is not scientific because it is nonobservable is irrelevant, since exactly the same objection applies to any of the evolutionary models. Who has ever *observed* a star evolve, or a "big bang," or an evolution of matter out of nothing?

Comparison of Evolutionist and Creationist Models

Although *no* model of origins can be scientifically tested—since one cannot repeat history—any such model can be used to predict and correlate the *observable* data which result from that history. The model which most effectively fits the data is the one most likely to be correct.

Any evolutionary model of the universe must conflict with one of the most fundamental laws of science, namely the **Second Law of Thermodynamics.** This law formalizes the observed fact that, within those regions of space and time which are accessible to observation, the universe is *decreasing* in complexity and in availability of energy. The evolutionary model must, however, postulate a universe that has instead *evolved upwards* toward higher states of order and availability. Since the Second Law always appears to hold true in *observable* space and time, an evolutionary model must include some component which negates the Second Law in *nonobservable* space and time. The *steady state theory* supposes that energy or matter somehow came into existence out of nothing (or at least out of some state of things completely incommensurate with the present state of things) far out in *nonobservable space*. The *big bang theory* postulates a tremendous increase in order in a gigantic explosion far back in *nonobservable time*. There is, of course, no way of testing any process which operates in nonobservable space or time!

In recent years, the discovery of a ubiquitous "background radiation" in space has been widely interpreted as proving the big bang cosmology, which is thus currently in favor. Some of the leading astronomers, however, are now again raising doubts.

The claim that this radiation lends strong support

to hot big bang cosmologies is without foundation.[1]

Suddenly it seems new cosmological theories and new twists on old ones are coming up all over the place. All the ideas that the big bang seemed to have put to rest are back.[2]

Perhaps, astronomers may even be willing to consider the creation model one of these days! At least it will not be embarrassed by the actual laws of science. All evolutionary models of cosmogony specifically contradict at least the Second Law of Thermodynamics.

The creation model, on the other hand, specifically predicts the conditions described by the two laws of thermodynamics. It postulates a primeval perfect and complete creation, preserved in quantity (First Law) but decaying in quality (Second Law). As a matter of fact, the two laws point directly back to a period of special creation. The Second Law says the universe must have had a beginning—otherwise it would already be completely disordered. The First Law (conservation of mass-energy) says it could not have begun itself. Thus, the Cause of its beginning must be greater than the universe—and external to it. The omnipotent, omniscient, eternal God of the Bible is the only Cause adequate to produce the universe as we know it.

The Nature of the Universe

The creation model must attempt to explain the various aspects of the universe, not in terms of evolutionary development (for this model assumes they did not evolve at all but were created), but rather in terms of creative purpose. This is no small task, in view of the infinite variety of stellar systems, but it is no more difficult, nor less susceptible to empirical test, than imaginary evolutionary explanations for the same things.

Why, for example, is the universe so big, and why are there so many different kinds of stars and galaxies and interstellar phenomena? Why are the moon and the other planets barren of life? What is the purpose of pulsars and quasars? And so on. It is obviously much easier to raise such questions than to answer them, whether in terms of evolutionary mechanisms or

1. Hannes Alfven and Asoka Mendis, "Interpretation of Observed Cosmic Microwave Background Radiation," *Nature,* Vol. 266, April 21, 1977, p. 698.

2. Dietrick V. Thomsen, "Cosmology against the Grain" *Science News,* Vol. 114, August 26, 1978, p. 138.

of creative purposes.

We can see a number of reasons for the *visible* stars at least. They are useful for light, for navigation, and for chronology. They are a source of beauty and inspiration for mankind. Furthermore, every new discovery in the stellar heavens adds that much more to our amazement at the vastness of power and variety in the Creation. "The heavens declare the glory of God, and the firmament showeth His handiwork" (Psalm 19:1). Surely the enlargement of our appreciation of Him is a worthwhile purpose for the stars.

The barrenness of the moon and planets, as well as the intense heat of the stars, emphasizes the Biblical teaching that "the heavens are the Lord's, but the earth hath He given to the children of men" (Psalm 115:16). U.F.O. enthusiasts to the contrary notwithstanding, there is no evidence, either in science or Scripture, that biological life exists elsewhere in the universe. Life was created specifically for the earth, and the earth for life. Of all other bodies in the universe, the moon would be expected to have most nearly the same (evolutionary) origin as the earth, but the lunar explorations have eliminated such a notion.

> To the surprise of scientists, the chemical makeup of the moon rocks is distinctly different from that of rocks on earth. This difference implies that the moon formed under different conditions . . . . and means that any theory on the origin of the planets now will have to create the moon and earth in different ways.[1]

The same situation apparently exists with respect to all the other planets in the solar system.

Thus the earth is unique in the solar system and, for all we know, the solar system is unique in the universe. So far as we can *observe,* there are not even any planets anywhere else, let alone a planet equipped to sustain biological life. And even if there were, with even the nearest star being four light-years distant, presently there is no rational possibility of our ever being able to communicate with such hypothetical space people on such hypothetical planets.

Amazing though it may seem to evolutionary naturalists, the evidence favors the conclusion that man is unique in the universe and, furthermore, that he is the apex, not of the

---

1. Jerry E. Bishop: "New Theories of Creation," *Science Digest,* Vol. 72, October, 1972, p. 42.

evolutionary process, but of God's creative purposes! Even the galaxies, therefore, are inferior to man. Isaac Asimov, certainly not a creationist, has nevertheless recognized this fact.

> In man is a three-pound brain which, as far as we know, is the most complex and orderly arrangement of matter in the universe.[1]

The physical universe of space and time—and all the phenomena of energy and matter and life that occur in space and time—must somehow be related to man and to God's purpose for man. In the present economy of things, however, man is inescapably confined to only a tiny corner of the vast universe. The fulfillment of the Creator's purposes for man in the universe (and they *will* be fulfilled, since an omnipotent and omniscient God, by definition, cannot fail in His purposes) must therefore await the establishment of a new economy of things, in an age to come.

The Heavenly Host

In the meantime, there is still another "host of heaven," described in the Bible as an "innumerable company of angels" (Hebrews 12:22). The frequent indentification of angels with stars in the Bible (note Job 38:7, Revelation 12:4, and many others) is most intriguing, especially in view of the fact that there is no obvious similarity between angels and stars! The same mysterious correlations are found everywhere in ancient mythology. The gods and goddesses (Jupiter, Venus, Orion, etc.) were identified with various stars, planets, and constellations. The age-long influence of astrology, even on people of intelligence and culture, is another strange phenomenon. And now, in an almost unbelievable return to these ancient pagan mysteries, modern scientific speculations about the evolution of life in other worlds have been transmuted into a weird celestial drama of ancient astronauts, flying saucers, little green men, and "chariots of the gods."

The reality behind all these "fearful sights and great signs from heaven" (Luke 21:11) can only be that there really is life in outer space! But these living inhabitants of the heavenly bodies are neither supermen in spaceships nor blobs of protoplasm in various stages of evolution. They are, rather, "angels that excel in strength" (Psalm 103:20), "ministering spirits, sent forth to minister for them who shall be heirs of salvation"

---

1. Isaac Asimov: "In the Game of Energy and Thermodynamics You Can't Even Break Even," *Smithsonian Institute Journal,* June 1970, p. 10.

(Hebrews 1:14)—none other than God's holy angels. There
exists also in the heavens a vast horde of rebel angels, following
"that old serpent, called the Devil, and Satan, which deceiveth
the whole world" (Revelation 12:9).

These are all real beings, living a real existence in this real
physical cosmos. However, they are spiritual beings, not
physical, and thus are not constrained by the gravitational and
electromagnetic forces which control bodies formed of chemical
elements. On occasion, however, the faithful angels have been
known to have power to "materialize" themselves in human
form (Hebrews 13:2)—and the fallen angels, or demons, to
"possess" human or animal bodies (Matthew 8:28-32).

Thus, there is a host of stars without number in the heavens
and also an innumerable angelic host of heaven. The latter
apparently inhabit the former and are thus, in both Scripture
and mythology, intimately interrelated.

But if only angels can ever reach the stars, why has God
placed such a strange fascination and yearning for the heavens
in the heart of man? Jesus answers: "For in the resurrection
they . . . are as the angels of God in heaven" (Matthew 22:30).
To the prophet Daniel, the angel said: "And many of them that
sleep in the dust of the earth shall awake, some to everlasting
life, and some to shame and everlasting contempt. And they
that be wise shall shine as the brightness of the firmament, and
they that turn many to righteousness *as the stars for ever and
ever*" (Daniel 12:2, 3).

In resurrection bodies, unfettered by gravity, the redeemed of
the Lord will thus have an eternity of time to explore the
infinitude of space! Though the earth will still be his home, man
will finally reach the stars.

MAN ON EARTH

Despite all the evidence, evolutionists continue wistfully to
hope that some evidence will eventually support their dreams of
the evolution of life on other planets. The results of their space
program have been a bitter disappointment—first on the moon,
then Mars and Venus and Jupiter, in turn. Creationists, on
the other hand, have long maintained that this is exactly
what would happen—the space probes would find no evidence
of extraterrestrial life, because there wasn't any such life
(except the angels, of course).

For example, the following paragraphs were written by the
author shortly before the Viking spacecraft landed on Mars,

and were published in *Acts and Facts,* the monthly newsletter
of the Institute for Creation Research. At the time, its predictions were in sharp contrast to those in all the standard
science journals.

The I.C.R. Prediction (*Acts and Facts,* August, 1976)

"Evolutionists have been eagerly awaiting the results of the
landing of the Viking spacecraft on Mars, hoping to find some
evidence of life there. In a symposium (published before the
Martian landing), several scientists tell why they are so concerned. James Christian, of Santa Ana College, says:

> Biochemical evolution already implies that life is
> all over the universe. It seems to me . . . if the
> theories are correct, that any time we have a con-
> genial environment and some of the right chemicals
> are there, including carbon, that given enough time,
> life will evolve. [1]

"Evolutionists reason that, since life has evolved on *this*
planet, it must also have evolved elsewhere in the universe,
wherever there is a planet with conditions comparable to those
on Earth. However, there was no life on the Moon, and the
evidence is all against any life on Venus or any of the other
planets in the solar system. Mars is just about the evolutionist's
last chance of finding support for his ideas of universal bio-
chemical evolution, except for the rather forlorn hope of
receiving some kind of intergalactic radio message from some
unknown intelligence out there in space.

"Astronomer Carl Sagan, who has been speculating about
extraterrestrial life for many years, is hopeful that Martian
life will convince people once and for all that life has evolved:

> If it turns out that there is life there as well, then,
> I would say, it would convince large numbers of
> people that the origins of life exist. [2]

"But suppose that the Martian landing does not produce
evidence of life. Even the most convinced evolutionists agree
that the odds against it are very high. Since finding life on Mars
would be strong evidence *for* evolution, would failure to find
life on Mars be strong evidence *against* evolution? Not at all!
Says Viking Project Biologist Gerald Soffen:

> If we don't find life, it doesn't prove anything

1. "Life on Mars: What Could It Mean?", *Science News,* Vol. 109, June
   5 & 12, 1976, p. 378.
2. *Ibid,* p. 379.

other than that it's difficult to find life on Mars. That's all.[1]

"Whatever of real scientific value may be learned from the Martian landing remains to be seen, but it is disturbing that the main purpose of this immensely costly tax-supported project is to *prove* evolution, *with no consideration for the possibility of disproving it!* Since evolution is not true, however, the entire venture (except for certain spin-off values) is redundant.

"I am writing these words prior to the actual landing but, by the time you read them, it should be apparent once again that there is no evidence of biological life on Mars—or anywhere else, except on earth. I have been maintaining for many years— as have most other creationists—that all such searches for extraterrestrial life are bound to turn out negatively. (See, for example, *That You Might Believe,* 1946, pp. 123-124; *The Bible Has the Answer,* 1976, pp. 76-78; *Scientific Creationism,* 1974, p. 30; *The Troubled Waters of Evolution,* 1974, pp. 168-171; etc.)

"One does not have to be a prophet to make such predictions, of course. The simplest living organism is so complex that it could never evolve by chance processes anywhere in the universe in astronomic time (see the writer's *Scientific Creationism,* pp. 59-69). Wherever life exists, it must have been created by God! Refusal to believe in God as Creator is the only reason for believing that life has evolved from nonlife—on the Earth or anywhere else.

"The only real question, then, is: 'Where has God created life?' The answer must be based on the revealed truth that God has created the earth uniquely for man (Psalm 115:16; Acts 17:20), and that all other forms of biological life were created to be under man's dominion (Genesis 1:28).

"It is on the Earth alone that God, Himself, became man (John 1:14), where He died for the sins of every man (Hebrews 2:9), from which He arose and ascended into heaven (Ephesians 4:8-10), and to which He will return (Acts 1:11). It is on this earth—not somewhere else in the universe—that He will live and reign in the ages to come (Revelation 21:1-3). The Earth—not Mars or Alpha Centauri or Orion—is the center of God's interest in this universe. It is man on Earth who is the object of God's creative and redemptive work, a fact *proved beyond question when He became man on Earth Himself!*"

---

1. *Ibid*

The foregoing paragraphs in this section were written prior to the actual landing on Mars. *Since* the landing, most evolutionary scientists have grudgingly accepted the uniqueness of human life on the earth, as far as the solar system is concerned. The Biology Department Chairman at Cal Tech, for example, has summarized the case as follows:

> Even though some ambiguities remain, there is little doubt about the meaning of the observations of the Viking landers: At least those areas on Mars examined by the two spacecraft are not habitats of life.[1]

Current searches for extraterrestrial life focus on the forlorn hope that life may exist in other galaxies, but this is also doomed to failure. The Earth, and only the Earth, was prepared by God for biological life.

CREATION AND THE BIRTH OF CHRIST

The Mystery of the Incarnation

The incarnation of Jesus Christ, in which the transcendent King of creation actually entered His own creation, and God became man, is such an important doctrine of the New Testament that without it there can be no true Christianity. "Every spirit that confesseth that Jesus Christ is come in the flesh is of God: And every spirit that confesseth not that Jesus Christ is come in the flesh is not of God" (I John 4:2,3).

But how can the one who "was God" (John 1:2) from the beginning be the same one who "was made flesh, and dwelt among us?" (John 1:1,14). How can He truly be "Emmanuel, which being interpreted is, God with us?" (Matthew 1:23). How can the infinite, eternal God become finite and temporal? Such a concept seems impossibly paradoxical, yet millions quite properly believe it to be a real and vital truth.

Perhaps the most amazing aspect of the incarnation is that a God who is absolute holiness could reside in a body of human flesh. Is it not true that "they that are in the flesh cannot please God?" (Romans 8:8). Our human bodies have been formed through many generations of genetic inheritance from Adam himself, and "in Adam all die" (I Corinthians 15:22).

The paradox is partially resolved, of course, when it is realized that Jesus Christ came in a body which was not of

---

1. Normal H. Horowitz, "The Search for Life on Mars," *Scientific American,* Vol. 237, November, 1977, p. 61.

sinful flesh. His body was truly "in the flesh," but only in "the *likeness* of sinful flesh" (Romans 8:3).

But even this doesn't resolve the dilemma completely, for how could His body be of flesh (carbon, hydrogen, amino acids, proteins, etc.), received by the normal process of reproduction of the flesh of his parents, without also receiving their genetic inheritance, which is exactly what makes it *sinful* flesh? "Behold, I was shapen in iniquity; and in sin did my mother conceive me" (Psalm 51:5). "Man that is born of a woman is of few days, and full of trouble . . . . Who can bring a clean thing out of an unclean? no one" (Job 14:1,4).

The Problem of Inherited Physical Defects

Not only is there the problem of inherent sin, but also of inherent physical defects. Over many generations, the human population has experienced great numbers of genetic mutations, and these defective physical factors have been incorporated into the common genetic pool, affecting in some degree every infant (except Jesus) ever born. Yet the Lamb of God, to be an acceptable sacrifice for the sins of the world, must be "without blemish and without spot" (I Peter 1:19). The very purpose of the incarnation was that God could become the *Savior* of men as well as their *Creator,* but this required that in His humanity He must be "holy, harmless, undefiled, separate from sinners" (Hebrews 7:26), and this would have been absolutely impossible by the normal reproductive process.

The solution could only be through a mighty miracle! He could not be conceived in the same manner as other men, for this would inevitably give him both a sin-nature and a physically defective body, and each would disqualify Him as a fit Redeemer. And yet He must truly become human. "Wherefore in all things it behoved Him to be made like unto His brethren, that He might be a merciful and faithful high priest in things pertaining to God, to make reconciliation for the sins of the people" (Hebrews 2:17).

It is not surprising, therefore, that the Christian doctrine of the Virgin Birth of Christ has always been such a watershed between true Christians and either non-Christians or pseudo-Christians.[1] Without such a miraculous birth, there could have been no true incarnation and therefore no salvation. The man

---

1. For answers to the various objections to the doctrine of the virgin birth, see the writer's discussion in *Many Infallible Proofs* (San Diego, Creation-Life Publishers, 1974.), pp. 54-63.

Jesus would have been a sinner by birth and thus in need of a Savior Himself.

On second thought, however, one realizes that it was not the virgin birth which was significant, except as a testimony of the necessity of the real miracle, the supernatural conception. The birth of Christ was natural and normal in every way, including the full period of human gestation in the womb of Mary. In all points, He was made like His brethren, experiencing every aspect of human life from conception through birth and growth to death. He was true man in every detail, except for sin and its physical effects.

The miracle was not His birth, but His conception. And here we still face a mystery. Conception normally is the result of the union of two germ cells, the egg from the mother and the seed from the father, each carrying half the inheritance and thus each, of course, sharing equally in the transmission of the sin-nature, as well as all other aspects of the human nature.

> Each individual gets exactly half of his chromosomes and half of his genes from his mother and father. Because of the nature of gene interaction, the offspring may resemble one parent more than the other, but the two parents make equal contributions to its inheritance.[1]

Each parent thus also makes an equal contribution of defective physical and mental characteristics, due to inherited mutations. Both mental and physical traits are inherited in this way.

Some writers have tried to make the virgin birth appear more amenable to human reason by comparing it to the process of *parthenogenesis,* which has been known to occur in some insects and even in some mammals, by which process the female egg begins to divide and grow into a mature animal without ever being fertilized. Others have compared it to the process of *artificial insemination,* by which the sperm is artificially introduced into the egg without actual copulation.

In addition to the rather crude concept of the work of the Holy Spirit which such suggestions involve, neither solves the problem of how the contribution of inherent defects contained in the *mother's* germ cell are kept from the developing embryo. If genetic inheritance in any degree is received from either parent, there seems to be no *natural* way by which the

1. Claude A. Villee (Harvard University), *Biology* (Philadelphia, W.B. Sanders, Co., 1962), p. 462.

transmission of the sin-nature, as well as physical defects, could have been prevented.

The Necessity of Special Creation

Therefore, even though He was nurtured in Mary's womb for nine months and born without her ever knowing a man, it was also necessary for all this to have been preceded by supernatural intervention, to prevent His receiving any actual genetic inheritance through her. The body growing in Mary's womb must have been specially created in full perfection, and placed there by the Holy Spirit, in order for it to be free of inherent sin damage. Christ would still be "made of the seed of David according to the flesh" (Romans 1:3), because His body was nurtured and born of Mary, who was herself of the seed of David. He would still be the Son of Man, sharing all universal human experience from conception to death, except sin. He is truly "the seed of the woman" (Genesis 3:15), His body formed neither of the seed of the man nor the egg of the woman, but grown from a unique Seed planted in the woman's body by God Himself.

That is, God *directly* formed a body for the second Adam just as He had for the first Adam (Genesis 2:7). This was nothing less than a miracle of creation, capable of accomplishment only by the Creator Himself. "That holy thing which shall be born of thee shall be called the Son of God" (Luke 1:35).

Surely God would devote no more attention to the design and construction of the body of "the first man, of the earth, earthy" than He would to that of "the second man, the Lord from heaven" (I Corinthians 15:47)!

The Marvel of Inheritance and Prenatal Growth

For that matter, the formation of every human body is a marvelous testimony to the power and wisdom of the Creator of the first human body, and so is His provision for its reproductive multiplication into the billions of bodies of distinctive individuals who have lived through the ages. "I will praise thee; for I am fearfully and wonderfully made" (Psalm 139:14).

The 139th Psalm contains a remarkably beautiful and scientifically accurate description of the divine forethought in the processes of heredity and embryonic growth. Verses 15 and 16 of this psalm (with explanatory comments interspersed) are as follows:

My substance (literally, *my frame*) was not hid

from thee, when I was made in secret, and curiously wrought (literally *embroidered*—probably a foregleam of the intricate double-helical structure of the DNA molecule as it carries out its function of template reproduction of the pattern provided by the parents) in the lowest (or *least seen*) parts of the earth (God originally made the dust of the earth—the basic elements—then man's body from those elements, and then the marvelous ability to multiply that body). (Verse 15)

Thine eyes did see "my substance yet being unperfect" (all one word, meaning *embryo,* in the original; note the embryo is not *imperfect,* but *unperfect,* still in the process of being completed); and in thy book all my members were written, which in continuance (literally *which days*—that is, all the days of development and growth were planned from the beginning) were fashioned (same word as *formed,* used in Genesis 2:7 for the formation of Adam's body) when as yet there was none of them (the whole amazing process was written into the genetic code even before actual conception). (Verse 16)

The Body of Christ

With such careful divine care and attention given to the development of every one of the billions of human bodies conceived since the days of Adam and Eve, how much greater must have been the extent of the divine preparation of the body of God's own Son! As a matter of fact, the design for His body was prepared before the very foundation of the world itself (I Peter 1:20; Hebrews 10:5). It is probable that, in some degree at least, God had this very body in mind when He undertook to make Adam "in our image after our likeness" (Genesis 1:26). That is, God formed for Adam a body patterned after that perfect body which had already been planned for the divine incarnation, when the time would come.

Then, "when the fulness of the time was come, God sent forth His Son, made of a woman—that we might receive the adoption of sons" (Galatians 4:4,5).

"Wherefore when He cometh into the world, He saith, sacrifice and offering thou wouldest not, but a body hast thou prepared me" (Hebrews 10:5). The verb "prepared" in this verse is striking. It is the same word in the Greek (i.e., *katartizo*) as used in the next succeeding chapter in Hebrews, in one of the greatest of all those verses in the Bible describing the Creation. "Through faith we understand that the worlds were framed by the word of God, so that things which are seen were not made of things which do appear" (Hebrews 11:3).

The "preparation" of Christ's body by God was the same process as the "framing" of the worlds by God! As the latter were created *ex nihilo* ("not out of things which do appear"), so must have been the former. The word is also translated "make perfect" (Hebrews 13:21, etc.).

To the possible question as to whether such a specially-created human body could be a truly *human* body, the conclusive answer is that the *first* Adam had a specially-created human body, and he was true man—in fact, the very prototype man. It is entirely gratuitous to say that God could not create a second human body which would be truly human in every respect (except for the inherent defects associated with the sin-nature). Furthermore, nothing less than a true miracle of creation could really accomplish the formation of a true human body which would not be contaminated with sin and its marks.

Thus, the body of Christ, was prepared by the great Creator, with no dependence on prior materials, and was made in total perfection, ready to receive Him as its occupant. In that perfect body, which would one day be "made sin" and would "bear our sins" on the tree (II Corinthians 5:21, I Peter 2:24), He would dwell forever after its resurrection and glorification (Revelation 1:14-18).

When God created the world, it was only a little thing (Isaiah 40:15-17), but the formation of any human body required the special planning of divine omniscience, eliciting the inspired testimony, "How precious also are thy thoughts unto me, O God! how great is the sum of them!" (Psalm 139:17).

The greatest of all creations, however, was that of the body in which His Son would take up His eternal abode. Miraculously created and conceived, then virgin-born, God's eternal Son became the perfect Son of Man.

There is yet another "body of Christ," of which all believers become members, now in process of formation, with Christ the head (Ephesians 4:15, 16). This body also is being supernaturally formed by the Holy Spirit (I Corinthians 12:13), with no genetic inheritance from sinful flesh. Its members are "born, not of blood, nor of the will of the flesh, nor of the will of man, but of God" (John 1:13), so that when complete it also will be a body "not having spot, or wrinkle, or any such thing; but that it should be holy and without blemish" (Ephesians 5:27).

Here is another mighty act of special creation, repeated again and again whenever a new member is added to Christ's body, when a new son of God is born. "But as many as received Him, to them gave He power to become the sons of God, even to them that believe on His name" (John 1:12). "Therefore if any man be in Christ, he is a new *creation*" (II Corinthians 5:17). These have "put on the new man, which after God is *created* in righteousness and true holiness" (Ephesians 4:24). "Ye have put off the old man with his deeds; and have put on the new man, which is renewed in knowledge after the image of Him that *created* him" (Colossians 3:10). "For we are His workmanship, *created* in Christ Jesus unto good works" (Ephesians 2:10).

The virgin birth of Jesus Christ thus testifies of the marvelous creation of His human body, which then speaks symbolically of the marvelous member-by-member creation of His spiritual body.

THE MIRACLE OF GOD IN MAN

In the previous section, it was pointed out that God must have performed a miracle of creation at the time of the conception of Christ in Mary's womb. Some, however, may believe that such a miracle of creation would somehow dilute the doctrine of the true humanity of the Lord Jesus. They may feel that Jesus would have to have possessed Mary's genes in order to be really human. If His body had been specially created, then how He could really have been "touched with the feeling of our infirmities" and "in all points tempted like as we are" (Hebrews 4:15)?

Such doubts, however, are merely due to our limited confidence in God's ability to *create!* To say that God could not create a truly human body for the Lord Jesus is to deny His omnipotence. Was the body which He created for Adam not a human body? Adam had no genetic inheritance from either mother or father, but he was surely a man! Why could this not be as true of the second Adam as of the first Adam?

That God did indeed in some miraculous way form such a

human body (*perfectly* human, in fact) is evident from the Scriptures. "Wherefore in all things it behoved Him to be *made like* unto His brethren . . . " (Hebrews 2:17). He was "*made* in the likeness of men" (Philippians 2:7). "The Word was *made* flesh . . . " (John 1:14).

Note, however, that this flesh was not *sinful* flesh. Rather, He was "in the *likeness* of sinful flesh" (Romans 8:3). In every other way, it was real human flesh. Prior to the entrance of sin into the world and prior to the curse on the ground, Adam's divinely formed body needed food and rest, and this was true of the divinely-formed body of the second Adam as well. Furthermore, since all of the very elements of the earth later came under the curse (Genesis 3:17, Romans 8:22), that curse must have affected those atoms and molecules which were gradually added to Jesus' body as it grew from the embryonic state into maturity, as well as the food He ate and air He breathed. He was, indeed, "touched with the feeling of our infirmities."

It is certain, however, that these infirmities did not include sin—either acts of sin or a sin-nature. He "did no sin," He "knew no sin," and "in Him is no sin" (I Peter 2:22; II Corinthians 5:21; I John 3:5). Neither can we allow even the bare possibility that He *could* have sinned. Though He is true man, He also is very God, and He did not in any wise relinquish His deity when He became man. He is not part man and part God, or sometimes man and sometimes God. Once He became incarnate in human flesh, He became *eternally* the God-man— all man and all God! Since "God cannot be tempted with evil" (James 1:13), the temptation of Christ (though a real *testing,* in the sense that His impeccability had to be demonstrated to all creation as genuine) could not possibly have resulted in sin on His part. For if He *could* have sinned, then God *might* indeed have been defeated by Satan. But this is unthinkable to one who truly believes in God as the omnipotent Creator of all things.

It was absolutely essential, therefore, that His human body be free of an inherited sin-nature, and even from mental or physical defects resulting from inherited mutations. Biologically and genetically, there was no way this could be assured except by a miraculous conception, accomplished in such a way that none of the sinful and defective attributes of *either* parent could be transmitted to Him.

The question is—how could this be done? All who believe in the virgin birth recognize that a miracle was required—but what kind of miracle? Could it be merely a providential statistical juggling of Mary's genes so that those which carried the "sin-factor," as well as specific physical and mental defective mutations were somehow screened out? Hardly, because *all* of Mary's genes (no less than those of Joseph) would have been carriers of sin. There is neither biological nor theological basis for thinking that sin affects only certain genes and chromosomes and not others.

No, a "Grade A" miracle[1] is absolutely required, a miracle of creation. Some suggest that this miracle was performed on Mary herself so that all her genes were made immaculate. Others suggest that the miracle was performed only on the genes in the particular egg cell which the Holy Spirit "artificially inseminated" with an immaculate sperm cell of His own creating. Still others think that Mary's egg cell was somehow purified by the Holy Spirit of all inherent sin and defects and then, caused to grow by a process of parthenogenesis.

Actually, any or all of these amount to the same thing as direct creation! The body formed in Mary's womb either must have been specially created or else all of the genes in Mary's egg must have been specially **re**-created, one or the other. In either case, there could have been no direct transmission of physical, mental, or spiritual characteristics (all of which, in every man and woman, are contaminated by sin) from Joseph or Mary or David or Adam. To say otherwise is to imply that the Lord Jesus Christ received a sin-nature by inheritance, and this would disqualify Him as Savior.

But this wonderful miracle of creation in no way detracts from His full humanity. He experienced the same complete human life experienced by every other person, from the moment of conception to the moment of death—*except for sin!* Furthermore, He still occupies His human body, now resurrected and glorified. He is "holy, harmless, undefiled, separate from sinners, and made higher than the heavens." "Wherefore He is able also to save them to the uttermost that come unto God by Him" (Hebrews 7:25, 26).

---

1. A "Grade A" miracle involves setting aside one or both of the two laws of thermodynamics, creating either matter or energy or a higher degree of order. A "Grade B" miracle involves a providential control of the various factors affecting a particular phenomenon, but operating within the framework of the two laws of thermodynamics. For a discussion of this subject, see *Biblical Cosmology and Modern Science,* Baker Book House, 1970, p. 37-45.

Thus, the great King of Creation became a part of His creation. The King became a servant, and God became man. This is a great mystery and a mighty miracle, but without it there is no salvation.

CREATION AND REDEMPTION—
A TALE OF TWO WEEKS

The two greatest events in all history are the creation of the world and the redemption of the world. Each of these events involved a great divine Week of work and a Day of rest. Creation Week accomplished the work of man's formation; the week that is called Holy Week or Passion Week (perhaps a better term would be Redemption Week) accomplished the work of man's salvation.

Creation Week, which culminated in a perfect world (Genesis 1:31), was followed by man's fall and God's Curse on the world, (Genesis 3:17). Passion Week, which culminated in the death and burial of the maker of that perfect world, is followed by man's restoration and the ultimate removal of God's Curse from the world (Revelation 22:3). A Tree (Genesis 3:6) was the vehicle of man's temptation and sin; another Tree (I Peter 2:24) was the vehicle of man's forgiveness and deliverance.

The Two Weeks

It is fascinating to compare the events of the seven days of Creation Week and Redemption Week, respectively. The chronology of the events of Redemption Week has been the subject of much disagreement among scholars, and it is not possible to be certain on a number of the details. The discussion below is not meant to be dogmatic, but only to offer a possible additional dimension to their understanding and harmony. The traditional view that Friday was the day of the crucifixion is further strengthened by the correlations suggested in this study.

First Day. The first day of creation involved the very creation of the universe itself (Genesis 1:1). An entire cosmos responded to the creative fiat of the Maker of heaven and earth. Initially this Space-Mass-Time (i.e., heaven, earth, beginning) continuum was created in the form of basic elements only, with no structure and no occupant (Genesis 1:2), a static suspension in a pervasive, watery matrix (II Peter 3:5). When God's Spirit began to *move,* however, the gravitational and electromagnetic force systems for the cosmos were energized. The waters and their suspensions coalesced into a great spherical planet and, at the center of the electromagnetic spectrum of forces, visible light was generated (Genesis 1:3).

In a beautiful analogy, on the first day of Passion Week, the Creator King of the universe entered His chosen capital city (Zechariah 9:9, 10; Matthew 21:1-9) to begin His work of redemption, as He had long ago entered His universe to begin His work of creation. Even the very elements He had created (Luke 19:39, 40) would have acknowledged His authority, though the human leaders of His people would not.

Second Day. Having created and activated the earth, God next provided for it a marvelous atmosphere and hydrosphere in which, later, would live the birds and fishes. No other planet, of course, is equipped with air and water in such abundance, and this is strong evidence that the earth was uniquely planned for man and animal life. The hydrosphere was further divided into waters below and waters above "the firmament." The waters above the firmament (the Hebrew word for firmament means, literally "stretched-out space") probably comprised a vast blanket of transparent water vapor, maintaining a perfect climate worldwide, with ideal conditions for longevity.

Paralleling the primeval provision of life-sustaining air and water, on the second day of Redemption Week, He entered again into the city (having spent the night in Bethany) and taught in the temple. As He approached the city, He cursed the barren fig tree (Mark 11:12-14) and then, in the temple, overthrew the tables of the money changers (Mark 11:15-19). This seems to have been the second time in two days that He had turned out the money changers (the parallel accounts in Matthew and Luke indicate that He also did this on the first day). Both actions—the cursing of the fig tree and the cleansing of the temple—symbolize the purging of that which is barren or corrupt in the Creator's kingdom. He had created a world prepared for life (air for the breath of life and water as the matrix of life), but mankind, even the very teachers of His chosen people, had made it unfruitful and impure. As physical life must first have a world of pure air and water, so the preparations for a world of true spiritual life require the purifying breath of the Spirit and the cleansing water of the Word, preparing for the true fruit of the Spirit and the true temple of God's presence, in the age to come.

Third Day. The next day, the sight of the withered fig tree led to an instructive lesson on faith in God, the Lord Jesus assuring the disciples that real faith could move mountains into the sea (Mark 11:19-24). In parallel, on the third day of creation, God had literally called mountains up out of the sea (Genesis 1:9, 10)!

It was also on this day that the Lord had the most abrasive of all His confrontations with the Pharisees and Saducees. He spoke many things against them and they were actively conspiring to destroy Him. It is appropriate that His challenges to them on this day began with two parables dealing with a vineyard (Matthew 21:28-32 and Matthew 21:33-43; see also Mark 12:1-11 and Luke 20:9-18), in which He reminded them that they had been called to be in charge of God's vineyard on the earth and had failed. Like the fig tree, there was no fruit for God from their service, and therefore, they would soon be removed from their stewardship.

Likewise, the entire earth was on the third day of Creation Week prepared as a beautiful garden, with an abundance of fruit to nourish every living creature (Genesis 1:11, 12) and it had been placed in man's care (Genesis 1:28-30; 2:15). But mankind in general, and the chosen people in particular, had failed in their mission. Before the earth could be redeemed and made a beautiful garden again (Revelation 22:2), it must be purged and the faithless keepers of the vineyard replaced.

This third day of Passion Week was climaxed with the great Sermon on the Mount of Olives in which the Lord promised His disciples that, though Jerusalem must first be destroyed, He would come again, in power and great glory, to establish His kingdom in a new Jerusalem (Matthew 24 and 25; Mark 13; Luke 21). It was appropriate that He should then spend the night following that third day, with the handful of disciples who were still faithful to Him, on the Mount of Olives (Luke 21:37), for the Mount would call to memory that far-off third day of Creation Week when He had drawn all the mountains out of the sea. Also, the Garden of Gethsemane on its slopes, with its little grove of vines and fruit trees, would bring to mind the beautiful Garden of Eden and the verdant world He had planted everywhere on the dry land on that same third day. Because of what He was now about to accomplish at Jerusalem (Luke 9:31), the ground would one day be cleansed of its Curse, and all would be made new again (Revelation 21:5).

Fourth Day. On the fourth day of Creation Week, the Lord Jesus had formed the sun and the moon and all the stars of heaven. There had been "light" on the first three days, but now there were actual *lights!* Not only would the earth and its verdure be a source of beauty and sustenance to man, but even the very heavens would bring joy and inspiration to him. Furthermore, they would guide his way and keep his time.

But instead of the stars of heaven turning man's thoughts and affections toward his Creator, they had been corrupted and identified with a host of false gods and goddesses. Furthermore, instead of creating a sense of awe and reverence for the majesty of the One who could fill all heavens, they had bolstered man's belief that the earth is insignificant and meaningless in such a vast, evolving cosmos. Perhaps thoughts such as these troubled the mind of the Lord that night as He lay on the mountain gazing at the lights He had long ago made for the darkness.

When morning came, He returned to Jerusalem, where many were waiting to hear Him. He taught in the temple (Luke 21:37, 38), but the synoptic gospels do not record His teachings. This lack, however is possibly supplied in the apparently parenthetical record of His temple teachings as given only in the fourth gospel (John 12:20-50) because there the Lord twice compared Himself to the Light He had made: "I am come a light into the world, that whosoever believeth in me should not abide in darkness.""Yet a little while is the light with you. Walk while ye have the light, lest darkness come upon you; for he that walketh in darkness knoweth not whither he goeth" (John 12:46, 35). He who was the true Light must become darkness, in order that, in the new world, there would never be night again (Revelation 22:5).

Fifth Day. There is little information given in the gospels about the fifth day of Redemption Week. When there were yet "two days until the Passover" (Mark 14:1), right after the bitter confrontation with the scribes and chief priests on the Third Day, the latter began actively seeking a means to trap and execute Jesus, though they feared to do it on the day on which the Passover Feast was to be observed (Mark 14:2). It was either on the Fourth Day or possibly on this Fifth Day, which was the feast day, that Judas went to them with his offer to betray Jesus. He had apparently been seriously thinking about this action ever since the night when the Lord had rebuked him for his cupidity. This had been in the home in Bethany, on the night of the Sabbath, just before the day when Christ entered Jerusalem riding on the ass (John 12:1-8). This seems to have been the same supper described in Matthew 26:6-13 and Mark 14:3-9, even though in these it is inserted parenthetically after the sermon on the Mount of Olives, probably in order to stress the direct causal relation of this supper to Judas' decision to betray his Master (Matthew 26:14-16; Mark 14:10-11).

On this day of the Passover, the Lord Jesus instructed two of His disciples to make preparations for their own observance of the feast that night (Mark 14:12-17). So far as the record goes; this is all that we know of His words during that day, though there is no doubt that He was teaching in the temple on this day as well (Luke 21:37, 38). Perhaps this strange silence in the record for this Fifth Day is for the purpose of emphasizing the greater importance of these preparations for the Passover. The fact that John indicates the preparation day to have been the following day (John 19:14) is probably best understood in terms of the fact that, at that time, the Galileans are known to have observed the Passover on one day and the Judeans on the following day.

Multitudes of sacrificial lambs and other animals had been slain and their blood spilled through the centuries, but this would be the last such acceptable sacrifice. On the morrow, the Lamb of God would take away the sins of the world (John 1:29). He would offer one sacrifice for sins forever (Hebrews 10:12). With the blood of His cross, He would become the great Peace Maker, reconciling all things unto the Maker of those things (Colossians 1:16, 20).

As the Lord thought about the shedding of the blood of that last Passover lamb on that Fifth Day of Holy Week, He must also have thought of the Fifth Day of Creation Week, when He had first created animal life. "God created every living creature (Hebrew *nephesh*) that moveth" (Genesis 1:21). This had been His second great act of creation, when He created the entity of conscious animal life (the first had been the creation of the physical elements, recorded in Genesis 1:1). In these living animals, the "life" of the flesh was in their blood, and it was the blood which would later be accepted as an atonement for sin (Leviticus 17:11). Note that the words "creature," "soul," and "life" all are translations of the same Hebrew word *nephesh*. Surely the shedding of the innocent blood of the lamb that day would recall the far-off day when the "life" in that blood had been created. And because He, the Lamb of God, was about to become our Passover (I Corinthians 5:7), death itself would soon be swallowed up in victory and life (I Corinthians 15:54).

Sixth Day. On the Sixth Day, man had been created in the image and likeness of God, the very climax and goal of God's great work of creation (Genesis 1:26, 27). But on *this* Sixth Day, God, made in the likeness of man, finished the even greater work of redemption.

Under the great Curse, the whole creation had long been groaning and travailing in pain (Romans 8:22). But now the Creator, Himself, had been made the Curse (Galatians 3:13; Isaiah 52:14), and it seemed as though the Creation also must die. Though He had made heaven and earth on the First Day, now He had been lifted up from the earth (John 3:14) and the heavens were silent (Matthew 27:46). Though He had made the waters on the Second Day, He who was the very Water of Life (John 4:14), was dying of thirst (John 19:28).

On the Third Day He had made the dry land, but now "the earth did quake and the rocks rent" (Matthew 27:51) because the Rock of salvation had been smitten (Exodus 17:6). He had also covered the earth with trees and vines on that third day, but now the True Vine (John 15:1) had been plucked up and the Green Tree (Luke 23:31) cut down. He had made the sun on the Fourth Day, but now the sun was darkened (Luke 23:45) and the Light of the World (John 8:12) was burning out. On the Fifth Day He had created life, and He Himself *was* Life (John 11:25; 14:6), but now the life of His flesh, the precious blood, was being poured out on the ground beneath the cross, and He had been brought "into the dust of death" (Psalm 22:15). On the Sixth Day He had created man and given him life, but now man had despised the love of God and lifted up the Son of Man to death.

Seventh Day. But that is not the end of the story, and all was proceeding according to "the determinate counsel and fore-knowledge of God" (Acts 2:23). "On the seventh day God ended His work which He had made" (Genesis 1:21). Furthermore, everything that He had made "was very good" (Genesis 1:31). God's majestic work of Creation was complete and perfect in every detail.

And so is His work of salvation! This is especially emphasized in John's account: "After this, Jesus knowing that all things were now *accomplished,* that the Scripture might be *fulfilled,* saith, "I thirst . . . . When Jesus therefore had received the vinegar, He said, it is *finished;* and He bowed His head, and gave up the ghost" (John 19:28, 30) (the emphasized words are all the same word in the Greek original). Jesus had finished all the *things* He had to do, and then He finished the last of the prophetic *scriptures* that must be carried out. Then, and only then, was the work of redemption completed and the price of reconciliation fully paid, so that He could finally shout (Matthew 27:50) the great victory cry, *"It is finished."*

The record of Creation stresses repeatedly that the entire work of the creation and making of all things had been *finished* (Genesis 2:1-3). In like manner does John's record stress repeatedly the *finished* work of Christ on the cross.

Furthermore, as the finished creation was "very good," so is our finished salvation. The salvation which Christ thus provided on the cross is "so great" (Hebrews 2:3) and "eternal" (Hebrews 5:9), and the hope thereof is "good" (II Thessalonians 2:13).

Then, finally, having finished the work of redemption, Christ rested on the seventh day, His body sleeping in death in Joseph's tomb. He had died quickly, and the preparations for burial had been hurried (Luke 23:54-56), so that He could be buried before the Sabbath. As He had rested after finishing His work of Creation, so now He rested once again.

On the third day (that is the First Day of the new week), He would rise again, as He had said (Matthew 16:21, *et al*). His body had rested in the tomb all the Sabbath Day, plus part of the previous and following days, according to Hebrew idiomatic usage, "three days and three nights" (Matthew 12:40)—but death could hold Him no longer. He arose from the dead, and is now alive forevermore (Revelation 1:8).

THE AGES TO COME

The Bondage of Decay

According to the Second Law of Thermodynamics, this planet on which we live is going to die. The sun which supplies its energy will someday burn out and the entire solar system will then quickly perish. Indeed, so far as we can tell, the universe itself is dying. The great agnostic, Bertrand Russell, sadly comments:

> Some day, the sun will grow cold, and life on earth will cease. The whole epoch of animals and plants is only an interlude between ages that will be too cold . . . . This, at least, is what science regards as most probable, and in our disillusioned generation, it is easy to believe. From evolution, so far as our

present knowledge shows, no ultimately optimistic philosophy can be validly inferred.[1]

Long before the sun grows cold, as a matter of fact, the earth could die biologically. The hydrosphere and atmosphere are becoming polluted, the soil is being eroded, the nutrients in the soil are being leached away, and food supplies are increasingly contaminated.

> Man has long been aware that his world has a tendency to fall apart. Tools wear out, fishing nets need repair, roofs leak, iron rusts, wood decays, loved ones sicken and die, relatives quarrel, and nations make war.[2]

This universal tendency toward decay and death seems obvious to everyday experience, but was only formalized as a law of science a little over a century ago. It is significant, therefore, that this principle has been noted in the Bible for thousands of years.

> Of old hast thou laid the foundation of the earth: and the heavens are the work of thy hands. They shall perish, but thou shalt endure: yea, all of them shall wax old like a garment; as a vesture shalt thou change them, and they shall be changed. (Psalm 102:25-26).

> . . . for the heavens shall vanish away like smoke, and the earth shall wax old like a garment, and they that dwell therein shall die in like manner (Isaiah 51:6).

> Heaven and earth shall pass away (literally "are passing away"), but my words shall not pass away (Matthew 24:35).

> For we know that the whole creation groaneth and travaileth in pain together until now (Romans 8:22).

This universal law of decay is considered today as among the most certain of all scientific principles. As the Second Law of Thermodynamics, or the Law of Increasing Entropy, it governs all natural processes. It is also called "Time's Arrow." As time goes on, the arrow points down!

The Testimony of Creation

But the same Law that prophesies eventual disintegration

---

1. Bertrand Russell, *Religion and Science,* Oxford University Press, 1961, p. 81.
2. Van Rensselaer Potter, "Society and Science," *Science* Vol. 146, October 20, 1964, p. 1018.

also testifies of primeval creation. Instead of a message of consummate pessimism as interpreted by Bertrand Russell, therefore, the entropy principle really speaks of ultimate divine purpose in creation. Since the universe is now "running down" it must once have been "wound up." There must be a great First Cause able to create a universe. Thus the real message of the Second Law of Thermodynamics is: "In the beginning God created the heavens and the earth" (Genesis 1:1).

God is omniscient and omnipotent and certainly cannot fail in His purpose in creation. Even though the whole creation is groaning and travailing together in pain, its present "bondage of decay" cannot possibly continue forever. Long before it reaches ultimate death, God will intervene and "the creation itself also shall be delivered from the bondage of corruption into the glorious liberty of the children of God" (Romans 8:21).

Just as the study of present processes cannot tell us anything about the past events of the creation period, neither can present processes give us any information about the future events of the deliverance period. The processes of the present are the only processes accessible to the scientific method, and they all operate within the framework of the Second Law. Thus, present processes can give us no information about any processes of creation—past or future—since they are diametrically opposite to the decay processes as specified by the Second Law. Biblical revelation is required for information about both the first creation and the new creation.

Fortunately, however, "we have also a more sure word of prophecy; whereunto ye do well that ye take heed, as unto a light that shineth in a dark place, until the day dawn, and the day star arise in your hearts" (II Peter 1:19).

The Eternal Earth
There is much revealed in Scripture about the future of Planet Earth, but we first need to resolve what seems at first to be an apparent contradiction in these prophecies. That is, the Bible teaches both that the earth is to last forever and also that the earth is to be destroyed. As is always true with apparent conflicts in Scripture, however, the contradiction is only superficial. There is complete harmony when both Biblical and scientific considerations are more carefully analyzed.

Such passages as the following speak of the eternal permanence of the earth and of the entire created universe:

And He built His sanctuary like high palaces, like

the earth which He hath established for ever (Psalm 78:69).

Who laid the foundations of the earth, that it should not be removed forever (Psalm 104:5).

Praise ye Him, sun and moon: praise Him, all ye stars of light. Praise Him, ye heavens of heavens, and ye waters that be above the heavens. Let them praise the name of the Lord: for He commanded, and they were created. He hath also stablished them for ever and ever: He hath made a decree which shall not pass (Psalm 148:3-6).

One generation passeth away, and another generation cometh: but the earth abideth for ever (Ecclesiastes 1:4).

And they that be wise shall shine as the brightness of the firmament; and they that turn many to righteousness as the stars for ever and ever (Daniel 12:3).

There are other Scriptures to the same effect, but it should not surprise us that when God creates anything, it will endure forever. Otherwise, His purpose in creation would have been defeated, and that is impossible for the Creator.

I know that, whatsoever God doeth, it shall be for ever: nothing can be put to it, nor any thing taken from it: and God doeth it, that men should fear before Him (Ecclesiastes 3:14).

As far as the physical creation is concerned, its permanence has been confirmed by the most important and universal of all scientific laws. The First Law of Thermodynamics, or the Law of Conservation of Matter and Energy, states that the total amount of matter and energy stays constant with time. Nothing can be created, but neither can anything be annihilated. For the earth to be annihilated, it would require a miraculous intervention by the Creator to uncreate His creation!

The Destroyed Earth

But then, what about such Scriptures as the following?

Heaven and earth shall pass away (Mark 13:31; Luke 21:33).

And I saw a great white throne, and Him that sat on it, from whose face the earth and the heaven fled away; and there was found no place for them (Revelation 20:11).

But the day of the Lord will come as a thief in the

night; in which the heavens shall pass away with a great noise, and the elements shall melt with fervent heat, the earth also and the works that are therein shall be burned up (II Peter 3:10).

The reconciliation of these two apparently contradictory teachings of the Scriptures is obvious when the relation of matter and energy is considered. The First Law of Thermodynamics states that it is the *totality* of matter and energy which is conserved. When matter is converted into energy (as per the Einstein equation $E = Mc^2$, c being the velocity of light), matter is not annihilated but merely transformed into other kinds of energy.

The marvelous prophecy of II Peter 3:10 speaks of such a nuclear reaction on a gigantic scale, when the earth's "elements" will be "dissolved" (literally "unloosed"—II Peter 3:12). Thus, although the earth did not *begin* with a "Big Bang", as evolutionist astronomers allege, it will indeed *end* (in its present form) with a Big Bang! There will be a *great noise* and *fervent heat,* as the atoms of earth disintegrate in a great nuclear explosion, converted into tremendous sound and heat energy, with light and radiation as well.

The earth and its heaven (i.e. atmosphere) will thus "flee away" (Revelation 20:11). This, however, is not their annihilation but their purification! The very "dust of the earth"—that is the very elements out of which God had formed all things, even man's body, in the primeval week of creation—had been placed under the great Curse (Genesis 3:17) when man sinned. The sedimentary crust of the earth is also the burial ground of vast numbers of animals fossilized in the great Flood, not to mention the human and animal bones since the Flood. All this evidence of suffering and death and the Curse must be purged out, and the only way to do this is by disintegration of the very elements themselves.

The Earth Renewed

But then God's great creative power will be exercised once again, as in the original creation!

For, behold, I create new heavens and a new earth: and the former shall not be remembered, nor come into mind (Isaiah 65:17).

Behold, I make all things new (Revelation 21:5).

Because the creation itself also shall be delivered from the bondage of decay into the glorious liberty of the children of God (Romans 8:21).

Atomic disintegration of the present earth is soon to be followed by atomic integration of the new earth, as God causes the unleashed energy to reassemble into new material substances by His creative power. In the new (or, more literally, "renewed") earth, there will be "no more curse" (Revelation 22:3), and everything in the creation will be "very good" once again (Genesis 1:31).

These will be the "times of restoration of all things" (Acts 3:21), and "there shall be no more death, neither sorrow, nor crying, neither shall there be any more pain: for the former things are passed away" (Revelation 21:4). All of God's purposes in the first creation will finally be accomplished in the new creation, one that will never again be interrupted by sin and death. "We, according to His promise, look for new heavens and a new earth, wherein dwelleth righteousness" (II Peter 3:13). The new earth will last forever. "The new heavens and the new earth, which I will make, shall remain before me, saith the Lord" (Isaiah 66:22).

The new earth will actually be, therefore, the *renewed* earth—the old earth made new again. There will be certain significant differences, however. The first earth was suitable for human *probation;* the new earth is planned for full human *occupation.* Thus, in the primeval earth, there was a division between night and day (Genesis 1:4, 5), but in the new earth, there will be "no night there" (Revelation 22:5). In the first earth there was a division of land and sea (Genesis 1:9, 10); in the coming earth, there will be "no more sea" (Revelation 21:1). That is, there will be human activity, everywhere and always, on the earth. "His servants will serve Him" (Revelation 22:3).

Nor will this glorious service of the redeemed for their Savior need to be limited to the earth. Even though interstellar space travel will continue to be impossible in this present order of things (even the nearest star is four light-years away from the earth!), it will not be impossible in the future age. Our present bodies and all other physical systems are limited in movement by the ever-present gravitational and electromagnetic forces which govern their behavior. All believers will then, however, have new bodies which are spiritual bodies (I Corinthians 15:44) no longer subject to the constraints of these present forces, and thus will be able to fly throughout the universe unimpeded by gravity, lack of oxygen, or any other physical restriction of the present. Yet these bodies will be as real and physical as was the body of Jesus Christ in His resurrection (Philippians 3:20, 21). The resurrected Christ could move rapidly from earth to heaven and back again (John 20:17; Acts 1:9-11), could pass through closed doors (John 20:19), and yet was recognizable as in the same body He had possessed before His death and resurrection (John 20:27). He was capable of eating food (Luke 24:43), handling objects (Luke 24:30), and uttering speech (Matthew 28:19, 20); and our immortal bodies will be like His (I John 3:2).

Perhaps it is appropriate, therefore, to look forward, in Christ, to exploring and developing God's created universe extending into infinite space, throughout ages continuing through eternal time. We can now only dimly see this wonderful life of the eternal future, and there is, no doubt, far more than we even dream of. One thing is sure, however! The infinite God who created the magnificent universe in which we live surely has a glorious purpose in mind for those who were created in His image and whom He died to redeem. "But God, who is rich in mercy, for His great love wherewith He loved us. Even when we were dead in sins, hath quickened us together with Christ, (by grace ye are saved;) and hath raised us up together, and made us sit together in heavenly places in Christ Jesus: That in the ages to come He might shew the exceeding riches of His grace, in His kindness toward us, through Christ Jesus" (Ephesians 2:4-7).

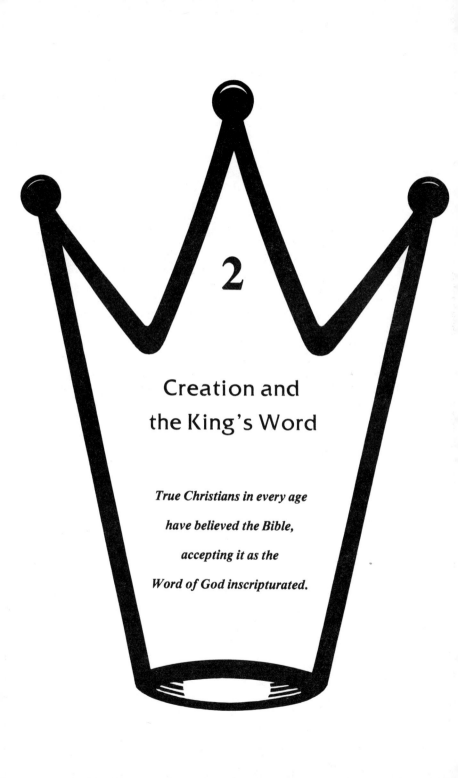

2

Creation and
the King's Word

True Christians in every age
have believed the Bible,
accepting it as the
Word of God inscripturated.

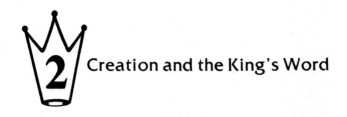

Creation and the King's Word

BIBLICAL INERRANCY AND
SPECIAL CREATION

True Christians in every age have believed the Bible, accepting it as the Word of God inscripturated. Believing it to be divinely inspired even in the very words themselves, Christians have taken the Bible as their absolute authority on all matters with which it deals . . . or so they claim!

This is what they say: "The Scriptures Alone!" "The Bible our only Rule of Faith and Practice!" "Where the Bible Speaks, We Speak; Where the Bible is Silent, We are Silent!" "We Stand Without Apology on the Old Book!" "We Believe in Plenary Verbal Inspiration." Slogans and claims of this sort abound in denominational and institutional advertisements, and the officials who make them no doubt sincerely believe them.

To creationists, however, such assertions often sound less than convincing. Sad experience has shown again and again that the plain teaching of Scripture on the most important doctrine of the Bible is being inexcusably compromised by multitudes of Christian people and their organizations. The doctrine of the special creation of all things by the one true God, who alone is eternal and transcendent, is the most important doctrine in the Scriptures because all other doctrines ultimately depend on it.

Hermeneutical Dissimulation

The writer can speak from personal experience in this connection, having spent much of his time during the past forty years trying to convince Christians that the Genesis record of creation really means what it says! But since what it says sharply contradicts what the modern scientific and educational establishments say about the origin and history of the cosmos, many Christians have in effect decided that, at this point, the Bible was not their real authority after all. The device by which their rejection of Genesis is reconciled with the doctrine of Biblical inerrancy is called *hermeneutics*. Hermeneutics is a formal quasi-Biblical discipline (the "science" of Bible interpretation, it is called) whereby it is possible to make any unacceptable Bible teaching to be something other than what its writer intended it to teach.

By some such procedure (very similar to that employed by evolutionists in interpreting the facts of science to teach evolution, when the actual *facts* plainly speak of creation), the straightforward histories of Genesis can be converted into a beautifully irrelevant allegory, the days of creation become transmuted into geological ages, the initial condition of the created cosmos is made into a mysterious global cataclysm, and the worldwide deluge of Noah becomes either a slight rise in sea-level after the ice age or else a heavy flood on the River Euphrates! Adam's creation from the dust is translated as the implantation of a human soul into a hominid body, and Adam's fall into sin "pictures" the experience of "everyman," when he yields to the voice of temptation in his frontal lobe, as symbolized by the idea of Satan indwelling a serpent in a garden.

Of course hermeneutics can be imposed on other parts of Scripture, as well. Uncomfortable commandments can be relegated to future, or former, dispensations. The warnings of eternal hell can be sublimated to a comfortable annihilationism. The wrath of God on unrepentant sinners can be waived in favor of His all-encompassing divine love. The necessity of conversion and regeneration is obviated by church membership and a Christian upbringing. Examples of hermeneutical transmutations are legion.

But it is in the early chapters of Genesis, especially Genesis 1-11, that it has been most destructive of the real authority of the Word of God. It is at this point that the fundamental integrity of God Himself, as sovereign Creator and Ruler of the universe, is being continually compromised in deference to the humanistic philosophies of His mortal enemies. If He can be dethroned as King of Creation, then His salvation becomes meaningless and His promises void. Man would become his own god (or so he supposes—actually he will eventually bow to Satan when he comes to realize the oppressive emptiness of real humanism).

Many will think the above indictment is too broad. Surely most people who believe the Bible believe in creation and in the historicity of the Genesis record, do they not? Maybe theological "liberals" don't, but conservatives, evangelicals, and fundamentalists do, surely! But *do* they?

It is these very people who continually resort to the gap theory, the day-age theory, the local flood theory, theistic evolution, progressive creation, and so on, or who (even worse) ignore the whole issue, in order to dodge the *real* conflict between the Bible and humanism. Liberals, on the other hand, don't bother with hermeneutics at all. They merely reject the Bible and creationism forthrightly, in favor of total evolutionism (perhaps with certain slight religious overtones).

The Plain Testimony of Scripture

It has been almost forty years since the writer first became concerned about this issue and set about to determine exactly how to reconcile Genesis and modern science. Every Scripture dealing with this issue in any way was thoroughly examined and catalogued. Commentaries were consulted, along with every book and article that could be uncovered on the subject. Practically all the latter took the position that the geological ages must be accepted as the starting point and then proceeded to devise various hermeneutical devices by which they hoped to interpret Scripture to fit them (the geological ages).

The Scriptures alone, however, (when they were studied apart from these various commentaries and harmonizations) unequivocally taught that the universe itself was only a few thousand years old and that God the Creator had begun and finished His work of creating and making all things in six natural days.

All the Scriptures were consistent with this "literal" interpretation. (Actually a *literal interpretation* is a contradiction in terms—there is no need to "interpret" a statement if it is taken "literally"!) Especially cogent was the direct assertion by God Himself, in Exodus 20:8-11:

> Remember the sabbath day, to keep it holy. Six days shalt thou labor, and do all thy work: But the seventh day is the sabbath of the Lord thy God . . . For in six days the Lord made heaven and earth, the sea, and all that in them is, and rested the seventh day: wherefore the Lord blessed the sabbath day, and hallowed it.

A similar passage is Exodus 31:15-18:

> Six days may work be done; but in the seventh is the sabbath of rest, holy to the lord . . . . It is a sign between me and the children of Israel for ever: for in six days the Lord made heaven and earth, and on the seventh day He rested, and was refreshed. And He gave unto Moses, when He had made an end of communing with him upon Mount Sinai, two tables

> of testimony, tables of stone, written with the finger
> of God.

It would be impossible to say it more clearly. The days of God's work week were the same as the days of man's work week, and all things in the universe were created and made in that first six-day period. This statement was included in the stone tables of the Ten Commandments, written by God's own hand. All of the Bible is divinely inspired, but this unique portion was divinely inscripturated! If any part of Scripture must be taken literally and seriously, this is it.

And yet most evangelical leaders continue to reject this emphatic teaching of Scripture in favor of the imaginary evolutionary ages of geology, all the while protesting their belief in Biblical inerrancy. There is no legitimate Biblical exegesis which can accommodate the standard geologic age system, and there are irreconcilable conflicts with both science and Scripture in all such "wrestings of Scripture" (II Peter 3:16) as these. The writer has pointed this out in detail in book after book and in lecturing all across the country for over 30 years. Evangelical pastors and professors, scientists and laymen have been urged to answer these numerous and serious objections to the various accommodationist theories to no avail. Furthermore, he has repeatedly emphasized and documented the necessary identity of these "ages" with evolutionism, and of evolutionism, in turn, with humanism in all its deadly forms—but no one has attempted to answer these evidences either. Most evangelical spokesmen still continue either to ignore or to reject these unanswerable evidences documenting the factual reality and vital importance of *real* creationism, as taught in Scripture.

The writer, for example, on several occasions (both in print and in person) has challenged the leaders of the American Scientific Affiliation to answer and refute these evidences and arguments, but they make no attempt to do so. This organization, which purports to be an organization of Bible-believing scientists serving as the scientific arm of evangelicalism, continues to ridicule "recent creationism" and "flood geology," but without facing the Biblical evidence at all. Many of the leading Christian liberal arts colleges in the evangelical orbit continue to promote so-called "progressive creationism" (a semantic circumlocution designed to mask its essential identity with theistic evolutionism). Even many fundamentalist colleges and seminaries continue to endorse the scientifically and

Biblically indefensible "gap theory," a futile compromise which they hope will enable them to avoid facing the real issue.

Creation and the "Battle for the Bible"

In recent years, leaders of conservative Christianity have become increasingly concerned about Biblical inerrancy. Dr. Harold Lindsell's best-selling book, *Battle for the Bible,* documented the growing dilution of the inerrancy doctrine among faculties of many supposedly orthodox seminaries and other institutions, including Fuller Seminary, where he himself had once served. His book stirred evangelical circles more than any other had done in a generation.

Amazingly, however, Dr. Lindsell made practically no reference to the creation issue, which is the primary cause of these increasing doubts about inerrancy. At Fuller Seminary, for example, the day-age theory, as advocated by Wilbur Smith and other charter members of the faculty, soon gave way to the more overt theistic evolutionism of its successive presidents and other key faculty members. Its current president, David Hubbard, as a member of California's State Board of Education, cast the key vote in 1972 which prevented creationism from being implemented in the state's science textbooks.

Creationism was also a key issue at Concordia Seminary in St. Louis, a situation finally resulting in a complete split in the Missouri Synod Lutheran denomination. Practically all Southern Baptist colleges and seminaries teach evolutionism, and this has effectively eliminated Biblical inerrancy as a belief of their faculties. The same cycle has repeated itself over and over again in churches, schools, missions, denominations, and all sorts of Christian institutions. A compromise position on the Bible's strict creationism inevitably undermines and eventually destroys belief in its inerrancy, and then it becomes only a matter of time until the other key doctrines of Christianity are also lost.

A current (1979) aspect of the "battle for the Bible" is the recently organized International Council on Biblical Inerrancy, which is attempting to call together all those diverse groups in conservative Christian circles who desire to maintain a firm stand on inerrancy. However, the leadership of this group includes many who accept either theistic evolution or progressive creation, as well as many who prefer to ignore the creation issue altogether. Consequently, unless the I.C.B.I. can somehow become convinced of the foundational importance of strict creationism for maintaining a consistent belief in inerrancy, its efforts will likely prove of only ephemeral effectiveness. The writer and others were able to persuade the I.C.B.I. to incorporate a brief article on creation and the flood into its "Chicago Statement on Inerrancy," but the Council leadership felt it could not stand on literal-day creationism and a worldwide flood, so the article was mostly innocuous.

The writer is convinced, from long experience and observation, that there can be no real and effective unity among evangelical Christians on the doctrine of Biblical inerrancy until there is first agreement on the doctrine of true creationism. As long as Bible teachers insist on accommodating evolutionists and their geological age system, in effect thus acknowledging grave errors in the Biblical record in its first and foundational chapters, their protests against those evangelicals who frankly reject inerrancy because of these same Biblical "mistakes" are going to seem either hypocritical or foolish to most people.

As a matter of fact, the doctrines of special creation and Biblical inerrancy are logically inseparable and it is difficult to assign a priority of importance to either one. In one sense, we believe in creation because the inerrant Bible teaches it, with its unequivocal assertion that God created and made the entire universe in six literal days. On the other hand, we believe in inerrancy because God, as Creator, both can and logically must provide an authoritative revelation concerning Himself to His creatures.

In fact, if *pressed* to assign a priority between the two doctrines, it would be necessary to start with creationism, because that was God's order. He first created, (Genesis 1:1), then spoke (Genesis 1:3). There were many years in the world's primeval ages when men did not have God's written Word, but they did have the witness of God's creation (Psalm 19:1; Romans 1:20). Furthermore, the pattern of apostolic evangelism was always to begin with the witness of creation (Acts 14:15-17; 17:22-31) when preaching to people who did not know or believe the Bible. Today, when a similar pagan unbelief again pervades the world, it is more necessary than ever to lay the foundation of real creationism first of all.

THE FOUNDATIONAL IMPORTANCE
OF CREATIONISM

One of the most frustrating problems which creationist scientists encounter in trying to encourage and strengthen belief in creationism is the indifference of so many Christian people to the importance of this issue. "I don't believe in evolution anyhow, so why should I waste time in studying creationism?" "Why get involved in peripheral and controversial issues like that—just preach the Gospel!" "The Bible is not a textbook of science, but of how to live." "It is the Rock of Ages which is important—not the age of rocks!" "Winning souls is the principal thing—not winning debates."

Platitudes such as the above, however spiritual they sound, are really cop-outs. They usually serve subconsciously as excuses for avoiding serious thought and the offense of the cross. In the name of evangelism and the desire for large numbers of "decisions," a "least-common-denominator" emphasis on emotional experience, with a nominal commitment of some kind, has become the dominant characteristic of most Christian teaching and activity today. This situation is almost as true in fundamentalist and conservative circles as it is among religious liberals.

This attitude seems to date largely from the after-effects of the infamous Scopes Trial in 1925. The fundamentalists and creationists were made to look so ridiculous by the news media covering that trial at the time (and evolutionists are still exploiting it today!) that Christians in general retreated altogether from the battle for the schools and the minds of their young people. Avoiding any further attempt to relate science and history to an inspired Bible, Christian teachers and preachers thenceforth emphasized evangelism and the spiritual life almost exclusively. The "gap theory" which supposedly allowed the earth's billions of years of evolutionary history to be pigeonholed between the first two verses of Genesis and then ignored, provided a convenient device for saying the entire question was irrelevant.

As a consequence, in less than a generation, the entire school system and the very establishment itself—educational, scientific, political, military, industrial, and religious—was taken over by the evolutionary philosophy and its fruits of naturalism, humanism, socialism, and animalistic amoralism.

For the past decade, happily, a noteworthy revival of creationism has been taking place, both in the churches and, to some extent, in the schools. Thousands of scientists have become creationists, and the interest among teachers and students in creationism is higher than it has ever been.

Nevertheless, although many churches and Christian people have become actively involved in the creation issue, it is still sadly true that the majority of Christians are indifferent, or even antagonistic, to creationism. They think it is only a peripheral biological question, of no concern in the preaching of the Gospel. Even most fundamentalists, who themselves may believe in creation, think evolution is a dead issue.

Such an attitude is based on wishful thinking, to say the least. Evolution is not a dead issue to the humanistic establishment. An important article in *Science,* the official journal of the prestigious American Association for the Advancement of Science, says, for example:

> While many details remain unknown, the grand design of biologic structure and function in plants and animals, including man, admits to no other explanation than that of evolution. Man therefore is another link in a chain which unites all life on this planet.[1]

Not only did man evolve, but so did "the religions of Jesus and **Buddha**"[2] That being so, not only are the *supernatural* aspects of Christianity open to question, but so are its *ethical* teachings.

> An ethical system that bases its premises on absolute pronouncements will not usually be acceptable to those who view human nature by evolutionary criteria.[3]

Ethics and morals must evolve as well as organisms! And so must social and political systems. There are no absolutes, according to the leaders of education.

This is the logical and inevitable outgrowth of evolutionary teaching. This is also the logical and inevitable outgrowth of Christian indifference to evolutionary teaching.

The doctrine of special creation is the foundation of all other Christian doctrines. The experience of belief in Christ as Creator is the basis of all other Christian experience. Creationism is not peripheral or optional; it is central and vital. That is why God placed the account of creation at the beginning of the Bible, and why the very first verse of the Bible speaks of the creation of the physical universe.

Jesus Christ was Creator (Colossians 1:16) before He became

---

1. A.G. Motulsky, "Brave New World," *Science,* Vol. 185, August 23, 1974, page 653.
2. *Ibid*
3. *Ibid*, p. 654

Redeemer (Colossians 1:20). He is the very "beginning of the creation of God" (Revelation 3:14). How then can it be possible to really know Him as Savior unless one also, and first, knows God as Creator?

The very structure of man's time commemorates over and over again, week by week, the completed creation of all things in six days. The preaching of the Gospel necessarily includes the preaching of creation. " . . . the everlasting gospel to preach unto them that dwell on the earth . . . worship Him that made heaven, and earth, and the sea, and the fountains of waters" (Revelation 14:6,7).

If man is a product of *evolution,* he is not a *fallen* creature in need of a Savior, but a *rising* creature, capable of saving himself.

The "gospel" of evolution is the enemy of the Gospel of Christ. The Gospel of Christ leads to salvation, righteousness, joy, peace, and meaning in life. Evolution's "gospel" yields materialism, collectivism, anarchism, atheism, and despair in death.

Evolutionary thinking dominates our schools today—our news media, our entertainment, our politics, our entire lives. But evolution is false and absurd scientifically! How long will Christian people and churches remain ignorant and apathetic concerning it?

IN PRAISE OF CREATION'S CREATOR

One of the greatest blessings of the study of God's creation is the increasing sense of wonder and gratitude that it generates. The planning and fabrication of the infinite array of beautiful animals in the heavens and on the lands and in the seas, with systems of incredible complexity and marvelous symbiosis, can only be explained in terms of an omniscient Creator.

One of the greatest mysteries of human nature is the fact that intelligent scientists, familiar with these phenomena, can actually attribute them to blind chance, acting through random mutations and a random walk through natural processes operating on eternal matter. The only explanation of this strange fact is, as the Apostle says, they " . . . became vain in their imaginations . . . .Professing themselves to be wise, they became fools . . . . they did not like to retain God in their knowledge . . . " (Romans 1:21, 22, 28).

The normal response to the beauty and order of the creation, however, is one of thanksgiving and praise. This is one of the dominant themes of the writers of the Bible, especially in the Book of Psalms. A few of these passages are noted below:

For great is the Lord, and greatly to be praised: He also is to be feared above all gods. For all the gods of the people are idols: but the Lord made the heavens (I Chronicles 16:25, 26).

Rejoice in the Lord, O ye righteous: for praise is comely for the upright . . . . By the word of the Lord were the heavens made; and all the host of them by the breath of His mouth (Psalm 33:1,6).

Let us come before His presence with thanksgiving . . . . The sea is His, and He made it: and His hands formed the dry land. O come, let us worship and bow down: let us kneel before the Lord our Maker (Psalm 95:1, 5, 6).

Know ye that the Lord He is God: it is He that hath made us, and not we ourselves . . . . Enter into His gates with thanksgiving, and into His courts with praise: be thankful unto Him, and bless His name (Psalm 100:3, 4).

I will praise thee; for I am fearfully and wonderfully made: marvelous are thy works: and that my soul knoweth right well (Psalm 139:14).

O give thanks unto the lord of lords . . . . To Him that by wisdom made the heavens . . . . To Him that stretched out the earth above the waters . . . . To Him that made great lights: for His mercy endureth forever (Psalm 136:3-7).

Sing unto the Lord with thanksgiving; sing praise upon the harp unto our God: Who covereth the heaven with clouds, who prepareth rain for the earth, who maketh grass to grow upon the mountains (Psalm 147:7-8).

Let them praise the name of the Lord; for He commanded and they were created (Psalm 148:5).

And when those beasts give glory and honour and thanks to Him that sat on the throne, who liveth for ever and ever . . . . saying, Thou art worthy, O Lord, to receive glory and honour and power: for thou hast created all things, and for thy pleasure they are and were created (Revelation 4:9-11).

There are many other such references in the Bible ascribing praise and thanks to God for His magnificent work of creation and for His providential and loving care thereof. In contrast to those who offer such praises, however, those who refuse to acknowledge and thank God for His creation are condemned in words of bitter irony:

> For the invisible things of Him from the creation of the world are clearly seen, being understood by the things that are made, even His eternal power and Godhead; so that they are without excuse: Because that, when they knew God, they glorified Him not as God, neither were thankful; but became vain in their imaginations, and their foolish heart was darkened (Romans 1:20-21).

But there is another important teaching of Scripture on the theme of thanksgiving. There are a greater number of references in the Bible to giving thanks and praise for God's work of salvation and personal guidance than even for His work of creation. Christ's work of creation is foundational, but His work of salvation is motivational! We are "created in Christ Jesus unto good works" (Ephesians 2:10).

There is a beautiful study of "first mentions" in the Bible in this connection. The main Hebrew word for "give thanks" is *yadah,* which is also often translated "praise." It occurs first in Genesis 29:35, when Jacob's wife Leah gave birth to Judah; " . . . and she said, Now will I praise the Lord: therefore she called his name Judah."

As events later developed, Judah turned out to be the most Christlike of Jacob's sons (in his willingness to give up his life for his brethren—see *The Genesis Record,* pp. 611-619) and was selected as the one through whom Christ would come (Genesis 49:10). Thus, the first mention of giving thanks to the Lord introduces us, in type, to His coming work of salvation.

The New Testament word for "give thanks" is the Greek *eucharisteo.* It occurs first in Matthew 15:36, 37 in which the Lord Jesus manifested Himself as Creator and Sustainer, creating a great quantity of food for the multitude: "And He . . . gave thanks . . . . And they did all eat, and were filled."

The first recorded thanksgiving in the Old Testament was for Judah, whose very name means "thanks," looking forward to God's work of salvation. The first recorded thanksgiving in the New Testament was by the promised Son of Judah, the Lord Jesus, whose very name means "salvation," looking back to God's work of creation. Today, let us praise the Lord continually, first for His splendid creation, but even more for His gracious salvation!

THE LIVING WORD

Before the Creator could become the Savior, of course, He must become man. The Word must become flesh. He who inspired the written word must now be, for all eternity, the Living Word, and thus will he also "inhabit the praises" of His people, world without end.

There are many mysteries involved in God's dealings with men, but the greatest of all is that God could become man. Yet the evidence is overwhelming that Jesus Christ is both wholly God and also fully man (that is, man without sin—man as God intended man to be).

This is the ultimate fascination of Christmas. Despite all the pagan trappings and worldly emphasis, the great message is still getting through—every year, everywhere—that "there is one God, and one mediator between God and men, the man Christ Jesus" (I Timothy 2:5). The "one God," the "one mediator," and "the man Christ Jesus" are all one, the God-Man!

Consider again the unfathomable mystery in just three marvelous Biblical truths:

1. *The Creator has become flesh.*

   "In the beginning was the Word, . . . and the Word was God . . . . All things were made by Him; . . . And the Word was made flesh, and dwelt among us" (John 1:1, 3, 14). The God of creation had, after creating and making all other things, finally formed the most complex system in the universe, the human body, composed of "flesh" (Genesis 2:21). And then, in the fulness of time, God formed another body of flesh (Hebrews 10:5) and dwelled therein, that He might "His own self bare our sins in His own body on the tree" (I Peter 2:24).

2. *The Eternal One has entered time.*

   "But, thou, Bethlehem . . . out of thee shall He come forth unto me . . . whose goings forth have been from of old, from everlasting" (Micah 5:2). The "high and lofty One that inhabiteth eternity" (Isaiah 57:15) was born and lived and died in time, so that those whose "days are passed away in thy wrath" (Psalm 90:9) "might not perish, but have everlasting life" (John 3:16).

3. *The Omnipotent God became a helpless babe.*

   "For unto us a child is born, . . . and His name shall be

called . . . the mighty God" (Isaiah 9:6). The resurrected Lord has "all power . . . in heaven and in earth" (Matthew 28:18), but in His incarnation, He "made himself of no reputation, and took upon Him the form of a servant" (Philippians 2:7). This was so that those who were themselves helpless could be saved "for when we were yet without strength, in due time Christ died for the ungodly" (Romans 5:6).

Thus, the Almighty became powerless, the Eternal became temporal, the Infinite One entered a finite body, the Creator suffered as a creature, the Holy One was made sin, and the Living One died. We are unable to comprehend such mysteries with our minds, but we can understand in our souls and believe in our hearts, thus to receive forgiveness and eternal salvation.

"And without controversy, great is the mystery of godliness: God was manifest in the flesh, justified in the Spirit, seen of angels, preached unto the Gentiles, believed on in the world, received up into glory" (I Timothy 3:16).

JESUS THE CREATIONIST

When God became man, He became man as God *intended* man to be. He lived as God wanted man to live (I Peter 2:21), and He thought as God intended man to think (Philippians 2:5). What He believed, His disciples must believe, if they are truly His disciples. Thus, so-called "Christian evolutionists" in effect are denying His Lordship. It may indeed be possible for a Christian to be an evolutionist (either through ignorance or deliberate disobedience), but evolution itself cannot be Christian, for the obvious reason that Christ was not an evolutionist. Thus, there is no such thing as Christian evolution!

True Christians, of course, accept the authority of the Lord Jesus Christ, so they certainly should no longer accept evolution—once they realize that He believed and taught the historicity and accuracy of the literal Genesis record of special creation. The following quotations from His own words indicate how clear and comprehensive was this teaching of Jesus.

1. *He accepted the compatibility of the two supposedly contradictory accounts of creation in Genesis 1 and Genesis 2.*

"Have you not read that He . . . made them male and female [quoting Genesis 1:27], And said, For this cause shall a man leave father and mother, and shall cleave to his wife; and, they twain shall be one flesh? [quoting Genesis

2:24]'' (Matthew 19:5).

2. *He accepted the historicity of the creation record, basing His teaching concerning the integrity of the home, the most basic of all human institutions, on its truthfulness.*

"Wherefore they are no more twain, but one flesh. What therefore, God hath joined together, let not man put asunder" (Matthew 19:6).

3. *He believed that the creation of man and woman was at the beginning of the creation, not four billion years after the beginning.*

"From the beginning of the creation God made them male and female" (Mark 10:6).

4. *He believed that the cosmos actually had a beginning, and not that matter was eternal.*

" . . . such as was not since the beginning of the world [Greek *kosmos*] to this time" (Matthews 24:21).

5. *He believed that it was God who did the creating, not some natural process.*

" . . . from the beginning of the creation which God created . . . " (Mark 13:19).

6. *He believed in the fixity of the created kinds.*

"Do men gather grapes of thorns, or figs of thistles? . . . . A good tree cannot bring forth evil fruit, neither can a corrupt tree bring forth good fruit" (Matthew 7:16, 18).

7. *He believed in the Sabbath as a rest day in commemoration of God's completed creation.*

"The sabbath was made for man, and not man for the sabbath" (Mark 2:28).

8. *He believed that the world had been "founded," not just accidentally condensed from agglomerations of particles.*

" . . . for thou lovedst me before the foundation of the world" (John 17:24).

9. *He believed that even the sun belonged to God.*

" . . . He maketh His sun to rise . . . " (Matthew 5:45).

10. *He accepted the record that God had made even the fowls of the air and had made provision for their food (as noted in Genesis 1:30).*

"Behold the fowls of the air . . . your heavenly Father feedeth them" (Matthew 6:26).

These and other teachings of Christ, plus the complete absence of any reference by Him either to evolution or long ages (both of which beliefs were universally accepted by the pagan philosophers of His day) make it certain that He accepted the account of special creation recorded in Genesis as completely authoritative and accurate in the most literal sense. Therefore, no true believer in *His* authority and integrity can afford to do less.

CREATION AND THE SEVEN-DAY WEEK

An often-overlooked testimony to the fact of creation is the strange phenomenon of the seven-day week. Almost universally observed in the present world and often observed in the ancient world, it is so deeply rooted in human experience and so natural physiologically that we seldom think about its intrinsic significance.

Thus, God has given yet another witness to the absolute integrity of His Word, even the very first chapter of His Word, the chapter that has always been the central focus of the attacks of the great enemy of God's Kingdom. The structure of man's daily existence—the time framework in which he conducts his activities—continually bears witness that the King's Word is sure and can be ignored only at the peril of losing all meaning to life.

The Unique Week

All the other important time markers in human life are clearly based on astronomical and terrestrial constants. The *day*, for example, is the duration of one rotation of the earth on its axis; the *year* is the duration of one orbital revolution of the earth about the sun; the *month* is the approximate interval between new moons; the *seasons* are marked by the equinoxes and solstices.

But the *week* has no astronomical basis[1] whatever! Yet we order our lives in a seven-day cycle, doing certain things on Monday, certain other things on Tuesday, and so on through the week. Furthermore, the common pattern is one of six normal working days, then a day of rest or change, then six normal days again, and so on, with the special day regarded as either the last of the seven preceding it, or the first of the seven following it.

How could such a system ever have originated? Most encyclo-

---

1. Some have said the "four phases of the moon" provided the astronomical basis of the week. It should be obvious, however, that the prior existence of the week provides the only rationale for dividing the monthly cycle of the moon into *four* phases, instead of some other arbitrary number.

pedias and reference books treat the subject very superficially, if at all. One can easily find extensive discussions about the length of the year and the length of the month in different eras and cultures, but it is very difficult to locate information about the week. Most of the discussions that do try to deal with it attribute the origin of the week to the use of "market days," pointing out also that the interval between market days was different in different nations, though rarely varying more than a day or so above or below seven days. With the exception of an occasional Biblical scholar, almost none of these writers even consider the obvious explanation—namely, that the seven-day week was established by God Himself, at the beginning!

Every effect must have an adequate cause, and the only cause which is truly able to account for such a remarkable phenomenon as the week is that it was established at creation and has been deeply etched in the common human consciousness ever since. Even if the week is noted in some cultures in terms of regular market days, this still does not explain how the market days happened to cluster around every "seventh" day, instead of every fifteenth day or nineteenth day or something else? Besides, there were various ancient nations whose weeks were quite unrelated to any marketing customs.

A related phenomenon, equally remarkable, is the almost universal significance attached to the number "seven" as a number speaking of completeness, usually with special religious overtones. This number is not "natural" in any physical way. It would be more natural to use the number "ten" (the number of a man's fingers), or the number "twelve" (the number of months in the year), or perhaps the number "365," to represent fulness. Why "seven"? Yet "seven" is everywhere the number of completeness.

The Origin of Sabbath Observance

Many people believe that the custom of a weekly day of rest began with Moses, when he incorporated Sabbath observance into the Ten Commandments. Such an explanation is so superficial, however, that it merely raises questions about its own motivation. Not only is there considerable evidence that Sabbath observance existed in both Israel and in other nations long before Moses, but the Word of God makes it plain that it was established by God Himself, in commemoration of His completed creation, and that it has been observed as a special day, at least by some, ever since. Here is the record:

> Thus the heavens and the earth were finished, and
> all the host of them, and on the seventh day God
> ended His work which He had made; and He rested
> on the seventh day from all His work which He had
> made. And God blessed the seventh day, and sancti-
> fied it: because that in it He had rested from all His
> work which God created and made (Genesis 2:1-3).

God "rested" after finishing His work of creating and making all things in the universe in the six days just completed. His rest was not because of fatigue (note Isaiah 40:28), but was simply a cessation of His creative activity.

And then God *blessed and sanctified* the seventh day! He declared it to be a holy day, a day peculiarly the Lord's Day. The six days had been occupied with His creation; *one* day should be occupied with the Creator. He frequently referred later to the day as "my Sabbaths" (e.g., Exodus 31:13).

From Adam to Moses

It is clearly implied in the story of Cain and Abel that the children of Adam continued to regard every seventh day as a day of rest and worship, even after the expulsion from Eden.

> And in process of time it came to pass, that Cain
> brought of the fruit of the ground an offering unto
> the Lord. And Abel, he also brought of the firstlings
> of his flock and of the fat thereof (Genesis 4:3, 4).

On this particular day, Cain was not tilling the ground, as he normally did, nor was Abel tending his sheep. On this day, they met with the Lord and brought Him an offering.

And what day was that? The phrase "in process of time" is, literally, "at the end of the days" ("process" = Hebrew *gets* = "end"; "time" = Hebrew *yamin* = "days"). The day on which they brought their offerings was the day "at the end of the days," and this clearly can be nothing but the seventh day, the day which God had blessed and hallowed.

The story of Noah contains many allusions to the seven-day week. Note the following in Chapters 7 and 8 of Genesis:

1. "For yet seven days, and I will cause it to rain upon the earth" (7:4).
2. "And it came to pass after seven days that the waters of the flood were upon the earth" (7:10).
3. Forty weeks later (280 days—compare 7:11; 8:3,4,5,6) Noah sent forth the dove and the raven (8:7, 8).
4. "And he stayed yet other seven days; and again he sent forth

the dove" (8:10).
5. "And he stayed yet other seven days; and sent forth the dove" (8:12).
6. Noah and his family left the ark exactly 371 days, or 53 weeks, after they had entered it (compare verses 7:11, 8:3, 4; 8:14).

Whether these repeated references to actions taken every seven days imply that they all took place on God's rest day is not stated, although it does seem probable. In any case, it is clear that both God and Noah were ordering events in terms of a seven-day cycle.

During the centuries from Noah to Moses, there was little occasion to refer to the week as such. However, there seem to be at least two allusions to it, in the story of Jacob and Leah ("fulfill her week," Genesis 29:27, 28) and in the story of Jacob's burial (Genesis 50:10).

Whatever form of Sabbath observance might have been practiced by the early patriarchs, it is probable that the long servitude in Egypt caused many to forget its religious significance, even though the weekly cycle was still followed. When the time came for God to redeem His people, however, He began to remind them of its importance. In preparation for the great Passover deliverance, He commanded: "Seven days shall ye eat unleavened bread . . . . And in the first day there shall be an holy convocation, and in the seventh day there shall be an holy convocation to you; no manner of work shall be done in them, save that which every man must eat, that only may be done of you" (Exodus 13:15, 16). In this preparation for the incorporation of the Sabbath into the Ten Commandments, it is interesting to note that both the *First* Day and the *Seventh* Day were days of rest and worship!

The Ten Commandments

Soon after this, the Israelites were strongly reminded that a seventh day each week was intended to be a day of rest, as God illustrated with the manna (Exodus 16:4, 5, 25-30), which fell for six days each week and was withheld by God on the seventh. They were instructed to collect only what they needed for each day. Anything that was left over spoiled before the next day—but not the extra that they kept over from the day before the Sabbath, when God would send no manna. Finally, Sabbath observance was incorporated as the fourth in the array of Ten Commandments recorded for Israel by the very finger of God on tables of stone (Exodus 31:18).

> Remember the Sabbath Day to keep it holy. Six days shalt thou labour, and do all thy work: But the seventh day is the Sabbath of the Lord thy God: in it thou shalt not do any work . . . (Exodus 20:8-10).

It should be stressed again that the Sabbath observance was by no means established here for the first time. The Israelites, however, were now commanded to *remember* the Sabbath and to *keep it holy,* as it should have been since God so pronounced it following the creation. The Lord's holy day may have been neglected by God's chosen people, or even forgotten altogether by most other nations, but it was still God's primeval commandment. At this time, God stressed again that the basis for the commandment was not regional but universal, relating to the entire creation. "For in six days the Lord made heaven and earth, the sea, and all that in them is, and rested the seventh day: wherefore the Lord blessed the Sabbath Day, and hallowed it" (Exodus 20:11). A commandment intended for *all* people should certainly be obeyed by the *chosen* people!

Christ, the Lord of the Sabbath

With the passing of the centuries, the Sabbath eventually became almost exclusively associated with the religious ceremonies of the nation of Israel, even though the Creator had hallowed it originally for all men. When that Creator eventually became man, however, in the person of Jesus Christ, He stressed that it had never been intended as a mere Jewish religious ritual, as the Pharisees had distorted it, but for the good of all men. "The Sabbath was made for man, and not man for the Sabbath" (Mark 2:27). All men needed to have a day of rest (for their own *physical* good) and worship, and to regularly remind themselves of the great truth of creation (for their *spiritual* good). And they needed to remember continually that the one who came to redeem them is also the one who had created them. "Therefore, the Son of man is Lord also of the Sabbath," He said (Matthew 12:28).

It was appropriate, therefore, that after Christ's death and resurrection, Christians from every nation soon began once again to observe one day in every seven as a day of rest, as they heard and believed the gospel of Christ. Now, however, there were two great works of God to commemorate, the completion of creation and the completion of redemption. As Christ had long ago finished the work of creation (Colossians 1:16), so

He could now report once again to the Father: "I have finished the work which thou gavest me to do" (John 17:4). This work was climaxed with the great victory cry from the cross: "It is finished!" (John 19:30).

For a time, Jewish Christians continued to participate both in the synagogue services on the seventh day each week (e.g., Acts 17:2) and also in Christian services on the first day of the week (Acts 20:7). Eventually, as they were more and more excluded from the synagogue, they observed only the Lord's day, on the first day of the week (I Corinthians 16:2), thereby honoring Christ simultaneously as both Creator and resurrected Savior.

The Lord's Day

There was discussion for a long time (continuing in some degree even today) as to whether Christian churches, once they were completely separated from the Jewish assemblies, should observe the Lord's day on the seventh day of the week as the Jews did, or on the first day of the week, as the day of Christ's resurrection. Without entering into this particular discussion, the important point to note here is the fact that Christians never even *questioned* the necessity for a weekly "rest day" on which especially to honor the Lord. That need was taken for granted, regardless of whether the "Sabbath" was to be observed on Saturday or Sunday. ("Sabbath," in Hebrew means neither Saturday nor Sunday, neither seventh day nor first day, but *rest* day!). In view of the chaotic state of ancient chronology, there is obviously no way of knowing which day of the modern week is an exact multiple of seven days since God's first rest day.

Those Christians who worship on Saturday believe that the Sabbath cycle has been kept intact ever since the creation and so they follow the practice of today's orthodox Jews, who make the same assumption. Other Christians, however, point out that the present Jewish calendar was not established until the fourth century A.D., so there is neither historical nor scientific basis for insisting that our present Saturday was the primeval Sabbath. Some Christian writers have argued that our modern Sunday was the ancient Sabbath and others have maintained that the day of the week on which the Sabbath fell actually changed from year to year, being affected by Sabbaths other than the weekly Sabbath, including one which extended for two days each year. The "long day" of Joshua (Joshua 10:13, 14) also must have affected the weekly cycle in some as yet uncertain fashion. In any case, the important consideration is the *fact* of a weekly "Lord's Day," rather than the particular day of the modern weekly cycle on which it is observed.

It is significant that the Ten Commandments, representing God's ineffable and unchanging holiness as they do, even though specifically written down in the Mosaic law for Israel's sake, are also written in the consciences of all men (Romans 2:14, 15). Consequently, these commandments were accepted and applied in the New Testament, as well (e.g., Romans 13:9; Ephesians 6:2; etc.).

This affirmation is clearly implied for the Sabbath commandment in particular. "For He spake in a certain place of the seventh day on this wise, and God did rest the seventh day from all His works. . . . There remaineth therefore a rest to the people of God" (Hebrews 4:4, 9). In this passage in Hebrews (verses 1-11), the English word "rest" occurs nine times. All except one of these are translations of essentially the same Greek word *(Katapausis)*, implying rest from labor. The exception is in verse 9: "There is yet reserved therefore a Sabbath rest (Greek *sabbatismos*, derived from *sabbaton*, "Sabbath") to the people of God." This is the only occurrence of this particular word in the New Testament.

In context, the writer is showing that the ultimate "rest" for God's people, which was typically portrayed by God's rest after creation and which was therefore typified by every weekly Sabbath observance, was not attained in Canaan under either Joshua or David, and was still reserved for the future even after Christ had returned to heaven and the Christian era had begun. Since the *antitype* is yet future, therefore, the *type* must still be in operation, just as the animal sacrifices in the temple did not cease until Christ "had offered one sacrifice for sins for ever" (Hebrews 10:12). This fact, combined with the evident fact that all the early Christians continued to observe a weekly "Lord's day," and that nowhere in the New Testament was it stated that "Sabbath" observance should cease, makes it clear that this commandment, like all the Ten Commandments, applies in the Christian dispensation, as well as in the Mosaic dispensation, though not with the same applications and penalties that related specifically to the Mosaic ordinances. As a matter of fact, God's people will continue to observe a weekly Sabbath even in the coming kingdom age (note Isaiah 66:22, Ezekiel 46:3).

All of this is the tremendous testimony of the seven-day week and, especially, of the day of rest which marks its boundaries. *Its very existence can only be explained by the reality of a primeval six-day completed creation!* God desires that we never forget that He is both our Creator and Redeemer, and also that we continually look forward to the eventual fulfillment of all His creative and redemptive purposes, when they are finally consummated in that eternal Rest for all the people of God in the ages to come.

NOAH AND THE FAITH THAT SAVES

One of the most thrilling aspects of the study of the early chapters of human history has always been the story of Noah. The Scriptures speak of "giants in the earth in those days" (Genesis 6:4), and these were not only giants in physical stature but giants in wickedness—"the earth also was corrupt before God, and the earth was filled with violence" (Genesis 6:11).

But Noah was also a giant—a *spiritual* giant! "Noah was a just man and perfect in his generations, and Noah walked with God" (Genesis 6:9).

Neither Satan nor Adam had believed the Word of their Creator, and thus they rebelled against His Word and disobeyed His Word. The result was Satan's expulsion from heaven and Adam's expulsion from Eden. Sin came into the world, and death by sin. There finally came a time when the world was filled to the brim with unbelief and wickedness, and no one but Noah heeded any more the words of its King.

Christ said (Luke 17:26) that the last days before His coming would be like Noah's days. As we confront the secularized world of our generation, we can profit much by studying and emulating Noah's example in his generation. Consider the following:

1. First of all, "Noah found grace in the eyes of the Lord" (Genesis 6:8). This is the first mention of *grace* in the Bible. Before anyone can expect to be used by God in this generation, as in that generation, he must first be the recipient of God's saving grace, entering into the family of God through faith in the Savior, Jesus Christ. Such faith is, basically, simply a firm trust that what God says is true, and what He promises, He will do. In Noah's case, as in the case of every true believer who has exercised saving faith through the ages, such faith is warranted by virtue of the simple fact

that He is the Creator!

2. Twice it is stated (Genesis 6:22; 7:5) that "Noah did according to *all* that God commanded him." When God's Word directed him to build an immense boat, he proceeded to build it according to the exact instruction; when the Word told him to take two of every kind of land animal into the boat, that he did. By any measure of the science and experience of his day, such actions were altogether foolish, but Noah believed and obeyed God's Word. In our day, we are ill-advised if we try to pick and choose among the Scriptures, believing only those portions that seem acceptable to current human experience and scientific philosophy. We must live today "by *every* word of God" if we are to win victory over the devil (Luke 4:4).

3. Noah had to confront the uniformitarians of his day, as we do in ours. The meteorologists had never seen rain at all (Genesis 2:5) and the hydrologists knew nothing of even a local flood, let alone a worldwide flood. The geologists knew where to find metals and precious stones (Genesis 2:12), but it is unlikely they had ever seen any fossils or earth movements. Nevertheless, Noah believed and preached God's Word, though his "model" of coming catastrophism was so contrary to common scientific experience that he never gained any followers. He, "being warned of God of things not seen as yet" (Hebrews 11:7), simply continued to pattern his preaching and practice after God's precepts. And so should we.

4. Though Noah gained few (none, so far as the record goes) converts in the world, his faithfulness did at least result in the saving of his own household. "Come thou and all thy house into the ark: for thee have I seen righteous before me in this generation" (Genesis 7:1). "He prepared an ark to the saving of his house" Hebrews (11:7). Christian parents today are rightly exercised about the ungodly influences of the world—especially the educational system and the media of communication—on their own children. The easy way is to drift, to compromise, to seek worldly advantage and recognition for them. But this is the way to lose them! The way to save them is, like Noah, to stand strong, to preach righteousness, to pray much, to work hard, to believe and obey God's Word in all its fulness and simplicity.

Of all the great men of faith catalogued in the famous "faith chapter" (Hebrews 11), Noah's description stands out like a beacon, being the only one which both begins and ends with the phrase "by faith" (Hebrews 11:7). Noah's tremendous faith in the Word of his Creator God and in its saving power is an incomparable example for believers today.

Modern subjectivist Christianity often stresses the importance of "faith," and the Bible does teach that faith is essential for salvation. But saving faith is not merely an emotion. Faith must have an object, and saving faith must have an object with the ability to save. It is significant that the very first object of faith mentioned in the "faith chapter" is the fact of special creation (Hebrews 11:3) by the Word of God. Noah believed that His Creator God was telling the truth, and therefore he obeyed His instructions. Consequently, he and his family were saved through the judgment of the great Flood.

It is no different today. We are saved, like Noah, by grace through faith—faith in the trustworthy Word of the One who created us and who alone provides salvation.

THE GOSPEL OF CREATION

Before His return to heaven, after His resurrection, the Lord Jesus Christ gave the great commission to all His disciples: "Go ye into all the world, and preach the gospel to every creature" (Mark 16:15).

In order to obey this most important commandment, it is essential that believers understand exactly what the gospel is. The word itself (Greek *euaggelion*) as applied to the true Gospel, occurs 74 times in the New Testament, and a related word *(euaggelizo)* is translated "preach the gospel" 22 times and "bring glad (or good) tidings" 5 times. The word means "the good news," and in all 101 of the above occurrences is applied to the good news concerning the Lord Jesus Christ.

It seems very significant that, of these 101 references to the gospel of Christ, the *central* reference is I Corinthians 15:1. The passage (I Corinthians 15:1-4) is, above all others, the *definition* passage for the gospel. It is here defined as the good news "that Christ died for our sins according to the scriptures; and that He was buried, and that He rose again the third day according to the scriptures." Thus, the central focus of the true gospel is the substitutionary death, physical burial, and bodily resurrection of Jesus Christ.

Note also four vital facts concerning this gospel: (1) it is something to be "received" and "believed" by faith, once for all; (2) it is the means by which we are "saved," continually and forever; (3) it is the fact upon which we firmly "stand;" (4) it is emphatically to be defined, understood, and preached "according to the scriptures."

Although this is the central and key verse for the gospel, all other 100 occurrences are likewise important, if it is truly to be preached "according to the scriptures." It is especially important to study its first and last occurrences.

The first occurrence is in Matthew 4:23, which speaks of Jesus Himself "preaching of the gospel of Jesus Christ, the Son of God" (Mark 1:1), it was vital that those who believed and preached the gospel stress its final consummation, when Jesus Christ would finally be acknowledged by every creature to be "King of Kings and Lord of Lords" (Revelation 19:16).

The last occurrence of the word is in Revelation 14:6, which says the gospel is "the everlasting gospel" that must be preached to all nations and furthermore, that its greatest emphasis must be to "worship Him that made heaven, and earth, and the sea, and the fountains of waters" (Revelation 14:7). Thus, the first occurrence of "gospel" looks ahead to the consummation of all things and the last occurrence stresses the initial creation of all things. As the consummation approaches, it is increasingly important that men look back to the creation. But the creation was saved and the consummation assured when the great Creator and Consummator paid the infinite price for the world's redemption, when He died on the cross and rose again.

The gospel thus entails the full scope of the work of Jesus Christ, from creation to consummation, involving the whole sweep of His redemptive purpose in history. Only this is the gospel "according to the scriptures." One does not truly preach the gospel without emphasizing both the initial special creation of all things by the omnipotent Word of God and also the final consummation of God's purpose in creation itself, as well as the central core of the gospel, the atoning death and triumphant victory over death achieved by the incarnate Creator and Redeemer.

The same threefold work of Christ is expounded in Colossians 1:16-20. "By Him were all things created." Then, "by Him all things are being conserved (or saved)." Finally, "by Him all things are reconciled." Similarly, in Hebrews 1:2, He "made the worlds," then "upholds all things," and ultimately becomes "heir of all things." "For of Him, and through Him, and to Him, are all things: to whom be glory forever. Amen" (Romans 11:36).

The gospel of the Lord Jesus Christ therefore encompasses the threefold work of Christ—Creation, Conservation, Consummation—past, present, and future. One preaches a gospel with no foundation if he neglects or distorts the creation, a gospel with no power if he omits the cross and the empty tomb, and a gospel with no hope if he ignores or denies the coming kingdom. He preaches the gospel "according to the scriptures" only if all three are preached in fulness.

In light of these facts, how sadly mistaken are the great numbers of "evangelicals" (a word meaning "those who preach the gospel") who oppose or neglect the doctrine of creation. They tell us not to "waste time on peripheral controversies such as the evolution-creation question—just preach the gospel," not realizing that the gospel includes creation and *precludes* evolution! They say we should simply "emphasize saving faith, not faith in creation," forgetting that the greatest chapter on faith in the Bible (Hebrews 11) begins by stressing faith in the *ex nihilo* creation of all things by God's Word (verse 3) as preliminary to meaningful faith in any of His promises (verse 13). They advise us merely to "preach Christ," but ignore the fact that Christ was Creator before He became the Savior, and that His finished work of salvation is meaningful only in light of His finished work of creation (Hebrews 4:3-10). They may wish, in order to avoid the offense of the true gospel, to regard creation as an unimportant matter, but God considered it so important that it was the subject of His first revelation. The first chapter of Genesis is the foundation of the Bible; if the foundation is undermined, the superstructure soon collapses.

Furthermore, in light of Revelation 14:6,7, it becomes more important to emphasize creation with every day that passes. Satanic opposition intensifies as the end approaches. The antigospel of Antichrist, as discussed in the next chapter, can be effectively corrected only by the true gospel of the true Christ.

3

The

World Against Creation

*. . . evolution is nothing less than
the foundation of the
"anti-gospel" of antichrist.*

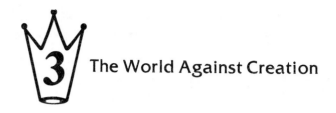

The World Against Creation

THE ANTIGOSPEL OF EVOLUTION

If creation is indeed the very foundation of the gospel of Christ, as demonstrated in the preceding chapter, then evolution is nothing less than the foundation of the "anti-gospel" of antichrist. Evolutionists often profess that evolution is the "scientific" way of looking at nature, whereas creation is "religious" requiring a naive faith in the supernatural. They thereby misidentify "naturalistic" with "scientific" and "super-naturalistic" with "unscientific," thus altogether ignoring the more rigorous definition of "science" as *knowledge,* or *truth!* As will be shown later, belief in evolution requires a high degree of credulous faith, not in the supernatural, but in the *anti-natural*—belief in processes which operate completely in contradiction to all the *actually observed facts* of science, and in contradiction to the basic scientific principle of causality.

The Evolutionary Religion

Evolutionism is, therefore, in every sense of the word a religion, not a science. It is a naive faith, a credulous belief, not based on scientific facts but on personal prejudice, an innate desire to find ultimate reality in *anything* except the true Creator. In contrast to the gospel according to the Scriptures, the evolutionary system is a religion diametrically in contrast to Christianity. The true gospel is "good news:" evolution is "bad news." Christ offers purpose and hope for eternity; evolution proffers randomness and uncertainty forever.

In the true gospel, the Lord Jesus Christ is the omniscient Creator. In evolution, God was replaced by natural selection.

> Darwin pointed out that no supernatural designer was needed; since natural selection could account for any known form of life, there was no room for a supernatural agency in its evolution.[1]

> For the devout of past centuries such perfection of adaptation seemed to provide irrefutable proof of the wisdom of the Creator. For the modern biologist

---

1. Julian Huxley in *Issues in Evolution,* Sol Tax, Editor, University of Chicago Press, 1960), p. 45.

it is evidence for the remarkable effectiveness of
natural selection.[1]

The essense of Darwinism lies in a single phrase:
natural selection is the creative force of evolutionary
change. No one denies that natural selection will play
a negative role in eliminating the unfit. Darwinian
theories require that it create the fit as well.[2]

Natural selection, however, is powerless to create or change
anything by itself, serving only to "select" and "save" those
features generated by the remarkable phenomenon known as
genetic mutation.

The process of mutation ultimately furnishes the
materials for adaptation to changing environments.
Genetic variations which increase the reproductive
fitness of a population to its environment are
preserved and multiplied by natural selection.[3]

However, mutations are not creative either. They have no
purpose or program, but occur strictly at random.

It remains true to say that we know of no way
other than random mutation by which new hereditary
variation comes into being.[4]

Natural selection was believed by evolutionists to have eliminated the need for an intelligent Creator, but natural selection
must wait for mutations, and mutations depend on chance! The
gospel of Christ is one of creative purpose; evolution bids us
worship the great god Chance!

The gospel of Christ is "according to the scriptures," which
were recorded as "holy men of God spake as they were moved
by the Holy Ghost" (II Peter 1:21). The antigospel of evolution
also has its scriptures, but instead of Moses, David, and Paul,
its prophets have names like Darwin, Huxley, and Dobzhansky—against whom none in the academic world dare speak lest
they be excommunicated.

The antigospel of evolution, while often professing to be
strictly empirical and scientific, is in reality a full-fledged

1. Ernst Mayr, "Behaviour Programs and Evolutionary Strategies," *American
   Scientist* (Vol. 62, November-December, 1974), p. 650.
2. Stephen Jay Gould, "The Return of the Hopeful Monsters," *Natural
   History,* Vol. LXXXVI, June-July 1977, p. 28.
3. Francisco J. Ayala, "Genotype, Environment, and Population Numbers,"
   Science, Vol. 162, December 27, 1968, p. 1456.
4. C. H. Waddington, *The Nature of Life* (New York, Anthenium, 1962),
   p. 98.

religious system, complete with cosmology, soteriology, ethics, and eschatology.

Since man is believed to be the highest achievement of evolution to date, its leading proponents have even elevated man to the position of deity. Evolution has become "incarnate" in man, and thus man can now worship himself, in a formal system of religion called humanism. He not only is the *product* of evolution, but can now even *control his future evolution,* so he believes.

> Humanism is the belief that man shapes his own destiny. It is a constructive philosophy, a nontheistic religion, a way of life.[1]

> Man created himself even as he created his culture and thereby he became dependent upon it.[2]

> In giving rise to man, the evolutionary process has, apparently for the first and only time in the history of the Cosmos, become conscious of itself.[3]

That humanism is nothing but evolutionism formalized as man-worship is indicated by one of the founders of the Humanist Association, leading evolutionist Julian Huxley:

> I use the word humanist to mean someone who believes that man is just as much a natural phenomenon as an animal or plant; that his body, mind, and soul were not supernaturally created but are products of evolution, and that he is not under the control or guidance of any supernatural being or beings, but has to rely on himself and his own powers.[4]

Another founding father of the American Humanist Association was John Dewey, the man more responsible than any other single individual for the secularization and antitheistic bias of the American public education system. Dewey was an evolutionary pantheist, regarding man as the most highly evolved animal and thus as the personification of evolution.

> There are no doubt sufficiently profound distinctions between the ethical process and the cosmic

1. Promotional brochure, American Humanist Association, distributed by Humanist Society of San Jose, California.
2. Rene Dubos, "Humanistic Biology," *American Scientist,* Vol. 53, March, 1965, p. 8.
3. Theodosius Dobzhansky, "Changing Man," *Science,* Vol. 155, January 27, 1967, p. 409.
4. Julian Huxley, American Humanist Association promotional brochure, *op cit.*

process as it existed prior to man and to the formation of human society. So far as I know, however, all of these differences are summed up in the fact that the process and the forces bound up with the cosmic have come to consciousness in man.[1]

Anticipation by Biblical Prophecy

Evolution, or evolutionary humanism, is thus in effect a state-established religion in which the true God of creation has been replaced by random forces and then by man himself. That this is essentially the philosophy of the coming antichrist and his world government is indicated by many of the prophetic Scriptures.

> Who changed the truth of God into a lie, and worshipped and served the creature more than the Creator, who is blessed forever. Amen (Romans 1:25).
>
> . . . there shall come a falling away first, and that man of sin be revealed who opposeth and exalteth himself above all that is called God . . . (II Thessalonians 2:3, 4).
>
> And he shall speak great words against the most High . . . and think to change times and laws (Daniel 7:25).
>
> Neither shall he regard the God of his fathers, nor the desire of women, nor regard any god; for he shall magnify himself above all. But in his estate shall he honor the God of forces (Daniel 11:37, 38).
>
> And he opened his mouth in blasphemy against God . . . and all that dwell upon the earth shall worship him (Revelation 13:6, 7).

In addition to its deification of man, evolutionary humanism incorporates all the other attributes of a complete system of religion. Consider the following facts.

1. It is not merely a theory of biology or anthropology, but rather is a complete *cosmology,* embracing everything in space and time in its system.

> Evolution comprises all the stages of the development of the universe: the cosmic, biological, and

---

1. John Dewey, "Evolution and Ethics," *Scientific Monthly,* Vol. 78, February, 1954, p. 66.

human or cultural developments.[1]

Most enlightened persons now accept as a fact that everything in the cosmos—from heavenly bodies to human beings—has developed and continues to develop through evolutionary processes.[2]

Our present knowledge indeed forces us to the view that the whole of reality *is* evolution—a single process of self-transformation.[3]

Man's worldview today is dominated by the knowledge that the universe, the stars, the earth, and all living things have evolved through a long history that was not foreordained or programmed . . . .[4]

In this picture of total evolution, the eternal God is replaced by *eternal matter,* which has through billions of years evolved itself from primeval randomly-moving particles into complex particular people and cultures. The process of "creation" is replaced by random mutations and natural selection.

2. Evolutionary humanism incorporates a system of *soteriology*—that is, a doctrine of salvation. In the gospel of Christ, salvation is obtained by grace through faith in the substitutionary death of Christ for man's sins. The anti-gospel, however, proposes that man must save himself.

Through the unprecedented faculty of long-range foresight, jointly serviced and exercised by us, we can, in securing and advancing our position, increasingly avoid the missteps of blind nature, circumvent its cruelties, reform our own natures, and enhance our own **values.**[5]

Evolutionary man can no longer take refuge from his loneliness by creeping for shelter into the arms of a divinized father figure whom he himself has **created.**[6]

1. Theodosius Dobzhansky, "Changing Man," *Science,* Vol. 155, January 27, 1967, p. 409.
2. Rene Dubos, "Humanistic Biology," *American Scientist,* Vol. 53, March, 1965, p. 6.
3. Julian Huxley, "Evolution and Genetics," in *What Is Man?* (Ed. by J.R. Newman, New York, Simon and Schuster, 1955), p. 278.
4. Ernst Mayr, "Evolution," *Scientific American,* Vol. 239, September, 1978, p. 47.
5. H.J. Muller, "Human Values in Relation to Evolution," *Science,* Vol. 127, March 21, 1958, p. 629.
6. Julian Huxley, Keynote address at Darwin Centennial Convocation, University of Chicago, November 27, 1959.

No deity will save us; we must save ourselves.[1]

3. Evolution also proposes and endorses a system of "scientific" *ethics*. The ethical system of the Christian gospel is based on love for Christ and one's fellow men. That of evolutionary humanism is based on whatever is judged, by the scientific and political establishments, to be conducive to further evolutionary progress in human societies. Since these establishments vary in space and time, so do their particular evolutionary ethical systems.

Suffice it to mention the so-called Social Darwinism, which often sought to justify the inhumanity of man to man, and the biological racism which furnished a fraudulent scientific sanction for the atrocities committed in Hitler's Germany and elsewhere . . . . [2]

The law of evolution, as formulated by Darwin, provides an explanation of wars between nations, the only reasonable explanation known to us.[3]

Unbridled self-indulgence on the part of one generation without regard to future ones is the modus operandi of biological evolution and may be regarded as rational behavior.[4]

The evolutionary basis of racism, imperialism, and economic exploitation are not commonly defended by evolutionists today, but modern evolutionists are no less ready to formulate their own ethical systems, usually in terms of evolutionary socialism.

The foregoing conclusions represent, I believe, an outgrowth of the thesis of modern humanism, as well as of the study of evolution, that the primary job for man is to promote his own welfare and advancement, both that of his members considered individually and that of the all-inclusive group in due awareness of the world as it is, and on the basis of naturalistic, scientific ethics.[5]

1. 1974 Manifesto of American Humanist Association.
2. Theodosius Dobzhansky, "Evolution at Work," *Science,* May 9, 1958, p. 1091.
3. Arthur Keith, *Evolution and Ethics* (New York, G.P. Putnam's Sons, 1947), p. 149.
4. W.H. Murdy, "Anthropocentrism: A Modern Version," *Science,* Vol. 187, March 28, 1975, p. 1172.
5. H.J. Muller "Human Values in Relation to Evolution," *Science,* Vol. 127, March 21, 1958, p. 629.

Christian standards of ethical behavior are, of course, codified and explained in the Bible, and are given by divine revelation for man's guidance and benefit. Evolutionary ethics can never be absolute, but must themselves evolve.

Thus, human "goodness" and behavior considered ethical by human societies probably are evolutionary acquisitions of man and require fostering . . . . An ethical system that bases its premises on absolute pronouncements will not usually be acceptable to those who view human nature by evolutionary criteria.[1]

4. Evolution even has an *eschatology,* a doctrine of future things. To considerable degree, of course, this merges with its soteriology, since salvation is not believed to apply to any future life but to this life and this world only. Humanists believe, however, that by manipulation of the evolutionary process, both genetically and sociologically, a glorious future awaits mankind.

We no longer need be subject to blind external forces but can manipulate the environment and eventually may be able to manipulate our genes.[2]

Man's unique characteristic among animals is his ability to direct and control his own evolution, and science is his most powerful tool for doing this.[3]

Thus, exactly as does the Christian gospel, the antigospel of evolution also has a doctrine of origins, a system of morals and ethics, a way of salvation, and a doctrine of consummation, all of which are polar opposites of the corresponding aspects of the true gospel. Evolution is nothing but a naturalistic religious system, erected in opposition to the gospel of supernatural creation, conservation, and consummation centered in Christ and revealed in Scripture.

THE MOTIVATIONS OF EVOLUTIONARY HUMANISM

The modern creationist movement and the resistance of secular educators to this movement have certainly brought into clear focus one very important fact. Our American public schools and secular universities are controlled by the religious philoso-

---

1. Arno G. Motulsky, "Brave New World?" *Science,* Vol. 185, August 23, 1974, p. 654.
2. *Ibid,* p. 653.
3. Hudson Hoagland, "Science and the New Humanism," *Science,* Vol. 143, January 10, 1964, p. 111.

phy of evolutionary humanism. Furthermore, through its pervasive influence on the graduate schools and the textbook publishers, this powerful concept has had significant impact even on most Christian schools.

Resistance to the proposed teaching of theistic creationism as an alternative to evolutionism commonly masquerades under the supposed authority of "science." The anti-creationist manifesto of the American Humanist Association proclaims the following:

> There are no alternatives to the principle of evolution, with its "tree of life" pattern, that any competent biologist of today takes seriously . . . . Evolution is therefore the only view that should be expounded in public-school courses on science.[1]

The Unscientific Nature Of Evolution

That evolution is *not* science, however, has not only been clearly demonstrated by the many modern publications of creationist scientists[2], but also is frequently recognized even by evolutionist scientists. For example, Loren Eisely says:

> With the failure of these many efforts, science was left in the somewhat embarrassing position of having to postulate theories of living origins which it could not demonstrate. After having chided the theologian for his reliance on myth and miracle, science found itself in the unenviable position of having to create a mythology of its own: namely, the assumption that what, after long effort could not be proved to take place today had, in truth, taken place in the primeval past.[3]

In fact there are now many evolutionists who recognize that

---

1. American Humanist Association, "A Statement Affirming Evolution as a Principle of Science," *The Humanist,* January-February, 1977, Vol. XXXVII, p. 4. This manifesto was prepared by a committee composed of Bette Chambers (A.H.A. president), Isaac Asimov, Hudson Hoagland, Chauncey Leake, Linus Pauling, and George Gaylord Simpson and signed by 163 others, most of whom are prominent humanistic educators—including psychologists Carl Rogers and B.F. Skinner, left-wing philosopher Corliss Lamont, anthropologist Sol Tax, and others.
2. For example, see *Scientific Creationism* (Ed. by Henry M. Morris; San Diego, Creation-Life Publishers, 1974, 277 pp.) Also note that the Creation Research Society has approximately 650 members, all with graduate degrees in science from accredited universities.
3. Loren Eisely, *The Immense Journey* (New York: Random House, 1957), p. 199.

the "theory of evolution" is really a tautology, with no predictive value.

> I argue that the "theory of evolution" does not
> make predictions, so far as ecology is concerned, but
> is instead a logical formula which can be used only
> to classify empiricisms and to show the relationships
> which such a classification implies . . . . these
> theories are actually tautologies and, as such, cannot
> make empirically testable predictions. *They are not
> scientific theories at all.*[1]

Even the writer of the Foreword of the 1971 edition of Darwin's *Origin of the Species,* himself a distinguished evolutionary biologist, has frankly recognized that evolution is simply a belief.

> [The theory of evolution] forms a satisfactory
> faith on which to base our interpretation of nature.[2]

Evolution is thus admittedly not scientifically testable, even though it is taught very dogmatically in most public schools. However, educators insist that creationism and theism must be excluded from education on the ground that they are not scientific!

This rejection is often emphatic and even slanderous. Dr. Preston Cloud of the University of California at Santa Barbara, for example, becomes quite melodramatic.

> Religious bigotry is abroad again in the land . . . .
> Although the creationists may be irrational, . . .
> they have proven themselves to be skillful tacticians,
> good organizers, and uncompromising adversar-
> ies . . . . And anyone who has studied their benign
> manner in public debate, their tortured logic and their
> often scurrilous expression in books and tracts for
> the faithful, has little difficulty in visualizing crea-
> tionist polemicists, given the opportunity, in the role
> of Pius V himself.[3]

This is not the language of objective science, of course, but of religious emotion. Dr. Cloud failed to mention that he had himself participated in such a debate on his own campus, before

---

1. R.H. Peters, "Tautology in Evolution and Ecology," *American Naturalist,* Vol. 110, No. 1, 1976, p. 1. Emphasis his.
2. L. Harrison Matthews, "Introduction to *Origin of Species"* (London, J.M. Dent, 1977), p. xii.
3. Preston Cloud, "Scientific Creationism. A New Inquisition," *The Humanist,* Vol. XXXVII, January-February, 1977, p. 67.

an audience composed mainly of university students, the large majority of whom had voted after the debate that the creationists had a better *scientific* case than the evolutionists. As a matter of fact, a common complaint at the debate was that the evolutionists had not presented a consistent scientific case at all, while the creationists had dealt *only* with science.

If creationists are, as Cloud declares, "bigots," he should recognize that there are other bigots also. One of the nation's top scientists has charged:

> One of the most astonishing characteristics of scientists is that some of them are plain, old-fashioned bigots. Their zeal has a fanatical, egocentric quality characterized by disdain and intolerance for anyone or any value not associated with a special area of intellectual activity.[1]

The fact is, however, that creationists are not attempting to oust evolutionary humanism from the public schools, but only to obtain a fair hearing for theistic creationism as an alternative. Both concepts involve faith and neither is scientifically testable in the ultimate sense.

> A hypothesis is empirical or scientific only if it can be tested by experience . . . . A hypothesis or theory which cannot be, at least in principle, falsified by empirical observations and experiments does not belong to the realm of science.[2]

Although the author of the above statement is a leading evolutionary biologist, it is obvious that his definition would exclude evolution, no less than creation, from the realm of science. In fact, a creationist might legitimately argue that evolution actually has been tested, *and disproved,* since it has never been observed in action and since it contradicts the scientific law of increasing entropy or disorder. One must, therefore, not only believe in evolution *without* evidence, *but in spite of the evidence.* Evolutionists walk by faith, not by sight!

Impact on Non-scientific Fields

Furthermore, not only is evolution taught in the schools as a scientific dogma, but as basic in all the social sciences and

1. Philip H. Abelson, "Bigotry in Science," *Science,* Vol. 144, April 24, 1964, p. 373.
2. Francisco J. Ayala, "Biological Evolution: Natural Selection or Random Walk?" *American Scientist,* Vol. 62, Nov.-Dec., 1974, p. 700.

humanities as well. It is, in fact, a complete worldview, purporting to explain the origin, development, and meaning of all
things.

The place of biological evolution in human thought
was, according to Dobzhansky, best expressed in a
passage that he often quoted from Pierre Teilhard
de Chardin. "[Evolution] is a general postulate to
which all theories, all hypotheses, and all systems
must henceforward bow and which they must satisfy
in order to be thinkable and true. Evolution is a light
which illuminates all facts, a trajectory which all lines
of thought must follow."[1]

Theodosius Dobzhansky, the subject of the eulogy from which
the above quotation was taken, was a church member and
claimed to be a creationist, but he meant by this that the
wonderful process of natural selection had "created" all things!

Dobzhansky was a religious man, although he
apparently rejected fundamental beliefs of traditional
religion, such as the existence of a personal God and
of life beyond physical death . . . . Dobzhansky held
that, in man, biological evolution had transcended
itself into the realm of self-awareness and culture.
He believed that mankind would eventually evolve
into higher levels of harmony and creativity. He was
a metaphysical optimist.[2]

Until his death, Dobzhansky had been probably the world's
leading spokesman for evolution.

From today's perspective, Dobzhansky appears as
perhaps the most eminent evolutionist of the twentieth century.[3]

His influence on the nation's schools has been profound, to
say the least, and he is typical of practically all leaders of
evolutionary thought.

Evolution as a complete system of life and meaning has, in
fact, dominated intellectual thought and the teachings in the
colleges since at least the last quarter of the nineteenth century.

. . . . after a generation of argument, educated

---

1. Francisco Ayala, " 'Nothing in Biology Makes Sense Except in the Light of
   Evolution.' Theodosius Dobzhansky, 1900-1975," *Journal of Heredity,*
   Vol. 68, No. 3, 1977, p. 3.
2. *Ibid,* p. 9.
3. *Ibid,* p. 6.

>Americans in general came to accept the fact of
>evolution and went on to make whatever intellectual
>adjustments they thought necessary.[1]

Once it came to be accepted by the intellectuals, the religious
liberals quickly, and typically, followed along. The most influential of these was the famous Henry Ward Beecher.

>Darwinian evolutionary science presented little or
>no challenge to Beecher's doctrinal beliefs, for
>Beecher's Christianity was already far removed from
>Biblical literalism into a vague poetic emotional
>realm of edifying thoughts, elevated feelings, and
>joyful noises unto the Lord.[2]

Beecher published his *Evolution and Religion* in 1883, and its
arguments are still being repeated almost verbatim by theistic
evolutionists today. Very quickly after that, evolution began
to dominate the public schools.

>In a nation that was undergoing a tremendous
>urban, industrial, and technological revolution, the
>evolutionary concept presented itself to intellectuals
>as the key to knowledge. And beyond that, the
>technical needs of industry called for a revolution in
>higher education away from the traditional classical
>and moral orientation and toward the sciences . . . .
>which were reclassifying man and society in evolu-
>tionary terms. In general the concept of education
>from kindergarten to graduate school was reoriented
>from the teaching of a fixed body of knowledge
>to the teaching of methods of inquiry to be applied
>to the continually changing facts of existence.[3]

This trend, of course, was tremendously accelerated under
the influence of John Dewey and his disciples in the first half
of the twentieth century, leading finally to the complete
dominance of the public schools by naturalistic evolutionism
and secular humanism at the present time.[4]

It was not always thus in our country or in our public
schools, however, and it is certainly in conformity with Ameri-

1. Gilman M. Ostrander, *The Evolutionary Outlook, 1875-1900,* (Clio,
Michigan, Marston Press, 1971), p. 2.
2. *Ibid,* p. 39.
3. *Ibid,* p. 2.
4. See the writer's book, *Education for the Real World* (San Diego:
Creation-Life Publishers, 1977, pp. 47-105) for further documentation on
the capture and current domination of the public schools by these systems.

can constitutionalism to seek to return the schools to their intended character and purpose.

> The American nation had been founded by intellectuals who had accepted a world view that was based upon Biblical authority as well as Newtonian science. They had assumed that God created the earth and all life upon it at the time of creation and continued without change thereafter. Adam and Eve were God's final creations, and all of mankind was descended from them. When Jefferson, in his old age, was confronted with the newly developing science of geology, he rejected the evolutionary concept of the creation of the earth on the grounds that no all-wise and all-powerful Creator would have gone about the job in such a slow and inefficient way.[1]

Jefferson's argument, of course, is perfectly valid today. The "god" of evolution (in the rationale of de Chardin and the other leaders of theistic evolutionary thought) is certainly not the God of the Bible, the omnipotent and omniscient God of orthodox Judaism and Biblical Christianity. Evolutionary humanism in our schools is not only a religion, but is a religion which opposes Judaism, Christianity, and the Bible in no uncertain terms.

> In cultures such as ours, religion is very often an alien form of life to intellectuals. Living as we do in a post-Enlightenment era, it is difficult for us to take religion seriously. The very concepts seem fantastic to us . . . . That people in our age can believe that they have had a personal encounter with God, that they could believe that they have experienced conversion through a "mystical experience of God," so that they are born again in the Holy Spirit, is something that attests to human irrationality and a lack of a sense of reality.[2]

With this type of attitude dominating the thinking of modern leaders in education, it is not surprising that there is so much resistance to allowing creationism to be returned to the schools. Neither is it surprising that a humanistic and atheistic religious

---

1. Gilman M. Ostrander, *op cit,* p. 1.
2. Kai Nielsen, "Religiosity and Powerlessness: Part III of 'The Resurgence of Fundamentalism,' " *The Humanist,* Vol. XXXVII, May-June, 1977, p. 46.

philosophy in the schools has generated an amoralistic attitude in society, increasing in influence with each emerging generation. A remarkable testimony has been published by Aldous Huxley, one of the most influential writers and philosophers of our day, grandson of evolutionist Thomas Huxley, brother of evolutionist Julian Huxley, and one of the early advocates of a "drug culture" (justifying drugs by the "religious" experiences they induced) and sexual permissiveness.

> I had motives for not wanting the world to have meaning; consequently assumed it had none, and was able without any difficulty to find satisfying reasons for this assumption . . . . The philosopher who finds no meaning in the world is not concerned exclusively with a problem in pure metaphysics; he is also concerned to prove there is no valid reason why he personally should not do as he wants to do . . . . For myself, as no doubt for most of my contemporaries, the philosophy of meaninglessness was essentially an instrument of liberation. The liberation we desired was simultaneously liberation from a certain political and economic system and liberation from a certain system of morality. We objected to the morality because it interfered with our sexual freedom.[1]

The following conclusions are clearly justified by the facts at hand: (1) A system of evolutionary humanism dominates our public schools and this system has produced devastating results in the moral and social realms; (2) neither the philosophy of humanism nor the evolutionary philosophy on which it is based is "scientific," in any proper sense of the term, though both are materialistic and essentially atheistic; (3) the system of evolutionary humanism is, therefore, merely a religious philosophy, a "non-theistic religion," as claimed by the American Humanist Association itself; (4) all the known facts of science (as well as the facts of human experience) correlate with belief in special creation and a personal Creator much better than belief in evolution and humanism correlate with those facts; (5) consequently, the "creation model," and its implications in all fields, should be taught equally and fairly with the "evolution model" in the public schools. All serious-minded and fair-

---

1. Aldous Huxley, "Confessions of a Professed Atheist," *Report: Perspective on the News,* Vol. 3, June, 1966, p. 19.

minded parents, teachers, and school administrators are urged to work diligently to that end.

EVOLUTION AND THE
ILLOGICAL THEOLOGICALS

It is inexcusable for evolutionary scientists to accept evolution as a scientific fact, when all the *facts* of science conflict with evolution and support creation, but at least we can understand their desire to find a naturalistic origin for everything. They feel it to be the peculiar mission of science to explain all physical reality without God. Though we disagree with this idea, we can comprehend it.

But what can we say about those *theologians* who are evolutionists? Why should those whose specialty is "the study of God" (for that is what "theology" means) attempt to explain things without God (for that is what evolution purports to do)? Is this strange behavior occasioned because "they love the praise of men more than the praise of God" (John 12:43)?

They apparently suppose that evolution may be God's method of creation, but this is a serious charge to bring against God. Evolution is the most wasteful, inefficient, cruel way that one could conceive by which to create man. If evolution *is* true, we certainly should not blame God for it!

The famous scientist-philosopher, Bertrand Russell, had some incisive comments to make about such evolutionist theologians in his well-known atheistic book, *Religion and Science:*

Religion, in our day, has accommodated itself to the doctrine of evolution, and has derived new arguments from it. We are told that "through the ages one increasing purpose runs," and that evolution is the unfolding of an idea which has been in the mind of God throughout. It appears that during those ages which so troubled Hugh Miller, when animals were torturing each other with ferocious horns and agonizing stings, Omnipotence was quietly waiting for the ultimate emergence of man, with his still more widely diffused cruelty. Why the Creator should have preferred to reach his goal by a process, instead of going straight to it, these modern theologians do not tell us. Nor do they say much to allay our doubts as to the gloriousness of the consummation.

But can't we be *Christian* evolutionists, they say. Yes, no doubt it is possible to be a Christian and an evolutionist. Likewise, one can be a Christian thief, or a Christian adulterer, or a Christian liar! Christians can be inconsistent and illogical about many things, but that doesn't make them right.

We are thankful for the great numbers of godly theologians who are true to the Scriptures, as well as to the real facts of science, and who therefore are strong creationists. We are concerned and sad for those out-of-character theologues who are not.

One of the most significant aspects of the modern revival of creationism is that it was spearheaded by scientists rather than theologians. As a matter of fact, it is usually easier to convert a scientist to belief in creation than it is to win a "liberal" theologian or philosopher. The latter are more committed to evolution than even evolutionary scientists. Scientists normally deal in facts, whereas liberal religionists, not being experienced in the factual approach to science and having long since rejected the factuality of the Bible, are completely adrift on a sea of metaphysical speculation.

Such liberal theologues (as well as their compromising conservative colleagues) suppose that evolution is God's "method of creation," ignoring the fact that this would make God out to be a monster. Evolution is certainly the most cruel and inefficient process conceivable by which to accomplish "creation." Most leading evolutionary scientists see this clearly, and consider such theologians to be misguided at best.

> The proponents of teleological theories, for all their efforts, have been unable to find any mechanism (except supernatural ones) that can account for their postulated finalism . . . . The frequency of extinction in every geological period is another powerful argument against any finalistic trend toward perfection.[1]

> Judged by scientists and others, much philosophy of science has been downright irrelevant, at best a series of brilliant axiomatic games, more often pretentious nonsense.[2]

Charles Darwin himself, once at least a nominal believer in God (the only degree he ever got was as a divinity student),

---

1. Ernst Mayr, "Evolution," *Scientific American*. Vol. 239, September, 1978, p. 50.
2. June Goodfield, "Humanity in Science," *Phi Beta Kappa Key Reporter*, Summer, 1977, p. 4.

was forced by the very nature of evolutionary theory to realize it was inconsistent with the concept of a wise and loving God. He stressed that, instead of man bringing death into the world, as the Bible teaches (Romans 5:12), death brought man into the world. In the very last paragraph of his *Origin of Species*, he wrote, "Thus, from the war of nature, from famine and death, the most exalted object which we are capable of conceiving, namely, the production of the higher animals, directly follows."

A brilliant young biologist of the present generation, in her book *The Center of Life*, notes the heartless and mindless character of evolution:

> Evolution is a hard, inescapable mistress. There is just no room for compassion or good sportsmanship. Too many organisms are born, so, quite simply, a lot of them are going to have to die, because there isn't enough food and space to go around. You can be beautiful, fat, strong, but it might not matter. The only thing that does matter is whether you leave more children, carrying your genes than the next person leaves. It's true whether you're a prince, a frog, or an American elm. Evolution is a future phenomenon. Are your genes going to be in the next generation? That is all that counts.[1]

This is the system which our illogical theologicals would seek to harmonize with Christianity! The essence of Darwinism is the survival of the fittest (or most prolific) in a life-and-death struggle for existence, with extermination of the weak and unfit. The Lord Jesus Christ, on the other hand, stressed that love and self-sacrifice, with special concern for the weak and helpless, must characterize true Christianity.

Evolutionism is compatible with communism, with fascism, with anarchism, imperialism, and all other systems based on struggle and hatred, but not with Christianity. It is a necessary component of atheism and materialism, but a very unnatural adjunct to theism.

> Marx admired (Darwin's) book not for economic reasons but for the more fundamental one that Darwin's universe was purely materialistic, and the explication of it no longer involved any reference to

1. Lorraine Lee Larison Cudmore, excerpts as quoted in *Science Digest,* Vol. 82, November, 1977, p. 46.

unobservable, non-material causes outside or "beyond" it. In that important respect, Darwin and
Marx were truly comrades.[1]
It is bad enough for theological "liberals" to embrace
evolutionism, but absolutely inexcusable for those who profess
to believe the Bible and to follow Christ. Yet there have been
many Christian leaders ever since Darwin who have led
multitudes down this path of compromise and eventual apos-
tasy, and the same cycle is repeating itself in much of so-
called evangelicalism today.

PROGRESSIVE CREATIONISTS AND
THE STRATEGY OF COMPROMISE

Many evangelicals today, aware of the theological and Biblical objections to theistic evolutionism, yet unwilling to abandon
its geologic-age framework, have resorted to a more subtle
compromise known as "progressive creationism." This system
more or less equates the geological ages with the six days of
creation of Genesis and so is essentially the same as the so-
called "day-age theory." It adopts the standard evolutionary
framework of history but allows God to "create" various
entities along the way, particularly at points where there are
gaps in the fossil record.

The God of the Gaps
Theistic evolutionists tend to ridicule progressive creationists
as relying on a "god-of-the-gaps" concept. That is, to postulate
a spurt of divine creative activity only where fossil gaps require
it, otherwise allowing His "creation" to proceed slowly by
standard evolutionary mechanisms. This is hardly worthy of an
omnipotent, omniscient God. He should certainly be both
powerful enough and intelligent enough either to specially create
all things in the beginning or else to plan and energize the
total evolutionary process from the beginning. Progressive
creationism makes Him appear as sort of a bumbler, having
to step down from heaven at various intervals during the ages
in order to re-direct and re-energize His lagging evolutionary
processes.
Nevertheless, since many Christian churches and schools have
looked upon straight-out evolution with some disfavor, consid-

---

1. Tom Bethell, "Burning Darwin to Save Marx," *Harper's,* December,
   1978, p. 37.

erable numbers of Christian intellectuals, hoping to please both the Christian community and the academic community, have adopted this futile compromise, thus pleasing nobody but themselves. Until the modern revival of creationism, in fact, it had appeared that practically all Christian educational institutions were well on the road to theistic evolutionism, perhaps stopping over tentatively at this half-way house of progressive creationism.

Now, however, large numbers of evangelical scientists have become strict creationists, advocating a commitment even to the recent creation of all things in the six literal days of the Genesis creation week. The number of creationist books, articles, research monographs, seminars, debates, etc. has far surpassed, both in quantity and quality, the efforts of the progressive creationists (including the theistic evolutionists) in recent years.

However, this development has now generated a new spurt of activity among the progressive creationists. Compromising Christians cannot abide Christians who don't compromise for very long, since the very existence of the latter is an indictment against them. True creationists have encountered their most bitter opposition, not from those who are strictly scientific evolutionists, but from those who are either theistic evolutionists or progressive creationists. The latter are much more vocal and vitriolic in their opposition to literal creationism than they are to naturalistic evolutionism. They are quite comfortable with the latter, but stand rebuked by the former.

"Christian" Attacks on True Creationism

A number of books have recently appeared written by progressive creationists attacking the scientific creationists, whom they prefer to identify as "young-earth creationists" or, perhaps, as "flood-geology creationists." Four books in particular may be mentioned, all by authors who are progressive creationists and who advocate the day-age interpretation of Genesis. Two are written by biologists *(God's Time Records in Ancient Sediments,* by Daniel Wonderly and *How to Deal with Evolution,* by Duane Thurman). One is written by two astronomers *(Genesis One and the Origin of the Earth* by Herman J. Eckelman, Jr., and Robert C. Newman).

The most important treatment, however, is written by a Christian Ph.D. geologist who, before he began his graduate studies, had accepted literal creationism and flood geology. This book is *Creation and the Flood*[1] by Davis A. Young, Associate Professor of Geology at the Wilmington branch of North Carolina University. Dr. Young advocates the venerable "day-age theory" as the best means for making the Genesis account of creation acceptable to geologists. Although he rejects theistic evolution, he does allow for much evolution in his system, with only a few possible acts of special creation that are essentially impossible to identify in the fossil record. Since Dr. Young is a Christian geologist, his book has been of great encouragement to those Christian intellectuals who have been deploring the modern creationist movement.

The only creationist book to which Young refers in any significant degree (and which he attacks vigorously) is *The Genesis Flood*.[2] He has practically ignored the numerous more recent books of this writer, as well as those of other creationists, not to mention the many relevant articles in the *Creation Research Society Quarterly*. Furthermore, his book contains neither an index nor a bibliography, unusual omissions for a purportedly scientific book.

He calls the day-age theory, the theory "that I have proposed" (p. 132), but there is nothing new in it except that he distorts Genesis more than most other advocates of the theory, as he tries unsuccessfully to make the order of creation correlate with the fossil record.

There are actually many contradictions[3] between these two sequences, but Young eliminates them merely by having the various days overlap each other. After providing in this way for these various discrepancies he says:

> If such overlap exists, then all apparent discrepancies between Genesis 1 and science would fall away (p. 131).

By such exegesis, one can, of course, make the Bible mean whatever he wishes.

Young's main Biblical basis for taking the creation days as ages is the idea that the seventh day is still going on, since God is still resting from His work of creation. But the Scripture

---

1. This book was published (1977) by Baker Book House, a firm that heretofore had committed itself to publishing only books advocating strict creationism and a literal interpretation of Genesis.
2. John C. Whitcomb and Henry M. Morris, *The Genesis Flood* (Philadelphia, Presbyterian and Reformed, 1961).
3. Henry M. Morris *Biblical Cosmology and Modern Science* (Nutley, N.J., Craig Press, 1970), pp. 56-62.

says that God *rested* (not "is resting") on the seventh day (Genesis 2:2, 3). In fact, Exodus 31:17 says "He rested, and was refreshed." Furthermore, even though God's rest from His work of creation is still continuing, this does not mean the seventh day is still continuing! The fact that God rested on the seventh day in no way precluded Him from continuing to rest on the eighth day and all future days. His one week of six days work followed by a day of rest was sufficient to set the pattern for all future weeks.

The testimony of the Fourth Commandment (Exodus 20:8-11) makes it very plain that the divine week was the pattern for man's week and that the "days" of the one were the same as the "days" of the other. Yet Young believes that the creation days not only lasted almost a billion years each but also that they "overlapped" each other by various amounts. This is a peculiar way for a Christian to deal with the words of God.

Furthermore, Dr. Young glosses over a gross inconsistency in "his" theory. He insists that God is still resting (in order to justify the long day interpretation) but also that the same processes God used to "create" and "make" all things in the six days are still going on (in order to justify his commitment to uniformitarianism). He confesses this to be a problem, but attempts to sidestep it by noting that certain later creative acts of God (e.g., the "creation" of Israel, as mentioned in Isaiah 43:1, 15) involved natural processes.

Such reasoning is specious. The fact that God has occasionally directly performed miracles of creation in human history (the acts of creation were supernatural in every case, though they were sometimes accompanied by God's concurrent use of natural processes) in no way changes the fact that He has said He rested from all His specific work of creating and making the heavens, the earth and all its living creatures (Genesis 2:1-3).

Space does not permit further discussion of Young's theory, though it is filled with many other distortions, both of Genesis and *The Genesis Flood*. He has by no means, answered the overwhelming scientific and Biblical case against the day-age theory.[1]

Young admits that the literal-day interpretation of Genesis not only is a "legitimate" interpretation (p. 44) of the Biblical

---

1. See for example *Scientific Creationism* (ed. by Henry M. Morris, San Diego, Creation-Life Publishers, 1974), pp. 214-230.

text, but also is "the obvious view" (p. 48). His real reason for rejecting it, therefore, is geological, not Biblical. He also rejects flood geology for the same reason, even though he admits the Bible does teach a universal flood (p. 172).

He offers four main geological proofs that a recent creation is impossible. These are: (1) the time required for hot magmas to cool and crystallize; (2) radiometric dating, especially the rubidium-strontium method; (3) the high pressures required to form metamorphic rocks; (4) the time required for continental drift.

"Mature creationists" (the term Young uses for those who accept the Biblical teaching of recent creation and its corollary of flood geology) have, of course, recognized that there are still unresolved *geological* problems in this model. This fact was stressed repeatedly in *The Genesis Flood*. Such problems, however, must not be used (as Young does) to warrant rejection of the plain Biblical record in favor of the model of evolutionary uniformitarianism, which *also* has serious unresolved geological problems. The remaining problems of the flood model can be solved by research—hence the formation of the Creation Research Society and the Institute for Creation Research. Creationists are at a disadvantage, because of their small numbers and financial resources, but they do have the one great advantage of knowing that God, who alone knows the full truth, has written His Word in such terms that its "obvious" implication is one of recent creation and cataclysmic geology.

In the meantime, one would think that Dr. Young could find better evidences for uniformitarianism than the four he proposes. There are few processes involving so many variables and unknowns (and thus so unsuited for determining process rates and time durations) as the formation of igneous and metamorphic rocks, systems of radiometric minerals in such rocks, and the spreading of continents! Uniformitarianism is supposed to be based on present processes, but who has ever measured a cooling batholith or the metamorphosis of a sedimentary rock or the expansion of a sea floor?

Young says (pp. 183-4) that the cooling of New Jersey's basaltic Palisades sill took several hundred years and that of the giant granitic southern California batholith took a million years! He does not indicate how these figures were calculated, but it is obvious they could only be guesses, because of the large number of unknown variables involved in any relevant heat flow and chemical reaction equations. As far as basaltic rocks are concerned, these are at least qualitatively comparable to modern volcanic lava flows, which of course do not take long to cool and crystallize. The cooling of granite batholiths is even more of an enigma, since no one knows for sure how granites are formed in the first place. Furthermore, the flood model would allow at least four thousand years for such cooling. As a matter of fact, the widespread occurence of geothermal springs and similar phenomena near igneous rocks indicate that the cooling is not yet complete in many cases, and this is hard to explain in terms of an old earth.

Metamorphic processes are even more variable and uncertain than magmatic processes. Temperature, compression, shearing forces, and chemical activity (especially the latter), as well as other factors, determine the rate of this metamorphism. It is absurd to say blandly, as Young does (p. 197), that the metamorphic rocks of California's Franciscan Formation had to be buried under eighteen miles of sediments in order to be metamorphosed from sedimentary rocks.

All such igneous and metamorphic rocks really seem to require some sort of catastrophic event for their formation. Heylmun says:

> We find certain rock types in the geologic column that are not being seen to form . . . anywhere on earth today. Where can granite be observed forming? . . . . Herz attributes the formation of anorthosite to . . . possibly a great cataclysm . . . . It is possible that other rock types were created during and following catastrophic events on earth.[1]

The current geological fad is plate tectonics and continental drift, and Young has endorsed this system also (p. 199). He should realize, however, that it has not yet been proved, to the satisfaction of many of his fellow uniformitarians.

> Why then do a few crabbed earth scientists refuse to accept some or all of the tenets of the "new global tectonics"? . . . . Strictly speaking, then, we do not have a scientific hypothesis, but rather a pragmatic model, reshaped to include each new observation . . . . Obviously, this kind of model is not testable in any rigorous scientific sense.[2]

---

1. Edgar B. Heylmun, "Should We Teach Uniformitarianism?" *Journal of Geological Education,* Vol. 19, January, 1971, p. 36.
2. John C. Maxwell, "The New Global Tectonics," *Geotimes,* V. 18, January, 1973, p. 31.

Like the evolutionary model itself, the plate tectonics model, incorporating sea-floor spreading and continental drift, is so flexible it can be made to fit anything. Like evolution, it has now become a bandwagon, on which all geologists are expected to ride.

> The theories of continental drift and sea-floor spreading are highly conjectural, but it is hard to stop anything as big as the floor of the ocean once it has been put into motion. [1]

It should be noted, however, that many highly-competent geophysicists, especially among the Russians, still vigorously reject the whole idea. One of these has said, for example:

> The foregoing discoveries led the author to one conclusion only, that paleomagnetic data are still so unreliable and contradictory that they cannot be used as evidence either for or against the hypothesis of the relative drift of continents or their parts. [2]

Since it was primarily the paleomagnetic data that led to the acceptance of continental drift in the first place, it is evident that the entire construct rests on a very tenuous foundation.

Nevertheless, the Biblical creationists will accept it when and if it is proved. It is not the idea of drift, but the rate of spreading of the continents that Young uses as a club against flood geologists. In the cataclysmic model, however, it would be possible to accommodate a rupture of the original continent followed by a rapid initial spreading, then a gradual deceleration to the present zero or near-zero velocity in, say, the past 4000 years (the flood model is quite flexible also!).[3] This would require only an average of about 5 inches per hour and this could not have been observed after the first century or so without sophisticated geodetic equipment.

As far as radiometric dating is concerned, Young does not even attempt to answer the many criticisms that have been leveled at such techniques by creationists. However, he insists that the rubidium-strontium isochron method eliminates the problem of unknown "initial daughter element" in a radio-

---

1. Daniel Behrman, *The New World of the Oceans* (Boston: Little Brown & Co., 1973) p. 209.
2. I.A. Rezanov, "Paleomagnetism and Continental Drift," *International Geology Review*, Vol. 10, July, 1968, p. 775.
3. For a brief review of evidences for and against moving continents see Stuart E. Nevins, "Continental Drift, Plate Tectonics, and the Bible," ICR *Impact* No. 32, February, 1976.

active mineral, and thus will give a true age (p. 186). That this is not necessarily the case, however, is now commonly recognized.

> One serious consequence of the mantle isochron model is that crystallization ages determined on basic igneous rocks by the rubidium-strontium whole-rock technique can be greater than the true age by many hundreds of millions of years.[1]

The problem, of course, is that the initial strontium indicated by the isochron method reflects conditions in the mantle from which the igneous rock material originally flowed, not the age of the rock itself. Data from young volcanic rocks in certain Pacific Islands, for example, indicated an "apparent age" well back in the Precambrian.

> The data from French Polynesia likewise imply that the source region from which Holocene to Miocene partial melts have been derived had previously maintained its rubidium/strontium heterogeneity for a period of from 1 to 1.5 billion years.[2]

Since all such minerals apparently have their ultimate source in the mantle, it would seem that this problem would render all rubidium dates too old by an indeterminate amount.

In spite of its endorsement by various evangelicals, therefore, this book is both unscientific and unscriptural. Dr. Young is to be commended for rejecting evolution, although even on this position he is inconsistent, being willing to accept the evolution of life from nonlife (p. 127) if necessary.

In spite of the continuing problem posed by such unnecessary evangelical compromises with evolutionary geology, the creationist movement (stressing the recent six-day creation and the worldwide cataclysmic flood) is on sound scientific and Biblical ground and thus will continue to grow, as God leads.

There is no need to discuss here the other recent books by progressive creationists. None of their arguments refute the overwhelming evidences against their day-age theory nor do they refute the strong scientific and Biblical arguments for a recent creation and worldwide flood.

---

1. C. Brooks, D.E. James & S.R. Hart, "Ancient Lithosphere: Its Role in Young Continental Volcanism," *Science,* Vol. 193, Sept. 17, 1976, p. 1093.
2. R.A. Duncan and W. Compston, "Strontium Isotope Evidence for an Old Mantle Source Region for French Polynesian Volcanism," *Geology,* Vol. 4, December, 1976, p. 732.

The Present Work of the Creator

However, a brief further discussion of God's "rest" after His creation may be helpful. The Biblical teaching that God "rested" from His work of creating and making all things (Genesis 2:1-3) after the six days of creation was stressed to show that the present processes of nature are not the same as those processes that developed the universe into its present form, as evolutionists allege. This inference is confirmed by the First and Second Laws of Thermodynamics, which state that these present processes are processes of *conservation* and *disintegration,* not processes of *innovation* and *integration* (as a consistent evolutionary structure would require).

A number of people have contended, however, that John 5:17 contradicts this teaching, showing that God is still working. In this passage, the Lord Jesus says: "My Father worketh hitherto, and I work." In context, Christ was justifying the healing of the crippled man at Bethesda on the sabbath day, stating in effect that God was no longer resting on the sabbath day when there was a work of healing to be accomplished.

This very fact, of course, further refutes the day-age theory, which requires the seventh-day "rest" to be still continuing in order to justify interpreting the first six days as "ages." As a matter of fact, however, it is obvious that the work spoken of in John 5:17 was not God's work of creation, but His work of redemption, of conservation and reconciliation, and salvation!

This work was frequently mentioned by Christ. For example:

My meat is to do the will of Him that sent me, and to finish His work (John 4:34). I must work the works of Him that sent me . . . (John 9:4). I have finished the work which thou gavest me to do (John 17:4).

This present work of the Creator should not be confused with His completed work of creation. That great work of the past was already perfected and finished; the Scriptures are very clear on this point.

And on the seventh day God ended His work which He had made; and He rested on the seventh day from all His work which He had made (Genesis 2:2). For in six days the Lord made heaven and earth, the sea, and all that in them is, and rested the seventh day (Exodus 20:11) . . . . the works were finished from the foundation of the world (Hebrews 4:3). For he that is entered into his rest, he also hath ceased from his own works, as God did from His (Hebrews 4:10).

The entrance of sin and death into the world (Romans 5:12) meant however, that God's rest and "refreshment" (Exodus 31:17) at the contemplation of His perfect creation would quickly be broken, and He would have to begin an age-long work of restoration. In fact the Bible teaches that there are *three* works of Christ—past, present, and future:

1. *Past work.* "For by Him were all things created, that are in heaven, and that are in earth" (Colossians 1:16).
2. *Present work.* " . . . and by Him all things consist" (literally, "are being sustained", Colossians 1:17).
3. *Future work.* " . . . by Him to reconcile all things unto Himself . . . whether they be things in earth, or things in heaven" (Colossians 1:20).

Following man's rebellion in Eden, God would have been justified in allowing man's entire dominion to collapse into chaos and even annihilation. In grace, however, He undertook to "sustain" it, "upholding all things by the word of His power" (Hebrews 1:3), until such time as the final work of reconciliation could be completed. Most of all, the price of redemption had to be paid—"the blood of His cross" (Colossians 1:20—and that required nothing less than God Himself becoming Man, in order to die in substitution for man's sin. God the Creator ("equal with God") "was made in the likeness of men . . . and became obedient unto death, even the death of the cross" (Phillipians 2:6-8).

Finally, on Calvary, the same good Creator who had "finished" His first great work, also finished His second and still greater work. On the cross, He shouted the greatest victory cry "It is finished!" (John 19:30), and the full price for the redemption of the universe had been paid. This fact has been sealed and assured forever by His victorious bodily resurrection on the first day of the New Week.

With the "whole creation still groaning and travailing together in pain" (Romans 8:22), the increasingly strong evidence of the completion of His great work of creation, combining with the already overwhelming proof of the completion of His greater work of salvation, gives us absolute assurance that His future work will likewise be finished one day, when "the creation itself also shall be delivered from the bondage of corruption into the glorious liberty of the children of God" (Romans 8:21).

ATHEISTS AND THE BATTLE
FOR EVOLUTION

Although Christian evolutionists and progressive creationists are currently more vocal in their opposition to literal creationism than are even atheistic evolutionists, there is no doubt that the real battle is ultimately with the latter. The leading scientific evolutionists are, with few exceptions, either atheists or humanists (if there is any difference), and it is only the "me-too" followers who usually comprise the theistic evolutionists. To most of these leaders of evolutionary thought, creationism, until recently, has been more of an irritant than an antagonist, and they have usually responded more by sarcasm than by serious opposition.

This situation is changing, however. I.C.R. scientists have now participated in probably 125 serious scientific creation/evolution debates with evolutionist professors on leading college and university campuses, and these have, without exception, resulted favorably for creationism. Consequently, scientific creationism is rapidly becoming a serious issue. Many young people, as well as many practicing scientists, have been converted to creationism. On the other hand, serious opposition is increasing also. It has now become almost impossible to persuade qualified evolutionary scientists to debate the subject in a public meeting, as the word has been widely circulated on campuses that this does the cause of evolution no good.

A 1978 lecture on scientific creationism at Auburn University drew over 600 students. They listened for an hour to the lecture by Dr. Duane Gish, Associate Director of I.C.R., and then for another hour to an audience question-and-answer session, following which Dr. Gish was given a standing ovation.

In the audience, however, was Dr. Delos B. McKown, Head of Auburn's Department of Philosophy. Dr. McKown was, apparently, profoundly disturbed by the experience. He later wrote:

> But modern, scientific, progressive America witnesses, at this very moment, a resurgence of Biblical literalism, fundamentalism, and evangelicalism that almost defies belief . . . . But of all the recent manifestations of old-time religion, I can think of none more intellectually impertinent or socially and politically ominous than that of the Creation Research Society and the Institute for Creation Research,

devoted to destroying the ideas of cosmic and organic evolution. The mischief that this organization is prepared to do to the life and earth sciences, particularly in elementary and secondary schools, staggers the scientific imagination.[1]

The American Humanist Association, along with many other scientific, educational, and other organizations, has gone on record as strongly opposed to creationism and its reintroduction into the public schools, even if it were taught strictly as a scientific model, with no reference to the Bible or religion. They well realize that creationism means a Creator and that means God! Their opposition is not directed at fundamentalist religion as such, but at God Himself.

There are many Christians who fail to realize the importance of the doctrine of special creation to Christianity, regarding it as a controversial matter of only peripheral significance. This myopic view is, however, not shared by atheists and humanists. They are well aware that the other vital doctrines of Christianity depend squarely on the doctrine of creation, and therefore they direct their major effort toward destroying creationism.

A recent article in the *American Atheist* (the journal of Madalyn Murray O'Hair's atheistic organization) makes this plain.

These "creation-science" textbooks, if allowed in our schools, can only serve to increase that mental anguish by teaching that the Genesis gibberish is a legitimate scientific theory . . . . Christianity is— must be!—totally committed to the special creation as described in Genesis, and Christianity must fight with its full might, fair or foul, against the theory of evolution . . . . It becomes clear now that the whole justification of Jesus' life and death is predicated on the existence of Adam and the forbidden fruit he and Eve ate. Without the original sin, who needs to be redeemed? Without Adam's fall into a life of constant sin terminated by death, what purpose is there to Christianity? None.[2]

1. Delos B. McKown, "Close Encounters of an Ominous Kind: Science and Religion in Contemporary America," *The Humanist,* Vol. XXXIX, January-February, 1979, p. 4.

2. G. Richard Bozarth, "The Meaning of Evolution," *The American Atheist,* September, 1978, p. 19.

This atheist leader (who has a letterhead proclaiming himself as "The Joyous Atheist") summarizes the importance of creationism in the battle of Christ against antichrist thus:

> What all this means, is that Christianity cannot lose the Genesis account of creation like it could lose the doctrine of geocentrism and get along. The battle must be waged, for Christianity is fighting for its very life.[1]

Christianity did not "lose the doctrine of geocentrism," of course, since the Bible does not teach such a doctrine, even though this ancient calumny has been repeated so often that most people have come to accept it. He is quite right, however, in pointing out that Christianity cannot long survive if it gives up the doctrine of special creation.

The writer of the above article sees the issue more clearly than most modern Christian leaders, who still view the creation/ evolution question as only of minor importance. However, he is happily confident that Christianity will lose. Then pure atheism will triumph, in all its glory!

Bogarth climaxes his article with an amazing assertion:

> Atheism is science's natural ally. Atheism is the philosophy, both moral and ethical, most perfectly suited for a scientific civilization. If we work for the American Atheists today, Atheism will be ready to fill the void of Christianity's demise when science and evolution triumph. Without a doubt, humans and civilization are in sore need of the intellectual cleanness and mental health of atheism.[2]

Thus is the battle joined. The religion of Atheism seeks to displace and destroy the Christian faith. Satan would dethrone the mighty King of Creation and proclaim himself the supreme lord of eternal matter, the most glorious product and representative of the natural order of the cosmos.

Thus so-called "Christian evolutionists" by giving aid and comfort to the evolution philosophy, could actually be making a vital contribution to their own destruction.

However, this atheistic assumption that evolution will soon destroy the Gospel is premature, to say the least. The modern revival of creationism is rapidly turning the tide of the battle.

---

1. G. Richard Bozarth, "The Meaning of Evolution," *The American Atheist,* September, 1978, p. 30.
2. *Ibid.*

College students and other young people have, in the past decade, been accepting Christ and the Gospel in greater proportions than in any time in living memory, and the increasing background awareness of the scientific strength of creationism has been a vital factor.

REVOLUTIONARY EVOLUTIONISM

An intriguing development in recent evolutionary thought has been the growing repudiation of neo-Darwinian orthodoxy (that is, the idea of slow and gradual evolution, accomplished by the mechanism of small random genetic mutations preserved by natural selection) in favor of the idea of rapid evolution caused by rapid environmental changes. Instead of contending solely against evolutionary uniformitarianism, the creationist now is having to battle also against catastrophic evolutionism!

In recent years, creationists have delivered telling blows against Darwinian paleontology by repeatedly citing the ubiquitous absence of transitional forms in the fossil record.

> Since 1859 one of the most vexing properties of the fossil record has been its obvious imperfection . . . . This lack has been taken advantage of classically by the opponents of organic evolution as a major defect of the theory . . . . The inability of the fossil record to produce the "missing links" has been taken as solid evidence for disbelieving the theory.[1]

Similarly, creationists have argued effectively against uniformitarianism by pointing out the widespread evidence of catastrophism in the actual rocks and fossil beds of the geological column.

> In fact, the catastrophists were much more empirically minded than Lyell. The geologic record does seem to require catastrophism: rocks are fractured and contorted; whole faunas are wiped out. To circumvent this literal appearance, Lyell imposed his imagination upon the evidence. The geologic record, he argued, is extremely imperfect and we must interpolate into it what we can reasonably infer but cannot see. The catastrophists were the hard-nosed

---

1. A.J. Boucot, *Evolution and Extinction Rate Controls* (Amsterdam, Elsevier Scientific Publishing Co., 1975), p. 196.

empiricists of their day, not the blinded theological apologists.[1]

So, all of a sudden, many—perhaps most—evolutionary biologists are no longer claiming that natural selection was a major factor in the development of basic categories of plants and animals. Many leading evolutionary paleontologists are aggressively proclaiming the absence of transitional forms in the fossil record, and many evolutionary geologists are advocating a return to catastrophism in the study of the rocks! What creationists have been vigorously contending, against heated denials, evolutionists now cheerfully admit to have been true all along!

The New Evolutionary Model

Does this mean they are all becoming creationists? No, of course not. Some, such as Pierre Grasse,[2] have simply stated that they have no idea how evolution could have occurred, even though they still believe in it. In the hands of others, however, evolutionism is a remarkably plastic philosophy. The model merely has to be changed to accommodate rapid evolution, instead of slow and gradual evolution. The reign of Huxley, Simpson, Mayr, Stebbins, and Dobzhansky has passed, and we enter the age of Lewontin, Gould, Ager, and others of the newer school. Long live evolution!

Probably the leading proponent of the new model is the young Harvard paleontologist and philosopher of science, Stephen Jay Gould. A brilliant writer, he has produced a stream of books and articles on many subjects in recent years and has all but demolished both traditional geological uniformitarianism and orthodox neo-Darwinism. The following statements are typical Gouldisms:

> Contrary to popular myths, Darwin and Lyell were not the heroes of true science . . . . Paleontologists have paid an exorbitant price for Darwin's argument. We fancy ourselves as the only true students of life's history, yet to preserve our favored account of evolution by natural selection we view

---

1. Stephen Jay Gould, "Catastrophes and Steady-State Earth," *Natural History,* February, 1975, p. 17.
2. Pierre Grasse, *The Evolution of Living Organisms* (English translation, New York, Academic Press, 1977, 297 pp.). Grasse was called "the most distinguished of all French zoologists" by America's leading evolutionist, Theodosius Dobzhansky.

our data as so bad that we never see the very process we profess to study.[1]

All paleontologists know that the fossil record contains precious little in the way of intermediate forms; transitions between major groups are characteristically abrupt.[2]

The history of life, as I read it, is a series of long stable states, punctuated at rare intervals by major events that occur with great rapidity and set up the next stable era . . . . My favorite metaphor is a world of occasional pulses, driving recalcitrant systems from one stable state to the next.[3]

Gould and his former Harvard colleague, Niles Eldredge (now at the American Museum of Natural History), have developed what they call their theory of "punctuated equilibrium," according to which large populations of organisms are normally genetically stable for a long time, except for **occasional evolutionary spurts, or "punctuations," during** which inbreeding within small "founder" populations, along with rapid environmental changes, stimulates rapid evolutionary change.

There can obviously be little experimental evidence for such a theory, but its critics grudgingly acknowledge its popularity.

The Eldredge-Gould concept of punctuated equilibria has gained wide acceptance among paleontologists . . . . The model is more *ad hoc* explanation than theory, and it rests on shaky ground. Paleontologists seem to be enthralled by small populations . . . . I hasten to point out that ecologists and geneticists have not elucidated macroevolutionary patterns: the gap has not been bridged from either side.[4]

Another prolific young geologist in Gould's camp has shown that the paleontological data, traditionally interpreted in terms of increasing adaptation and natural selection over the ages,

1. Stephen Jay Gould, "Evolution's Erratic Pace," *Natural History,* Vol. LXXXVI, May, 1977, p. 12, 14.
2. Stephen Jay Gould, "The Return of Hopeful Monsters," *Natural History,* Vol. LXXXVI, June-July, 1977, p. 24.
3. Stephen Jay Gould, "An Early Start," *Natural History,* Vol. LXXXVII, February, 1978, p. 24.
4. Robert E. Ricklefs, "Paleontologists Confronting Macroevolution," *Science,* Vol. 199, January 6, 1978, p. 59.

can be organized just as well in terms of pure chance assemblages of fossils:

> If we allow that natural selection works, as we almost have to do, the fossil record doesn't tell us whether it was responsible for 90 percent of the change we see, or 9 percent, or 0.9 percent.[1]

> The fossil record of evolution is amenable to a wide variety of models ranging from completely deterministic to completely stochastic.[2]

The term "stochastic" means essentially "random," and Raup and his colleagues have shown by computer simulations that the fossil patterns throughout the so-called geologic ages can be attributed to random variations and extinctions, without the need of natural selection—at least not in terms of a gradual step-by-step improvement. Ricklefs emphasizes this aspect of the record:

> Indeed, the success of Monte Carlo simulations of evolutionary patterns and R.H. MacArthur's "broken-stick" model of the relative abundances of species point out the similarities between natural patterns and randomly generated systems. It is not clear that an understanding of deterministic processes and both internally and externally imposed constraints will necessarily elucidate macroevolution.[3]

The explosive evolutionary "punctuations" which do occur from time to time in the postulated small populations are believed by Ager and others to be associated somehow with geological catastrophism. Derek Ager is past president of the British Geological Association and believes neither in the Bible nor in creationism. However, he has shown that all geologic features must be explained in terms of catastrophism, rather than uniformitarianism, and he maintains that this ties in with the fossil gaps stressed by Gould and Eldredge.

> The point emerges that, if we examine the fossil record in detail, whether at the level of orders or of species, we find—over and over again—not gradual evolution, but the sudden explosion of one group at

---

1. David M. Raup, "Conflicts Between Darwin and Paleontology," *Bulletin, Field Museum of Natural History,* Vol. 50, January, 1979, p. 26.
2. David M. Raup, "Probabalistic Models in Evolutionary Paleobiology," *American Scientist,* Vol. 166, January-February, 1977, p. 57.
3. Robert E. Ricklefs, *op cit,* p. 60.

the expense of another.[1]

In other words, the history of any one part of the earth, like the life of a soldier, consists of long periods of boredom and short periods of terror.[2]

Ager and other modern geologic catastrophists do not, of course, believe in the worldwide Flood of the Bible, but rather that intermittent regional catastrophes throughout the geological ages account for all the actual formations and structures in the geologic column.

But the idea that the marvelous array of intricately complex and highly adapted organisms in the world could have developed rapidly from simpler organisms in catastrophically changing environments is contrary to all experience and reason. Simple systems never evolve naturally into complex systems. By the Second Law of Thermodynamics, changes go in exactly the opposite direction—complex systems always *tend* to degenerate into simple systems. Furthermore, catastrophic environments merely accelerate the decay of such systems. By the standard thermodynamics of heat flow, for example, an influx of heat energy into an open system will increase the entropy of that system more rapidly than if it were an isolated system. How, then, is it even conceivable that evolution could proceed by any such mechanism as this?

As a matter of fact, however, Ilya Prigogine, who received a Nobel Prize in 1977 for his work in non-equilibrium thermodynamics, has made just such a proposal, based on his analyses. That is, he has developed a mathematical theory for what he calls "dissipative structures" in fluids, in which a high flow of energy through an open system (with consequent high energy dissipation) somehow generates a higher degree of order in that system, even in the midst of an over-all increase of entropy. This suggestion has been eagerly appropriated by evolutionists, since it seems to give them a slight ray of hope that the Second Law of Thermodynamics may not preclude evolution after all. However, Prigogine himself has acknowledged that his actual data had no direct confirmation from living systems at all, so that his ideas on the origin of life and on evolution in general, are mere speculations at this time.

---

1. D.V. Ager, "The Nature of the Fossil Record," *Proceedings of the British Geological Association,* (Presidential Address), Vol. 87, No. 2, 1976, p. 133.
2. D.V. Ager, *The Nature of the Stratigraphical Record* (New York, John Wiley & Sons, 1973), p. 100.

Prigogine's theory is couched in highly mathematical terminology and is difficult to follow in detail. Qualitatively, however, he speaks of "order through fluctuations" in systems "far from equilibrium," systems in which unusually chaotic conditions somehow may result in structures of higher order in small portions of those systems. (For a brief rebuttal of Prigogine's theories as a basis for evolution, see the Impact articles 57 and 58, in the Institute for Creation Research publication *Acts and Facts,* for March and April, 1978. Also see pages 120-123 in the following chapter.)

This theme occurs with increasing frequency in many diverse fields today. Richard Lewontin, leading population geneticist at Harvard, has rejected the Darwinist concept of unending struggle and survival, even at the genetic level,[1] and M.I.T.'s Noam Chomsky, recognized as the world's foremost linguist, stresses that there is no evolutionary transition between the noises of animals and the speech of humans.[2] The current concept of evolution at all levels (human and non-human) is, typically, one of large stable populations in which recombination and adaptation normally operate in an egalitarian milieu punctuated at rare intervals in small select groups by rapid evolution to a higher order, probably through large random mutations stimulated by catastrophically changing environments.

The amazing aspect of this emerging consensus is that it is not based on any direct scientific evidence, but only on *lack* of evidence! Since there are no intermediate forms, the reasoning goes, evolution must occur rapidly. All systems tend to become disordered, so higher order must somehow arise out of the chaos of a more rapidly disintegrating system! Where, pray tell, have all the scientists gone?

Evolution and Social Change
The answer may be that they have gone into politics! Russian-born Ilya Prigogine, for example, now at the University of Texas and the University of Brussels, has made a remarkable leap of faith with his dissipative structure equations, and he and his followers are seeking to apply them to problems of social change.

1. Richard Lewontin, "Adaptation," *Scientific American,* Vol. 239, September, 1978, pp. 213-230.
2. Noam Chomsky, *Language and Mind* (New York: Harcourt, Brace and Jovanovich, Inc., 1972), pp. 67, 68.

Prigogine's work has long been of interest to systems theorists seeking to apply the logic of their fields to global problems. One such scientist is Ervin Laszlo of the United Nations. "What I see Prigogine doing," says Laszlo, "is giving legitimization to the process of evolution—self-organization under conditions of change . . . . It's analogy to social systems and evolution could be very fruitful."[1]

Beyond its direct scientific application, Dr. Prigogine's work seems to him to imply a physical principle never fully perceived before—a fundamental impetus inexorably pushing life and humanity to further evolution and complexity, for better or worse, perhaps even against man's will.[2]

Even more overtly political is the Harvard-M.I.T. group whose spokesmen seem to be Gould and Lewontin.

Gradualism, the idea that all change must be smooth, slow and steady, was never read from the rocks. It was primarily a prejudice of nineteenth-century liberalism facing a world in revolution.[3]

If gradualism is more a product of western thought than a fact of nature, then we should consider alternative philosophies of change to enlarge our realm of constraining prejudices. In the Soviet Union, for example, scientists are trained with a very different philosophy of change—the so-called dialectical laws, reformulated by Engels from Hegel's philosophy. The dialectical laws are explicitly punctuational . . . . Eldredge and I were fascinated to learn that most Russian paleontologists support a model very similar to our punctuated equilibria. The connection cannot be accidental.[4]

Well, he said so himself! Gould is a self-proclaimed Marxist, as are Lewontin and Chomsky, so it is not overly surprising that their concepts of what might be called "revolutionary

1. Wil Lepkowski, "The Social Thermodynamics of Ilya Prigogine," *Chemical and Engineering News,* April 16, 1979, p. 30.
2. Malcolm W. Browne, "Scientists See a Loophole in the Fatal Law of Physics," *New York Times,* May 27, 1979, p. C-1.
3. Stephen Jay Gould, "An Early Start," *Natural History,* Vol. LXXXVII, February, 1978, p. 24.
4. Stephen Jay Gould, "Evolution's Erratic Pace," *Natural History,* Vol. LXXXVI, May, 1977, p. 16.

evolution'' coincide with the Marxian dialectic and with Soviet ''philosophies of change.''

Tom Bethell, of Harper's magazine, has written a penetrating analysis of these remarkable recent shifts in evolutionary philosophy.

> No longer is unrestrained competition, once perceived as beneficial to business production and animal production alike, considered acceptable. We now live in a time when lip service, at least, is paid to notions of collective effort and collective security. One can see why Darwinism would upset the Left . . . . Evolution was nature's eugenics program. How do you think our Marxist biologists like that idea? They don't like it at all.[1]

It is interesting that these current criticisms of Darwinism are essentially the same that creationists have been making for years and which evolutionists have, until recently, denied. When the racist connotations of neo-Darwinism, for example, are pointed out by creationists,[2] evolutionists often become indignant but now their own colleagues are making the same charge.

> As with genetic theories of race, (Darwinism) has been found to have implications contrary to the egalitarian spirit of the times, hence in need of revision. As one would expect, the attack on Darwinism has come from the Left.[3]

These younger evolutionists are even claiming that Darwin himself, as well as the other nineteenth century evolutionists, were politically motivated and were merely forcing their science to support their racial and economic prejudices. They are now doing the same thing themselves, of course, except that their own prejudices are tied to Karl Marx instead of Adam Smith. The remarkable feature of all this is that, despite all the bitterness with which the two evolutionary camps oppose each other, they are perfectly united in their devotion to evolutionary materialism and their opposition to creationism!

> The left-wing critique of Darwinian theory has by no means prevailed, but if it should do so, let us

---

1. Tom Bethell, ''Burning Darwin to Save Marx,'' *Harper's,* December, 1978, p. 38.
2. Henry M. Morris, ''Evolution and Modern Racism,'' *Acts and Facts,* Vol. II, Impact Series No. 7, 1973.
3. Tom Bethell, *op cit,* p. 36.

also enjoy the fantastic irony that the fundamentalists, who have been trying for more than a hundred
years to knock Darwin off his pedestal, without
success, will be indebted not to the right-wingers,
with whom they have always been aligned, but to
biologists whose god is **Marx**.[1]

And speaking of irony, please note the quandary faced by
evolutionists. The evidences continually cited by creationists
have finally been acknowledged and "uniformitarian evolutionism" is being abandoned. The only remaining alternative to
creationism is "revolutionary evolutionism," with its magical
apparatus of hopeful monsters, big bangs, black holes, dissipative structures, punctuational catastrophes, and Marxian dialectic: *"Quos Deus vult perdere prius dementat"* ("Whom the
gods would destroy, they first make mad").

---

1. Tom Bethell, *op cit*, p. 92.

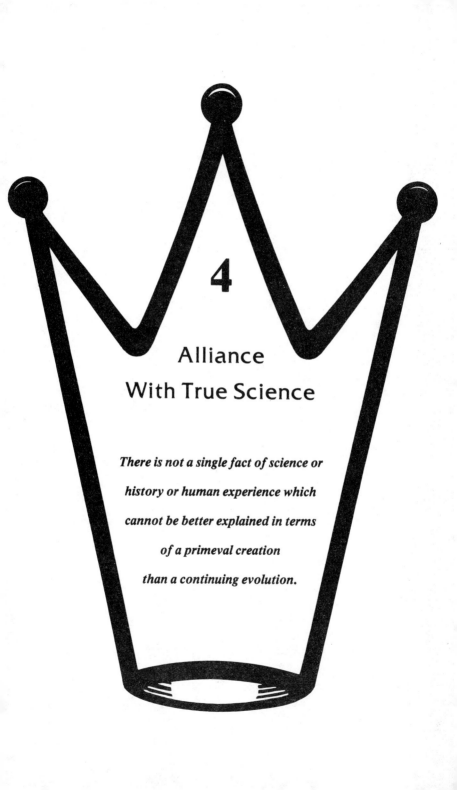

4

Alliance
With True Science

There is not a single fact of science or

history or human experience which

cannot be better explained in terms

of a primeval creation

than a continuing evolution.

Alliance With True Science

CREATION AND THE LAWS
OF SCIENCE

The most astounding anomaly in the history of human thought is the almost universal belief in evolution in spite of the almost universal absence of any evidence for evolution. There is not a single fact of science or history or human experience which cannot be better explained in terms of a primeval creation than a continuing evolution. Yet evolution is everywhere taught as the only *scientific* view of the origin, development, and meaning of all things. Creationism is universally derided as *"religious,"* evolution everywhere acclaimed as *"scientific."* Black is white and up is down, and we all live in a wonderland where the universe is its own Creator, and God is dead!

But when we return from wonderland and look again at the actual facts of science, their testimony is clearly of creation, not evolution! Men and devils may rebel against their Creator and His infallible Word, but the creation itself is faithful. "The invisible things of Him from the creation of the world are clearly seen, being understood by the things that are made, even His eternal power and Godhead, so that they are without excuse" (Romans 1:20).

In this chapter some of the important laws and systems of nature will be surveyed, in the light of their possible origin by evolution or creation. In these and all other cases, it quickly becomes apparent that evolution contradicts true science and creation explains true science.

The Law of Disorder

For example, a devastating and conclusive argument against evolution is the entropy principle. This principle—also known as the Second Law of Thermodynamics—implies that, in the present order of things, evolution in the "vertical" sense (that is, from one degree of order and complexity to a higher degree of order and complexity) is completely impossible.

The evolutionary model of origins and development requires some universal principle which *increases* order, causing random particles eventually to organize themselves into complex chemicals, non-living systems to become living cells, and populations of worms to evolve into human societies. However the only naturalistic scientific principle which is known to effect real changes in order is the Second Law, which describes a situation of universally deteriorating order.

> This law states that all natural processes generate entropy, a measure of disorder.[1]

> Entropy, in short, is the measurement of molecular disorder. The law of the irreversible increase in entropy is a law of progressive disorganization, of the complete disappearance of the initial conditions.[2]

It can hardly be questioned that evolution is at least superficially contradicted by entropy. The obvious prediction from the evolution model of a universal principle that *increases* order is confronted by the scientific fact of a universal principle that *decreases* order. Nevertheless evolutionists retain faith that, somehow, evolution and entropy can co-exist, even though they don't know how.

> In the complex course of its evolution, life exhibits a remarkable contrast to the tendency expressed in the Second Law of Thermodynamics. Where the Second Law expresses an irreversible progression toward increased entropy and disorder, life evolves continually higher levels of order. The still more remarkable fact is that this evolutionary drive to greater and greater order also is irreversible. Evolution does not go backward.[3]

> Back of the spontaneous generation of life under other conditions than now obtain upon this planet, there occurred a spontaneous generation of elements of the kind that still goes on in the stars; and back of that I suppose a spontaneous generation of elementary particles under circumstances still to be fathomed, that ended in giving them the properties that alone make possible the universe we know.[4]

---

1. David Layzer, "The Arrow of Time," *Scientific American* (Vol. 223, December, 1975), p. 56. Dr. Layzer is Professor of Astronomy at Harvard.
2. Ilya Prigogine, "Can Thermodynamics Explain Biological Order?" *Impact of Science on Society* (Vol. XXIII, No. 3., 1973, p. 162. Dr. Prigogine is Professor in the Faculty of Sciences at the University Libre de Belgique and is one of the world's leading thermodynamicists.
3. J.H. Rush, *The Dawn of Life* (New York, Signet, 1962), p. 35.
4. George Wald, "Fitness in the Universe," *Origins of Life* (Vol. 5, 1974), p. 26.

Life might be described as an unexpected force that somehow organizes inanimate matter into a living system that perceives, reacts to, and evolves to cope with changes to the physical environment that threatens to destroy its organization.[1]

When confronted directly with this problem (e.g., in creation/evolution debates) evolutionists often will completely ignore it. Some will honestly admit they do not know how to resolve the problem but will simply express confidence that there must be a way, since otherwise one would have to believe in supernatural creation. As Wald says:

In this strange paper I have ventured to suggest that natural selection of a sort has extended even beyond the elements, to determine the properties of protons and electrons. Curious as that seems, it is a possibility worth weighing against the only alternative I can imagine, Eddington's suggestion that God is a mathematical physicist.[2]

Some evolutionists try to solve the problem by suggesting that the entropy law is only statistical and that exceptions can occur, which would allow occasional accidental increases in order. Whether this is so, however, is entirely a matter of faith. No one has ever *seen* such an exception—and science is based upon observation!

There is thus no justification for the view, often glibly repeated, that the Second Law of Thermodynamics is only statistically true, in the sense that microscopic violations repeatedly occur, but never violations of any serious magnitude. On the contrary, no evidence has ever been presented that the Second Law breaks down under any circumstances . . . .[3]

The Vacuous Open System Argument

By far the majority of evolutionists, however, attempt to deal with this Second Law argument by retreating to the "open system" refuge. They maintain that, since the Second Law

1. Mars and Earth, National Aeronautics and Space Administration (Washington, U.S. Govt. Printing Office, NF-61, August, 1975), p. 5.

2. George Wald, *op. cit.,* p. 26. Wald is a famous humanistic biologist at Harvard.

3. A.B. Pippard, *Elements of Chemical Thermodynamics for Advanced Students of Physics* (Cambridge, England, Cambridge University Press, 1966), p. 100. Pippard was Professor of Physics at Cambridge.

applies only to isolated systems (from which external sources of information and order are excluded), the argument is irrelevant. The earth and its biosphere are open systems, with an ample supply of energy coming in from the sun to do the work of building up the complexity of these systems. Furthermore, they cite specific examples of systems in which the order increases —such as the growth of a crystal out of solution, the growth of a seed or embryo into an adult plant or animal, or the growth of a small Stone Age population into a large complex technological culture—as proof that the Second Law does not inhibit the growth of more highly-ordered systems.

Arguments and examples such as these, however, are specious arguments. It is like arguing that, since NASA was able to put men on the moon, therefore it is reasonable to believe cows can jump over the moon! Creationists have for over a decade been emphasizing that the Second Law really applies only to *open* systems, since there is no such thing as a truly isolated system. The great French scientist and mathematician, Emil Borel, has proved this fact mathematically, as acknowledged by Layzer:

> Borel showed that no finite physical system can be considered closed.[1]

Creationists have long acknowledged—in fact *emphasized*— that order can and does increase in certain special types of open systems, but this is no proof that order increases in *every* open system! The statement that "the earth is an open system" is a vacuous statement containing no specific information, since all systems are open systems.

The Second Law of Thermodynamics could well be stated as follows: "In any ordered system, open or closed, there exists a *tendency* for that system to decay to a state of disorder, which tendency can only be suspended or reversed by an external source of ordering energy directed by an informational program and transformed through an ingestion-storage-converter mechanism into the specific work required to build up the complex structure of that system."

If either the information program or the converter mechanism is not available to that "open" system, it will *not* increase in order, no matter how much external energy surrounds it or flows into it or through it. The system will proceed to decay in accordance with the Second Law of Thermodynamics.

---

1. Layzer, *op cit.*, p. 65.

To cite special cases (such as the seed, for which the genetic code and the conversion mechanism of photosynthesis *are* available) is futile, as far as "evolution" is concerned, since there is neither a directing program nor conversion apparatus available to produce an imaginary evolutionary growth in complexity of the earth and its biosphere.

It is even more futile to refer to inorganic processes such as crystallization as evidence of evolution. Even Prigogine recognizes this:

> The point is that in a non-isolated system there exists a possibility for formation of ordered, low-entropy structures at sufficiently low temperatures. This ordering principle is responsible for the appearance of ordered structures such as crystals as well as for the phenomena of phase transitions.
>
> Unfortunately this principle cannot explain the formation of biological structures. The probability that at ordinary temperatures a macroscopic number of molecules is assembled to give rise to the highly-ordered structures and to the coordinated functions characterizing living organisms is vanishingly small. The idea of spontaneous genesis of life in its present form is therefore highly improbable, even on the scale of the billions of years during which prebiotic evolution occurred.[1]

Another scientist has also pointed out the fallacy in comparing crystallization to evolution:

> Attempts to relate the idea of "order" in a crystal with biological organization or specificity must be regarded as a play on words which cannot stand careful scrutiny.[2]

Thus the highly specialized conditions that enable crystals to form and plants and animals to grow have nothing whatever to do with evolution. These special conditions themselves (that is, the marvelous process of photosynthesis, the complex information programs in the living cell, even the electrochemical properties of the molecules in the crystal, etc.) could never

---

1. Ilya Prigogine, Gregoire Nicolis & Agnes Babloyants, "Thermodynamics of Evolution," *Physics Today* (Vol. 25, November, 1972), p. 23.
2. Hubert P. Yockey, "A Calculation of the Probability of Spontaneous Biogenesis by Information Theory," *Journal of Theoretical Biology*, Vol. 67, 1977, p. 380.

arise by chance—their own complexity could never have been produced within the constraints imposed by the Second Law. But without these, the crystal would not form, and the seed would never grow.

But what is the information code that tells primeval random particles how to organize themselves into stars and planets, and what is the conversion mechanism that transforms amoebas into men? These are questions that are not answered by a specious reference to the earth as an open system! And until they *are* answered, the Second Law makes evolution appear quite impossible.

To their credit, there are a few evolutionists (though apparently very few) who recognize the critical nature of this problem and are trying to solve it. Prigogine has proposed an involved theory of "order through fluctuations" and "dissipative structures."[1]

But his examples are from inorganic systems, and he acknowledges that there is a long way to go to explain how these become living systems by his theory.

> But let us have no illusions—our research would still leave us quite unable to grasp the extreme complexity of the simplest of organisms.[2]

Another recent writer who has partially recognized the seriousness of this problem is Charles J. Smith.

> The thermodynamicist immediately clarifies the latter question by pointing out that the Second Law classicially refers to isolated systems which exchange neither energy nor matter with the environment; biological systems are open and exchange both energy and matter . . . . This explanation, however, is not completely satisfying, because it still leaves open the problem of how or why the ordering process has arisen (an apparent lowering of the entropy), and a number of scientists have wrestled with this issue. Bertelanffy (1968) called the relation between irreversible thermodynamics and information theory one of the most fundamental unsolved problems in biology. I would go further and include the problem of meaning and value.[3]

---

1. *Ibid*, pp. 23-28.
2. Ilya Prigogine, "Can Thermodynamics Explain Biological Order?" p. 178.
3. Charles J. Smith, "Problems with Entropy in Biology," *Biosystems* (Vol. 1, 1975), p. 259.

Whether rank-and-file evolutionists know it or not, this problem they have with entropy is thus *"one of the most fundamental unsolved problems in biology."* In fact it is more than a problem—it is a devastating denial of the evolution model itself. It will continue to be so until evolutionists can demonstrate that the vast imagined evolutionary continuum in space and time has both a program to guide it and an energy converter to empower it. Otherwise, the Second Law precludes it.

It is conceivable, though extremely unlikely, that evolutionists may eventually formulate a plausible code and mechanism to explain how both entropy and evolution could co-exist. Even if they do, however, the evolution model will still not be as good as the creation model. At the most, such a suggestion would constitute a secondary modification of the basic evolution model. The latter could certainly never predict the Second Law.

The evolution model cannot yet even explain the Second Law, but the creation model *predicts* it! The creationist is not embarrassed or perplexed by entropy, since it is exactly what he expects. The creation model postulates a perfect creation of all things completed during the period of special creation in the beginning. From this model, the creationist naturally predicts limited horizontal changes within the created entities (e.g., variations within biologic kinds, enabling them to adapt to environmental changes). If "vertical" changes occur, however, from one level of order to another, they would have to go in the downward direction, toward lower order. The Creator, both omniscient and omnipotent, made all things perfect in the beginning. No process of evolutionary change could improve them, but deteriorative changes could disorder them.

Not only does the creation model predict the entropy principle, but the entropy principle directly points to creation. That is, if all things are now running down to disorder, they must originally have been in a state of high order. Since there is no naturalistic process which could produce such an initial condition, its cause must have been supernatural. The only adequate cause of the initial order and complexity of the universe must have been an omniscient Programmer, and the cause of its boundless power an omnipotent Energizer. The Second Law of Thermodynamics, with its principle of increasing entropy, both repudiates the evolution model and strongly confirms the creation model.

THERMODYNAMICS AND THE ORIGIN OF LIFE

Evolutionists should, indeed, be embarrassed by the Second Law of Thermodynamics. Dr. V.F. Weisskopf, President of the American Academy of Arts and Sciences, has recently pointed up the problem in the following words:

> The evolutionary history of the world from the "big bang" to the present universe is a series of gradual steps from the simple to the complicated, from the unordered to the organized, from the formless gas of elementary particles to the morphic atoms and molecules and further to the still more structured liquids and solids, and finally to the sophisticated living organisms. There is an obvious tendency of nature from disorder to order and organization. Is this tendency in contradiction to the famous second law of thermodynamics, which says that disorder must increase in nature? The law says that entropy, the measure of disorder, must grow in any natural system.[1]

The "obvious tendency of nature from disorder to order and organization" is, of course, only an assumption of evolutionists. The real tendency in the natural world, as expressed by the Second Law of Thermodynamics, is from order and organization to disorder. This very obvious problem is commonly bypassed by evolutionists (including Weisskopf) with the naive statement that the earth is a system open to the energy of the sun and that this fact resolves the problem! Creationists in turn have reminded them that while an open system and available energy constitute *necessary* conditions before a growth in order (or information) can take place, they are not *sufficient* conditions. In addition, there must be a pre-coded program containing the necessary information to direct the growth of the system and one or more conversion mechanisms to convert the external energy into the highly specific work of internal growth. Since the vast system of the hypothetically evolving biosphere as a space-time continuum seems to lack both a program and mechanism, it is clearly precluded by the Second Law.

The Complexity of Living Systems

It has been especially difficult to imagine ways to get life

1. Victor F. Weisskopf, "The Frontiers and Limits of Science," *American Scientist,* Vol. 65, July-August, 1977, p. 409.

started in the first place. How can unordered non-living chemical elements be combined naturalistically into the extremely sophisticated ordered information in a replicating system? The common belief that this problem has been practically solved by modern biochemists is premature, to say the least. Freeman Dyson says:

> We are still at the very beginning of the quest for understanding of the origin of life. We do not yet have even a rough picture of the nature of the obstacles that prebiotic evolution has had to overcome. We do not have a well-defined set of criteria by which to judge whether any given theory of the origin of life is adequate.[1]

The nature of the problem in trying to account for the origin of a replicating system has been well expressed by Angrist and Hepler:

> Life, the temporary reversal of a universal trend toward maximum disorder, was brought about by the production of information mechanisms. In order for such mechanisms to first arise it was necessary to have matter capable of forming itself into a self-reproducing structure that could extract energy from the environment for its first self-assembly. Directions for the reproduction of plans, for the extraction of energy and chemicals from the environment, for the growth of sequence and the mechanism for translating instructions into growth all had to be simultaneously present at that moment. This combination of events has seemed an incredibly unlikely happenstance and often divine intervention is prescribed as the only way it could have come about.[2]

Small wonder! In the real world, every effect must have an adequate cause, but the usual laws of science do not seem to intimidate evolutionists. In the strange land of evolutionary credulity, wonderful things may happen—plans draw themselves, mechanisms design themselves, order generates itself from chaos, and life creates itself! Yet evolutionists call creationists unscientific because they postulate an adequate

---

1. Freeman Dyson, "Honoring Dirac," *Science,* Vol. 185, Sept. 27, 1974, p. 1161. Dyson is at Princeton's Institute for Advanced Study.
2. Stanley W. Angrist and Loren G. Hepler, *Order and Chaos* (New York: Basic Books, Inc., 1967), pp. 203-204.

Cause (divine intervention) to account for the marvelous Effect called life.

In creation/evolution debates, creationists commonly place great emphasis on the Second Law of Thermodynamics as an overwhelming evidence against evolution. Although there have been approximately 125 such debates held within the period 1972-78, with leading evolutionist professors on major college and university campuses, the latter have never yet been able to come up with an answer of any consequence to this problem. Even more amazingly, most of them do not even seem to understand the problem, either dismissing it as irrelevant or else making some vacuous reference to ice crystals or open systems!

Entropy and the Nobel Prize

There are apparently only a few evolutionists who realize the magnitude of the problem and have been trying to find a solution. By far the most important of these efforts has been the suggestion of a Belgian scientist named Ilya Prigogine. Dr. Prigogine is a widely-known chemist and thermodynamicist, with faculty appointments both at the University Libre de Bruxelles and at the University of Texas at Austin. An indication of the strategic significance of Prigogine's ideas, is that they have recently won for him the Nobel Prize in Chemistry. Judging from the popular announcements, the main reason for this award may well have been the ray of hope Prigogine has given evolutionists in their battle with entropy!

According to *Newsweek,* for example, the significance of Prigogine's work is as follows:

> Scientists who have sought to explain the origin of life as the result of chemical interactions have been confounded by the second law of thermodynamics: energy tends to dissipate and organized systems drift inevitably toward entropy, or chaos . . . . Prigogine's insights will give biologists new grounds for learning how the first random molecules organized themselves into life forms . . . . Prigogine thinks the Nobel committee recognized that his work is building a bridge between the physical and human sciences.[1]

According to an interview in a professional chemical journal, Prigogine himself was "really surprised" at the decision of the Nobel committee. He also said: "The fact that the Nobel

---

1. Chemistry: "The Flow of Life" *(Newsweek;* October 24, 1977), p. 87.

committee has chosen this one subject is a great encouragement."[1]

If, indeed, Prigogine had shown that the tremendous amount
of information necessary for molecular self-replication can be
produced naturalistically despite the entropy law, his achievement would be well worth the Nobel Prize. It would be all the
more remarkable in view of the fact that Prigogine himself
has "not actually worked in a chemistry lab for decades."[2] At
best, however, he has only offered a theoretical speculation,
not an experimental demonstration. It is hard to avoid the
suspicion that the Nobel award in this case was due less to
the scientific value of Prigogine's achievement than to the
urgent need of the evolutionary establishment for some kind
of answer, no matter how superficial, to the entropy problem.

Just how has Dr. Prigogine proposed to harmonize molecular
evolution with the Second Law? Here it is, in his own words:

> In all these phenomena, a new ordering mechan-
> ism . . . appears. For reasons to be explained later,
> we shall refer to this principle as *order through
> fluctuations.* The structures are created by the con-
> tinuous flow of energy and matter from the outside
> world; their maintenance requires a critical distance
> from equilibrium, that is, a minimum level of dissipa-
> tion. For all these reasons we have called them
> dissipative structures. [3]

These "dissipative structures" are supposed to exhibit a
higher degree of structure, or order, than they possessed
before being subjected to a large influx of outside energy,
while at the same time their generation is accompanied by a
large dissipation of energy in the form of heat. The main
example cited by Prigogine is the formation of convection
currents and vortices in a fluid subjected to a temperature
gradient.

Under such conditions, vortices (or other fluctuations or
instabilities) may be generated and maintained. These, supposedly, manifest higher "order" than the system possessed
previously, even though such order has been produced at
the cost of excessive over-all energy dissipation. This phenomenon has long been familiar to hydrodynamicists, but Prigogine

1. *Chemical and Engineering News;* October 17, 1977, p. 4.
2. *Newsweek, Ibid.*
3. Ilya Prigogine, Gregoire Nicolis, and Agnes Babloyants, "Thermodynamics
of Evolution," *Physics Today* (Vol. 25, November, 1972), p. 25.

suggested that it may also apply in certain chemical and biological reactions which are proceeding under non-equilibrium conditions.

That such vortices or any other analagous "dissipative structures" could actually be called a device for naturalistic generation of higher order, and then that such a description could be awarded a Nobel Prize is almost unbelievable! This writer's own Ph.D. dissertation over a quarter of a century ago described in quantitative and analytical form the generation of turbulent vortices in fluid flow over rough surfaces.[1] These, indeed, are dissipative structures, requiring the dissipation of much flow energy in the form of heat for their generation. Their own rotational energies in turn are soon dissipated by breaking up into smaller vortices, so that no permanent increase in order is produced, even if such vortices are assumed (very questionably) to possess a higher degree of order than the energy gradient which generated them. "Big whirls make little whirls that feed on their velocity; little whirls make tiny whirls, and so on to viscosity!"

In any case dissipative structures could hardly serve as a substrate for still *higher* order, since they themselves require an abnormally large input of energy just to maintain their own structures. Prigogine himself says that, as far as chemical or biological reaction are concerned, the generation of dissipative structures is apparently limited to "auto-catalytic" processes. But catalytic processes, like fluid vortices, do not generate higher order—they merely speed up reactions which themselves are already going downhill thermodynamically in the first place. And any imaginary "auto-catalytic" processes would certainly require already-living systems for their own generation, so they can hardly explain the generation of living systems!

Although Prigogine wistfully expresses the hope that his speculations may someday lead to an understanding of how life may have evolved from non-life, he is at least more cautious than those of his fellow evolutionists who are currently exuberating over it. He warns:

> It would be too simple to say that the concepts of life and dissipative structures are intermingled . . . . But it is not just one instability that makes it possible to cross the threshold between life and non-

1. Henry M. Morris, *A New Concept of Flow in Rough Conduits* (Minneapolis, University of Minnesota, 1951, 157 pp.).

life; it is, rather, a succession of instabilities of which we are only now beginning to identify certain stages.[1]

In a later section, he again suggests caution:

But let us have no illusions. If today we look into the situation where the analogy with the life sciences is the most striking—even if we discovered within biological systems some operations distant from the state of equilibrium—our research would still leave us quite unable to grasp the extreme complexity of the simplest of organisms.[2]

One thing is clear. Whatever of scientific value may be deduced from Prigogine's analysis, he has *not* solved the problem of harmonizing entropy with evolution and he certainly has *not* shown that life can evolve from non-living chemicals. His dissipative structures do not constitute either the required program or the required mechanism to enable any kind of permanently increased order to be produced in an open system. However, he should perhaps be commended for trying. Maybe next he can work on a perpetual motion machine!

The problem of the origin of life can really only be resolved by recognition of the omnipotent Creator. The only alternative to belief in special creation is credulous faith in impotent Chance.

We are faced with the idea that genesis was a statistically unlikely event. We are also faced with the certainty that it occurred. Was there a temporary repeal of the second law that permitted a "fortuitous concourse of atoms"? If so, study of the Repealer and Genesis is a subject properly left to theologians. Or we may hold with the more traditional scientific attitude that the origin of life is beclouded merely because we don't know enough about the composition of the atmosphere and other conditions on the earth many eons ago.[3]

Yes, not knowing how life could be formed would indeed becloud the understanding of the origin of life! The problem is why this should be called the *scientific* attitude when all the *scientific evidence* continues to support special creation.

---

1. Ilya Prigogine, "Can Thermodynamics Explain Biological Order? *Impact of Science on Society,* Vol. XXIII, No. 3, 1973, p. 169.

2. *Ibid,* p. 178.

3. Angrist and Hepler, *op cit,* p. 205.

Evolutionary Faith Versus Scientific Fact

Returning to the quotation from V.F. Weisskopf with which this section began, Dr. Weisskopf in no way intended to repudiate evolution because of its apparent conflict with the Second Law of Thermodynamics. However, he, like Prigogine, recognized that there is an apparent problem and felt he should at least contribute a suggestion as to how it might be resolved. His attempted harmonization, unfortunately, is even less viable than that of Prigogine.

Dr. Weisskopf, indeed assumed evolution to be so certain that its continual energizing by the sun could be elevated to the status of a *fourth law of thermodynamics*.[1] He suggested that "order" on earth continually increases as the earth cools from its primeval molten state, and that the continual influx of solar radiation provides the necessary energy for evolutionary work. Dr. Weisskopf also noted that since the cooling of dissolved substances promoted crystallization (and thus increased order), the cooling of the earth's primeval soupy sea would encourage the analogous "crystallization" of highly-ordered organic molecules.

If anyone thinks the writer has somehow misrepresented these remarkable suggestions, he should read the paper first-hand. Fortunately, there is no need to comment on them here, since Dr. George P. Stravropoulos has already done it so effectively, in a subsequent issue of the same journal.[2] Speaking of Dr. Weisskopf's ingenious suggestion about crystals and the first living molecules, Dr. Stravropoulos makes the following observation:

> He makes it appear as though crystals and highly ordered organic molecules belong in the same class, when in fact they do not. When a crystal is broken up, the smaller crystals are physically and chemically identical to the original. This is never observed with (organic) molecules; when the original molecule is split up, lesser molecules appear, and part of the original information is lost. To ignore such fundamental differences in an effort to arrive at some general overview or law is to create a false overview,

1. The third law describes zero entropy, or perfect order, as occurring at a temperature of absolute zero.
2. George P. Stravropoulos, Letters section, *American Scientist,* Vol. 65, November-December, 1977, pp. 675-676.

a pseudolaw.[1]

To which might be added the observation that such dead-end crystals actually contain less "information" than the solution out of which they crystallize. Rather than providing an exception to the second law they illustrate it.

Dr. Weisskopf's premature suggestion to make evolution a "fourth law" of thermodynamics is dismissed by Dr. Stravropoulos as follows:

> To say that "there is an obvious tendency of nature from disorder to order and organization" and to advance this idea to a "fourth law" is to misunderstand completely and to compromise all of thermodynamics.[2]

Thermodynamics is highly quantitative and its laws are as fully confirmed as any laws of science can be confirmed, but the notion of the sun's energy driving the evolutionary process is about as fully *unconfirmed* as any process ever imagined by human speculation.

Dr. Stravropoulos continues:

> . . . under ordinary conditions, no complex organic molecule can ever form spontaneously but will rather disintegrate, in agreement with the second law. Indeed, the more complex it is, the more unstable it is, and the more assured, sooner or later, is its disintegration. Photosynthesis and all life processes, and life itself, despite confused or deliberately confusing language, cannot yet be understood in terms of thermodynamics or any other exact science.[3]

The *coup de grace* to the facile notion that solar energy produces terrestrial evolution is administered when it is pointed out that the influx of raw heat energy to an open system increases (not decreases!) the entropy (disorder) of that system. This is a fundamental principle of thermodynamics. That is, unmodified, undirected solar energy impacting on the earth would cause internal disintegration, not evolution! Listen again to Dr. Stravropoulos:

> The thrust of Dr. Weisskopf's argument that order appears in a cooling body—runs against his statement that the flow of heat from the sun to the

---

1. *Ibid*, p. 675.
2. *Ibid*, p. 675.
3. *Ibid*, p. 676.

Earth resulted in photosynthesis and the development of "highly hierarchical" forms of organic
matter on earth. For one thing, why only Earth?
Why has Mars failed the test? And for another, the
sun cools and Earth necessarily warms up (if we
consider only the "sun-Earth system") and therefore
it is the sun that should be drawing toward order,
Earth toward disorder.[1]

The writer hopes, naively perhaps, that the discussion in
this and the previous section will permanently dispel the evolutionary misconception that the "open system" argument somehow harmonizes entropy and evolution. An open system is,
indeed, a *necessary* condition for a decrease of entropy in that
system, but it is far from being a *sufficient* condition!

Some writers use the term "negentropy," and talk about
negentropy entering a system to increase its complexity. Since
there is no such thing as negentropy, this idea is also fruitless.

Certain old untenable ideas have served only to
confuse the solution of the problem. Negentropy is
not a concept because entropy cannot be negative.
The role that negentropy has played in previous
discussions is replaced by "complexity" as defined
in information theory.[2]

Complexity and information do not flow into a system by
chance, of course. Once again, there must be both a control
system of some complex form and a storage-conversion mechanism of some kind before this will happen. Since evolution
has neither a control system nor a conversion mechanism,
evolution will not happen.

An uninvited guest at any discussion of the origin
of life and of evolution from the materialistic re-
ductionist point of view is the role of thermodyna-
mic entropy and the "heat death" of the universe
which it predicts.[3]

As far as the naturalistic evolution of life from non-living
chemicals is concerned, therefore, neither Weisskopf nor Prigogine nor anyone else has provided the slightest evidence of any
mechanism for overcoming the impregnable entropy barrier.

---

1. *Ibid*, p. 676.
2. Hubert P. Yockey, "A Calculation of the Probability of Spontaneous
   Biogenesis by Information Theory," *Journal of Theoretical Biology*, Vol.
   67, 1977, p. 377.
3. *Ibid*, p. 380.

Yockey's evaluation of this whole idea is a fitting summary:
> The "warm little pond" scenario was invented *ad hoc* to serve as a materialistic reductionist explanation of the origin of life. It is unsupported by any other evidence, and it will remain *ad hoc* until such evidence is found . . . . One must conclude that, contrary to the established and current wisdom, a scenario describing the genesis of life on earth by chance and natural causes which can be accepted on the basis of fact and not faith has not yet been written.[1]

THE TESTIMONY OF COMPLEX SYSTEMS

According to the dominant neo-Darwinian theory of evolution, the sole mechanism for producing evolution is that of random mutation and natural selection. Mutations are *random* changes in genetic systems. Natural selection is considered by evolutionists to be a sort of sieve which retains the "good" mutations and allows the others to pass away.

Random changes in ordered systems almost always will decrease the amount of order in those systems, and therefore, nearly all mutations are harmful to the organisms which experience them. Nevertheless, the evolutionist insists that each complex organism in the world today has arisen by a long string of gradually-accumulated, good mutations, preserved by natural selection.

No one has ever actually *observed* a genuine beneficial mutation occurring in the natural environment (and was, therefore, retained by the selection process). For some reason, however, the idea has a certain persuasive quality about it and seems eminently reasonable to many people—until it is examined *quantitatively,* that is!

The Improbability of Complexity

For example, consider a very simple organism composed of only 200 integrated and functioning parts, and the problem of deriving that organism by this type of process. Presumably, the organism must have started with only one part and then gradually built itself up over many generations into its 200-part organization. The developing organism, at each successive stage, must itself be integrated and functioning in its environment in order to survive until the next stage. Each successive stage, of course,

---

1. *Ibid,* p. 398.

becomes less likely than the preceding one, since it is far easier for a complex system to break down than to build itself up. A four-component integrated system can more easily mutate into a three-component system (or even a four-component non-functioning system) than into a five-component integrated system. If, at any step in the chain, the system mutates backward or downward, then it is either destroyed altogether or else moves backward.

Therefore, the successful production of a 200-component functioning organism requires, *at least,* 200 successive, successful mutations, each of which is highly unlikely. Even evolutionists recognize that true mutations are very rare, and beneficial mutations are *extremely* rare—not more than one out of a thousand mutations are beneficial, at the very most.

But let us give the evolutionist the benefit of every consideration. Assume that, at each mutational step, there is equally as much chance for it to be good as bad. Thus, the probability for the success of each mutation is assumed to be one out of two, or one-half. Elementary statistical theory shows that the probability of 200 successive mutations being successful is then $(½)^{200}$, or one chance out of 10^{60}. The number 10^{60}, if written out, would be "one" followed by sixty "zeros." In other words, the chance that a 200-component organism could be formed by mutation and natural selection is less than one chance out of a trillion, trillion, trillion, trillion, trillion! *Lest anyone think that a 200-part system is unreasonably complex, it should be noted that even a one-celled plant or animal may have millions of molecular "parts."*

The evolutionist might react by saying that even though any one such mutating organism might not be successful, surely some around the world would be, especially in the 10 billion years (or 10^{18} seconds) of assumed earth history. Therefore, let us imagine that every one of the earth's 10^{14} square feet of surface harbors a billion (i.e. 10^9) mutating systems and that each mutation requires one-half second (actually it would take far more time than this). Each system can thus go through its 200 mutations in 100 seconds and then, if it is unsuccessful, start over for a new try. Therefore, in 10^{18} seconds, there can be $10^{18}/10^2$, or 10^{16}, trials by each mutating system. Multiplying all these numbers together, there would be a total possible number of attempts to develop a 200-component system equal to $10^{14}(10^9)$ (10^{16}), or 10^{39} attempts. Since the probability against the success of any one of them is 10^{60}, it is obvious that the probability that even just one of these 10^{39} attempts might be successful is only one out of $10^{60}/10^{39}$, or 10^{21}.

All of this means that the chance that any kind of a 200-component integrated functioning organism could be developed by mutation and natural selection just once, anywhere in the world, in all the assumed expanse of geologic time, is less than one chance out of a billion trillion. What possible conclusion, therefore, can we derive from such considerations as this except that evolution by mutation and natural selection is mathematically and logically indefensible!

As noted in Chapter III, however, neo-Darwinism is today under attack by a new school of evolutionary thought, which postulates extremely rapid evolution from one stage of complexity to the next higher stage (the Eldredge-Gould theory of "punctuated equilibria"). By this model, the development of a 200-component system would not proceed by a step-by-step advance, but all at once!

There are 200! (200 "factorial"—explained in the following section, "Zero Probability") different ways in which 200 different components could be aligned. This number can be calculated as the product of every digit from 1 through 200, which works out to be the number 10^{375}, or the number one followed by 375 zeroes. This number is fantastically large, but it represents the odds against the chance alignment of the 200 components in just the right order on any one trial.

If, following the example above, we assume that each of the 10^{14} sq. ft. of the earth's surface carries a billion (10^9) 200-component mutating systems, with each mutation taking 1/10 second, there could be 10^{42} such mutations (or random shufflings of 200 components) in the 10^{18} seconds of earth history. The probability that one of these would be the one *right* mutation, which would be functional and therefore preserved by natural selection, would be only one chance in $10^{375}/10^{42}$ or one out of 10^{333}. For any practical purpose, this number is zero!

The conclusion is that the naturalistic evolution of even an impossibly simple 200-component system by random step-by-step mutation is infinitely unlikely (1 in 10^{21}), and evolution of the same system by a sudden "punctuational" mutation is impossible beyond all imagination (1 in 10^{333}). It is granted that the suggested calculations are vastly over-simplified, but only in the direction of providing every benefit possible in favor of chance evolution. Remember also that even the simplest imaginable living system is tremendously more complex than the postulated ordered aligment of just 200 components.

Thus, one of the strongest direct evidences for special creation is the existence of innumerable highly complex systems in the universe, systems composed of components occurring in a pattern of "order" rather than disorder. Creationists maintain that highly ordered systems could not arise by chance, since random processes generate disorder rather than order, simplicity rather than complexity, and confusion instead of "information."

Zero Probability

As another example, consider a series of ten flash cards, numbered from one to ten. If these are thoroughly and randomly mixed, and then laid out successively in a linear array along the table, it would be extremely unlikely that the numbers would fall out in order from one to ten. Actually, there are 3,628,800 different ways in which these numbers could be arranged, so that the "probability" of this particular ordered arrangement is only one in 3,628,800. (This number is "ten factorial," written as 10!, calculated simply by multiplying together all the numbers from one to ten.)

It is obvious that the probability of such a numerically ordered arrangement decreases rapidly as the number of components increases. For any linear system of 100 components in specified order, the probability is one in 100!, or one chance in 10^{158} (a number represented by "one followed by 158 zeroes").

A system requiring such a high degree of order could never happen by chance. This follows from the fact that probability theory only applies to systems with a finite possibility of occurring at least once in the universe, and it would be inconceivable that 10^{158} different trials could ever be made in our entire space-time universe.

Astrophysicists estimate that there are no more than 10^{80} infinitesimal "particles" in the universe, and that the age of the universe in its present form is no greater than 10^{18} seconds (30 billion years). Assuming each particle can participate in a thousand billion (10^{12}) different events every second (this is impossibly high, of course), then the greatest number of events that could ever happen (or trials that could ever be made) in all the universe throughout its entire history is only 10^{80} x 10^{18} x 10^{12}, or 10^{110} (most authorities would make this figure much lower, about 10^{50}). Any event with a probability significantly lower than one chance in 10^{110}, therefore, cannot occur. Its probability becomes zero, at least in our known universe.

This conclusion is intuitively obvious, but it has also been demonstrated mathematically by the great French mathematician, Emil Borel, who called it "the sole law of chance," the law which is the basis of all other laws of probability.

A French scientist, drawing on Borel's work, has defined this law as follows:

> A phenomenon whose probability is sufficiently weak—that is, below a certain threshold—will never occur, "never" meaning here within the limits of space and time at our disposal, that is to say within the limits within which it is possible to repeat the trials, for as long as a world, all of whose known dimensions are finite, allows.[1]

It should be observed also that we have been considering only the probability of a certain arrangement of a very specialized class of events—that is, the ordered linear alignment of 100 pre-specified components. There are also, of course, an unending series of altogether different other classes of events which might occur in space and time, each of which could be specified and studied probabilistically. All events of all categories and arrangements must be counted among the 10^{110} *possible* events. To say that a certain event in one given class of events has a probability in that class of only one in 10^{110} is to say that its probability is still infinitely lower when innumerable other classes of events also have to be crowded into the available space and time.

Thus, the above-suggested ordered arrangement of 100 components has a zero probability. It could *never* happen by chance. Since every single living cell is infinitely more complex and ordered than this, it is impossible that even the simplest form of life could ever have originated by chance. Even the simplest replicating protein molecule that could be imagined has been shown by Golay[2] to have a probability of one in 10^{450}. Salisbury[3] calculates the probability of a typical DNA chain to be one in 10^{600}.

---

1. Georges Salet, *Evolution in the Light of Modern Biology,* as reviewed by Louis Lafont in *Permanences,* Vol. 94, Nov., 1972. Translated from the French by Geoffrey Lawman, in *Approaches Supplement,* p. 7.
2. Marcel Golay, "Reflections of a Communications Engineer," *Analytical Chemistry,* V. 33, June, 1961, p. 23.
3. Frank B. Salisbury, "Doubts about the Modern Synthetic Theory of Evolution," *American Biology Teacher,* September, 1971, p. 336.

The Improbability of Any Kind of Order

However, when creationists use this evidence from probability while lecturing or debating on the creation/evolution question, evolutionists often dismiss the evidence as irrelevant, using the clever and confusing argument that no arrangement is more or less probable than any other arrangement, and *some* arrangement *must* exist! (See Figure 1)

For example, suppose the ten flash cards showed up as follows:

Figure 1.

(a)   3   8   1   10   4   7   9   6   2   5

This arrangement obviously is **unordered** in comparison with the **ordered** arrangement below:

(b)   1   2   3   4   5   6   7   8   9   10

Nevertheless, the evolutionist will say, the unordered arrangement has the same probability (one in 3,628,800, or 10!) as the ordered arrangement. Consequently, since some arrangement is necessary, and any arrangement is just as probable as any other, there is no reason to see any particular significance in the arrangement which happens to occur. Consequently, any argument for design based on probability, they say, is meaningless.

Superficially, this claim may seem logical, even though we immediately sense that something is wrong with it. We know intuitively, as well as experimentally, that ordered arrangements are much less probable than unordered arrangements. Random arrangements of boulders on a hillside, for example, are "natural," whereas the same boulders arranged in a circle would require explanation.

Closer consideration, of course, does quickly reveal that such evolutionary reasoning is specious. If arrangement **(a)** had, for some reason, been specified beforehand, then its actual occurrence in the shuffle would indeed have been surprising. It could then no longer be considered an unordered arrangement, since it had been "ordered" externally! But it was *not* specified ahead of time—it was just the luck of the draw. Arrangement **(b)**, however, has intrinsic order and its actual occurrence, therefore, would almost certainly not have been by chance.

This type of evolutionary equivocation crops up in various guises. One debater responded to the creationists' probability argument by calling attention to the particular combination of people in the audience. With all the people in the state, he noted, the probability that this specific group, rather than some other group, would come together by chance was extremely small, yet there they were! The answer, of course, was that the group had not come together by chance at all—each person had come by direct intent. Nor had the individuals in the group been pre-specified, as would have been the case in a designed system, where each component had to occupy a specific position in order for the system to function.

Once in a while, the objection is a little more subtle. The fact that a certain ordered structure, functioning in a specific way, seems to have an infinitesimal probability of origin by chance is side-stepped by asserting that if some other chance assemblage had come together, it may have functioned in some other way. Evolution might then have taken a different direction. The present functioning system is merely the natural development from the components that happened to come together, and this is no less probable than any other assemblage that might have evolved differently.

But this tenuous argument implicitly assumes that *any* chance aggregation of particles will contain some amount of "information" and, therefore, will have some kind of evolutionary potential. Such a belief is gratuitous and naive, to say the least, when all *real* experience indicates the exact opposite. That is, it is far easier and more common to generate something disordered and useless than something organized and functioning.

One cannot simply pull a working system out of a hat full of random particles. The system must possess the requisite "information" before it can get anywhere or do anything constructive. It must be organized in some kind of pattern, and patterns do not usually appear spontaneously. They are not inevitable, as the above evolutionary argument implies, but extremely rare.

For example, although one could arrange the ten flash cards in a number of possible "ordered" patterns, the number is quite limited. There seems to be a certain amount of "information" in each of the arrangements shown below, but it is obvious that arrangements **(b)** and **(c)** are more "ordered," containing more information than any of the others. Arrangement **(a)**, as noted earlier, contains *no* real order or information—it is strictly "random." No doubt a few other arrangements could be devised with a small amount of order to them, but only a few (see Figure 2).

Figure 2.

(a)	1	2	3	4	5	6	7	8	9	10
(b)	10	9	8	7	6	5	4	3	2	1
(c)	2	4	6	8	10	9	7	5	3	1
(d)	1	3	5	7	9	10	8	6	4	2
(e)	10	8	6	4	2	1	3	5	7	9
(f)	9	7	5	3	1	2	4	6	8	10
(g)	1	2	10	9	3	4	8	7	5	6
(h)	6	5	7	8	4	3	9	10	2	1
(i)	1	10	2	9	3	8	4	7	5	6
(j)	10	1	9	2	8	3	7	4	6	5

To be generous, however, let us assume that as many as 100 patterns could be devised for the ten cards which would contain some modicum of order. Each of these would have some amount of "information" and therefore, might theoretically be able to specify some sort of wobbly function. This is entirely speculative, of course, since the only one which is *known* to be functional is the ideal pattern, as defined in arrangement **(b)**.

Even at best, however, there would be only 100 possible functional arrangements, leaving 3,628,700 completely unordered, and, therefore, non-functional arrangements, a ratio of over 36,000 to one. That is, the odds are at least 36,000 to one against any random assemblage of ten components into a meaningful system, which could possibly serve as a base or pattern for anything.

This simple examination merely confirms that which is intuitively obvious anyhow, namely, that disorder in a system is tremendously more probable than *any kind* of order in that system—not only one specific pattern, but any kind of pattern! Furthermore, this improbability increases as the number of components in the system increases (See Figure 3).

Figure 3.

Number of Components	Number of Arrangements			Ratio of Disordered to Ordered Arrangements
	Possible	Ordered	Disordered	
2	2	2	0	0
3	6	2	4	2:1
4	24	6	18	3:1
5	120	10	110	11:1
—	—	—	—	—
—	—	—	—	—
10	3,628,800	100	3,628,700	36,287:1

The number of ordered arrangements shown in the table is somewhat arbitrary, of course, but certainly generous. In any event, it is very clear that the probability of the *chance* occurrence of any kind of "information" in a system is very small, and that this probability rapidly diminishes as the complexity of the system increases.

This means that, whenever one sees any kind of real ordered complexity in nature, particularly as found in living systems, he can be sure this complexity was *designed*.

One must conclude that, contrary to the established and current wisdom, a scenario describing the genesis of life on earth by chance and natural causes which can be accepted on the basis of fact and not faith has not yet been written.[1]

I believed we developed this practice (i.e., of postulating pre-biological natural selection) to avoid facing the conclusion that the probability of a self-replicating state is zero . . . . When for practical purposes the concept of infinite time and matter has to be invoked, that concept of probability is annulled.[2]

The Impotence of Natural Selection

There is still one other evolutionary equivocation to be noted, however. What chance cannot accomplish, evolutionists glibly attribute to natural selection.

So natural selection as a process is okay. We are also pretty sure that it goes on in nature although good examples are surprisingly rare. The best evidence comes from the many cases where it can be shown that biological structures have been optimized—that is, structures that represent optimal engineering solutions to the problems that an animal has of feeding or escaping predators or generally functioning in its environment . . . . The presence of these optimal structures does not, of course, prove that they developed through natural selection, but it does provide strong circumstantial argument.[3]

This is a rather typical example of the way evolutionists bypass even the strongest evidences for design. Dr. Raup, with his doctorate from Harvard, is a highly competent geologist, serving as Curator of Geology at Chicago's great Field Museum, and formerly as Professor of Geology at the University of Rochester. He candidly acknowledges the complete absence of transitional forms in the fossil record and the complete absence of evidence for observable progressive evolution.

Instead of finding the gradual unfolding of life, what geologists of Darwin's time, and geologists of

---

1. Hubert P. Yockey, "A Calculation of the Probability of Spontaneous Biogenesis by Information Theory," *Journal of Theoretical Biology*, V. 67, 1977, p. 398.
2. Peter T. Mora, "The Folly of Probability," in *The Origins of Prebiological Systems* (Sydney Fox, Editor, New York, Academic Press, 1965), p. 45.
3. David M. Raup, "Conflicts Between Darwin and Paleontology," *Bulletin of the Field Museum of Natural History*, V. 50, January, 1979, pp. 25-26.

the present day actually find is a highly uneven or jerky record; that is, species appear in the sequence very suddenly, show little or no change during their existence in the record, then abruptly go out of the record. And it is not always clear, in fact it's rarely clear, that the descendants were actually better adapted than their predecessors. In other words, biological improvement is hard to find.[1]

Thus, in spite of the utter lack of evidence in either living populations or the fossil record that natural selection ever generates higher orders of complexity (or "biological improvement," or "better adaptation") the mere existence of "optimal structures" is taken by evolutionists as confirmation of the remarkable power of natural selection! As a matter of fact, we have already shown, at the beginning of this section, the utter inability of the mutation-selection process to generate complex functioning systems.

And, of course, such a process as natural selection does not even *exist* at the prebiological level! Whatever effect selection may possibly have had on random processes in later biological reproduction, it is clear beyond any rational argument that chance processes could never have produced even the simplest forms of life in the first place. Without a living God to create life, the laws of probability and complexity prove beyond doubt that life could never come into existence at all.

MISSING LINKS AND HOPEFUL MONSTERS

The laws of thermodynamics and probability show that evolution, despite its almost universal acceptance, is essentially impossible. Therefore, it is not surprising that the fossil record clearly shows that it never happened. Even if the geological ages were real, so that life had been on the earth for billions of years, there is not the slightest evidence in the fossil record that the different forms of plants and animals have an evolutionary history tracing back to a common ancestor.

Nevertheless, it is commonly believed and taught that the fossils record the actual history of evolution, from the first primordial forms of one-celled life up through the invertebrates, then fishes, amphibians, reptiles, birds, and mammals. Finally, it is taught, man and the various apes evolved from

---

1. *Ibid*, p. 23.

a common ancestor back in the Tertiary period. The sequence of fossil forms considered significant in human evolution change from decade to decade, but the basic evolutionary faith remains intact.

Thirty years ago, the three main "proofs" of man's animal ancestry were Piltdown Man, Java Man, and Peking Man. These have all been abandoned in recent years for various reasons and now man's "ancestors" have names like *Ramapithecus, Australopithecus,* and *Homo erectus.* The fact remains, however, that there are *still* no real transitional forms between ape and man.

Time and Human Evolution

Few articles on evolution have been read more widely than the *Time* magazine cover story for November 7, 1977, featuring a photograph of Dr. Richard Leakey and a monstrous-headed superimposed black "man" imaginatively identified as *Homo habilis.* Since many asked how to evaluate this article, a "letter-to-the-editor" briefly summarizing our own reaction is reproduced below:

Editor
Time, *Inc.*

Dear Sir:

With reference to your cover article, "Puzzling Out Man's Ascent" (Time, *November 7, 1977, pp. 64-78), the real puzzle is why the news media continue to promote such evolutionary speculations as* science! *A sampling of the language of the article yields the following:* "many thought," "to suggest," "believed him to be", "seemed to show," "Also, if," "a tooth here, a bone fragment there," "If he isn't," "If they are right," "could have descended," "almost certainly," "We should think rather," "anthropologists now believe," "Leakey too believes," "may someday reveal," "most likely," "whatever the case," "probably," "most anthropologists believe," "new surprises," "could enable him," "anthropologists speculate," "some anthropologists believe," "others think," *"whatever the case," "generally agreed," "scientists believe," "may have been," "frequently undecipherable," "occasionally contradictory," "still incompletely understood," "raise more questions than they answer," "probably."*

Fortunately, all of the above phrases are taken out of context. When the entire article is read in context, it becomes still more amazing that anyone accustomed to basing conclusions on factual evidence could really believe in such modern mythology as human evolution. Why will not Time, *or any other prominent secular periodical ever devote a feature article to the solid scientific evidence for special creation and to the fact that there are today thousands of qualified scientists (most of whom once were evolutionists) who have rejected the whole theory of evolution? Is there some dark reason why this kind of information should continue to be kept hidden?*

There is, of course, one revealing paragraph in the article, and this bears repeating. Here it is:

Still, doubts about the sequence of man's emergence remain. Scientists concede that even their most cherished theories are based on embarrassingly few fossil fragments, and that huge gaps exist in the fossil record. "Anthropologists," ruefully says Alan Mann of the University of Pennsylvania, "are like the blind men looking at the elephant, each sampling only a small part of the total reality." His colleagues agree that the picture of man's origin is far from complete (page 77).

The reason why all the transitional forms between man and his hypothetical ape-like ancestor are still missing, even after 125 years of intensive search, is simply because they never existed. Man was created as man, and apes were created as apes, and all the evidence so far agrees completely with this premise.

Sincerely yours,
Henry M. Morris
Director, I.C.R.

The letter, of course, was never published by *Time,* nor was any other similar letter published. The establishment media, for some reason, seem absolutely determined to perpetuate and foster the myth of human evolution, at all costs.

The Vanishing Hominids

Nevertheless, the facts of the fossil record show no evidence whatever for man's evolution from either an ape or a common ancestor with the apes. As far as *Ramapithecus* is concerned, he also has now been abandoned as a true hominid form: The fossils, consisting only of teeth and jaw fragments, never were very good evidence for his assumed upright posture, but this is how *Ramapithecus* was depicted in millions of now outdated textbooks.

> What, finally, can we say about the position of *Ramapithecus* in primate evolution? One of several kinds of apes that lived during the Miocene, it may have fed in open country, developing jaws and teeth for chewing tough roots and fibers . . . . The case for *Ramapithecus* as an ancestral human has been weak from the start and has not strengthened with the passage of time. Now . . . nothing is left but his smile.[1]

What about *Australopithecus?* This is the current favorite candidate of many anthropologists for the first real ancestor to man. Nevertheless, the actual fossils negate this belief. Solly Zuckerman, Charles Oxnard, and a large team of technicians have devoted years to careful and systematic measurements and analyses of all the Australopithecine fossils, with the final conclusion that this creature did *not* walk upright, as commonly claimed, and could not have been related to man at all. Oxnard was originally a student and colleague of Lord Zuckerman, then later at the University of Chicago and currently (1979) is Dean of the Graduate School and University Professor in Biological Sciences and Anatomy at the University of Southern California. His evaluation is as follows:

> The new investigations suggest that the (Australopithecine) fossil fragments are usually uniquely different from any living form; when they do have

---

1. Adrienne L. Zihlman and Jerold M. Lowenstein, "False Start of the Human Parade," *Natural History,* Vol. 88, August-September, 1979, p. 91.

similarities with living species, they are as often as
not reminiscent of the orangutan.[1]

It is really now somewhat unlikely that australopithecines . . . can actually have had very much to
do with the direct human pathway.[2]

Australopithecus had only a gorilla-sized brain (about 500
cubic centimeters) and was only thought to be ancestral to man
because of his supposed bipedalism. Zuckerman, Oxnard, and
their co-workers have shown conclusively, however, from a
detailed multivariate computer analysis of all details of the
pelvic and limb bones, that *Australopithecus* could *not* have
walked upright at all. Oxnard criticized the "eye-balling"
method of comparing bone forms (as practiced by Leakey
and other leading paleontologists) as follows:

This is a time-honored method that can be extra-
ordinarily powerful (for the eye and the mind are
excellent computers of a kind). But we have merely to
remember cases like Piltdown Man, which turned out
to be a fraudulent composite of a genuine fossil
skull cap and a modern ape jaw, or *Hesperopithecus,*
the ape of the West, which eventually was discovered
to be a peccary, or even by the completely different
portraits that have been drawn for the facial features
of a creature such as *Zinjanthropus* to realize that
this method also has difficulties.[3]

Additional recent skeletal evidence has still further alienated
Australopithecus from any possible relation to man:

We report here the discovery of the first ear ossicle, an incus, of a Plio-Pleistocene hominid. It is
substantially different from that of a modern man,
and the dissimilarity exceeds that between the ear
bones of *Homo sapiens* and of the African apes.
The new incus is of interest particularly in view of
the unique advantages the ear ossicles have for taxo-
nomic and phylogenetic studies . . . . Although the
incus is tiny, its importance should not be over-
looked. Furthermore, this is one of the most complete
and undistorted bones of *Australopithecus robustus*

---

1. Charles E. Oxnard, "Human Fossils: New Views of Old Bones," *American Biology Teacher,* Vol. 41, May 5, 1979, p. 273.

2. *Ibid,* p. 274.

3. *Ibid,* p. 264.

yet discovered.[1]

Thus, it now seems that both *Ramapithecus* and *Australopithecus* must be discarded as human ancestors. That leaves only *Homo erectus* as a possibility. As a matter of fact, Richard Leakey and Carl Johanson, who between them have been in on the discoveries of most of the australopithecine fossils, have maintained for several years that *Homo erectus* and *Australopithecus* lived contemporaneously, with neither the evolutionary descendent of the other. Oxnard agrees.

> It is far more likely that the genus *Homo* is much older than currently believed and that the australopithecines of Olduvai and Sterkfontein represent only parallel evolutionary remnants.[2]

Now, *Homo erectus* means "Erect Man," and it may well be that some of these fossils are true men, perhaps physically degenerate or handicapped for some reason. They are believed to have been toolmakers and, except for their cranial capacity, to have been essentially indistinguishable from *Homo sapiens.* Because of their small brain size (about 900-1000 c.c., whereas the average in modern man is about 1500 c.c.), they have been assumed to be intermediates between modern man and his as-yet-missing apelike ancestor.

But this is not necessarily so. Assuming these to be true *Homo* fossils (actually many of them, such as *Homo habilis* and the Peking skulls, are more likely australopithecines or other apes or monkeys), there is no compelling reason to assume their small brain capacities are anomalous.

> In modern populations . . . there is such a wide range in variation that the lower end of the range is well below the capacity for certain fossil hominids, yet there is no evidence that these individuals are less intelligent than persons with larger cranial vaults . . . . In fact, there are many persons with 700 to 800 cubic centimeters.[3]

As far as Neanderthal Man and Cro-Magnon Man are concerned, we need not even discuss them, since all evolutionists now agree that these are truly *Homo sapiens* representatives, with cranial capacities averaging even higher than those of

---

1. Yoel Rak, "Ear Ossicle of *Australopithecus Robustus,*" *Nature,* Vol. 279, May 3, 1979, p. 62. Rak is in U.C.L.A.'s Department of Anthropology.
2. Charles E. Oxnard, *op cit,* p. 274.
3. Stephen Molnar, *Races, Types, and Ethnic Groups—The Problem of Human Variation* (Englewood Cliffs, N.J., Prentice-Hall, 1975), p. 56-57.

modern man. Thus, all the real fossil evidence indicates that man has always been man and the ape has always been an ape. There may well be some man-like apes (go to the zoo!) or some ape-like men (go to a university faculty meeting!), but there have never been any ape-men or man-apes.

One of the leading evolutionary anthropologists of our day has recently penned a remarkable confession. In a review of the book *Origins* (by Richard Leakey and Roger Lewin, Dutton, 1977), Dr. David Pilbeam of Yale says:

> . . . perhaps generations of students of human evolution, including myself, have been flailing about in the dark; our data base is too sparse, too slippery, for it to be able to mold our theories. Rather, the theories are more statements about us and ideology than about the past. Paleoanthropology reveals more about how humans view themselves than it does about how humans came about. [1]

In other words, evolutionists believe in evolution because they *want* to, not because there is any evidence for it. Otherwise they would have to believe in creation and this would mean acknowledging God as King, rather than man. This they cannot bring themselves to do, and so they go on imagining missing links that never existed.

The Universally Missing Fossil Transitions

And if there are no fossil transitions to be found leading up to the supposedly most *recent* evolutionary arrival—namely, man—what could we expect for earlier evolutionary transitions, the record of which has supposedly had far greater time to be obliterated? The fact is, of course, that there is no record in the fossil record of transitional forms anywhere!

This fact has already been briefly documented in the previous chapter, so here we will only take a brief look at the two most frequently claimed examples of fossil transitions—namely, the famous horse series and *Archaeopteryx*. The horse family tree, from the small three-toed *Eohippus* up to the single-toed large *Equus,* is frequently cited as the best example of a fossil transitional series, but it is actually more of a "bush", if anything.

The record of evolution is still surprisingly jerky and, ironically, we have even fewer examples of evolutionary transition than we had in Darwin's time.

---

1. David Pilbeam, *American Scientist,* Vol. 66, May-June, 1979, p. 378-379.

> By this I mean that some of the classic cases of Dar-
> winian change in the fossil record, such as the evolu-
> tion of the horse in North America, have had to be
> discarded or modified as a result of more detailed
> information—what appeared to be a nice simple pro-
> gression when relatively few data were available now
> appears to be much more complex and much less
> gradualistic.[1]

There is no real evidence that any member of this horse series
developed from any other—they might well all have been con-
temporaneous. Even if they are (or were) related, they would
still all be in the same family and would thus be more or less
like the dog family, or the human family, with variation being
"horizontal," rather than "vertical," and thus strictly in accord
with the principles of creationism.

Archaeopteryx, if genuine, however, represents a different
situation. It has been cited interminably as the best example
of a true transition—half bird, half reptile, with teeth like a
reptile and feathers like a bird.

Actually, all paleontologists acknowledge that *Archaeopteryx*
was really a true bird, though they call it a bird with reptilian
characteristics, newly evolved from a reptilian ancestry, and
probably unable even to fly. Now, however, even this assumption is no longer possible.

> Although *Archaeopteryx* is generally considered
> the earliest bird on record, a recent find suggests
> that the creature, which lived some 130 million years
> ago, may not have been the only bird alive then. A
> new fossil found by James Jensen of Brigham Young
> University dates back to the same period—the late
> Jurassic—and appears to be the femur (thighbone)
> of a bird . . . . The fossil resembles the thighbone of
> modern birds more closely than the comparable
> *Archaeopteryx* bone does . . . . The hypothesis that
> *Archaeopteryx* represents a direct link from reptiles
> to birds has been generally accepted. The existence
> of another bird—one that was an adept flyer and
> thus more advanced on the evolutionary scale—
> would present a challenge to that hypothesis.[2]

1. David M. Raup, "Conflicts between Darwin and Paleontology," *Bulletin,
   Field Museum of Natural History,* Vol. 50, January, 1979, p. 25.
2. "The Oldest Fossil Bird: A Rival for Archaeopteryx," *Science,* Vol. 129,
   January 20, 1978, p. 284.

Thus, whatever *Archaeopteryx* may have been, it was not the ancestor of modern birds, since modern birds were living at the same time as *Archaeopteryx*. As a matter of fact, *Archaeopteryx* itself was much more "modern" than most evolutionists have believed. Until recently, it was asserted that *Archaeopteryx* was so primitive that his wings were still incapable of true flight. Recent aerodynamic analyses have shown, however, that his wings and feathers were as efficient as those of modern birds.

The shape and general proportions of the wing and wing feathers in *Archaeopteryx* are essentially like those of modern birds. The fact that the basic pattern and proportion of the modern avian wing were present in *Archaeopteryx* and have remained essentially unchanged for approximately 150 million years (since late Jurassic time) and that the individual flight feathers showed the asymmetry characteristic of airfoils seems to show that *Archaeopteryx* had an aerodynamically designed wing and was capable of at least gliding.[1]

The Hopeful Monster Returns

Now, if the horse and *Archaeopteryx* do not represent transitional forms in the fossil record, there are *no* such intermediate forms. Nowadays, in fact, most knowledgeable evolutionists no longer even expect to find such transitional forms at all and have tried to make these gaps a part of their new evolutionary model.

For example, "The Return of the Hopeful Monsters" is the title of a remarkable recent article by Stephen Jay Gould. Dr. Gould is Professor of Geology and Paleontology at Harvard and is one of the world's current leaders of evolutionary thought. Along with a number of other modern evolutionists, Gould has recognized the failure of neo-Darwinism (slow and gradual evolution by small beneficial mutations preserved by natural selection) and has been advocating what he calls "punctuated equilibria" (rapid evolution in small populations followed by stability in large populations) to explain the universal gaps in the fossil record.

But now, in trying to imagine a mechanism for this rapid

---

1. Alan Peduccia and Harrison B. Turdoff, "Feathers of *Archaeopteryx:* Asymmetric Vanes Indicate Aerodynamic Function," *Science,* Vol. 203, March 9, 1979, p. 1022.

evolution, Gould is actually predicting a refurbishing of Richard Goldschmidt's long-ridiculed "hopeful monster" mechanism. Goldschmidt was an outstanding geneticist who, realizing that mutations normally produce monsters, nevertheless believed that occasional small genetic changes could generate *hopeful* monsters, by which, for example, a bird could suddenly be produced from a reptile's egg! Says Gould:

> As a Darwinian, I wish to defend Goldschmidt's postulate that macroevolution is not simply micro-evolution extrapolated and that major structural transitions can occur rapidly without a smooth series of intermediate stages.[1]

Of course, both Goldschmidt and Gould were driven to such an extremity as hopeful monsters by the intractable facts of the fossil record, which they have been honest enough to acknowledge. As Gould says in another article:

> The extreme rarity of transitional forms in the fossil record persists as the trade secret of paleontology . . . . We fancy ourselves as the only true students of life's history, yet to preserve our favored account of evolution by natural selection we view our data as so bad that we never see the very process we profess to study.[2]

The creationist, however, does not have to invent such bizarre explanations for the gaps in the fossils. The creationist *predicted* the gaps! They provide positive evidence for the creation model.

Creationists are not the only ones who recognize the absurdity of making this complete absence of evolutionary transitional forms a basic feature of the new evolution model! Evolutionist philosopher Larry Azar raises this question in *Bioscience:*

> I can understand the inherent difficulty in attempting to discover intermediate forms. My problem concerns the *methodology* of science: If an evolutionist accepts gaps as a prerequisite for his theory, is he not arguing from a lack of evidence? If a biologist teaches that between two existing fossils there was a non-existing third (and perhaps several others), is he not

---

1. Stephen Jay Gould, "The Return of the Hopeful Monsters," *Natural History,* Vol. LXXXVI, June-July, 1977, p. 24.
2. Stephen Jay Gould, "Evolution's Erratic Pace," *Natural History,* Vol. LXXXVI, May, 1977, p. 14.

really like the man of religious faith who says: "I believe, even though there is not evidence"?[1]

Two hundred years of systematic fossil collecting, with billions of fossils now known, yet all the supposed evolutionary links are still missing links! The laws of science demonstrate that evolution is impossible and the fossil record demonstrates that it never occurred even if it *were* possible. Evolution is nothing but a credulous religious faith in the omnipotence of Matter—a faith exercised blindly, in spite of the universal evidence against it.

FOSSILS AND THE FLOOD

Since the fossils do not, as evolutionists had hoped, really provide a record of evolution, what exactly do they represent? The answer is the great Flood. Instead of speaking of the world-wide evolution of life over many ages, they really speak of the worldwide destruction of life in one age—the age of the universal Deluge.

The Premature Rejection of Catastrophism

In the early days of geology, especially during the 17th and 18th centuries, the dominant explanation for the sedimentary rocks and their fossilized contents was that they had been laid down in the great Flood of the days of Noah. This was the view of Steno, the "father of stratigraphy," whose principles of stratigraphic interpretation are still followed today, and of John Woodward, Sir Isaac Newton's hand-picked successor at Cambridge, whose studies on sedimentary processes laid the foundation for modern sedimentology and geomorphology. These men and the other Flood geologists of their day were careful scientists, thoroughly acquainted with the sedimentary rocks and the geophysical processes which formed them. In common with most other scientists of their day, they believed in God and the divine authority of the Bible. Evolution and related naturalistic speculations had been confined largely to the writings of social philosophers and rationalistic theologians.

Toward the end of the 18th century, and especially in the first half of the 19th century, the ancient pagan evolutionary philosophies began to be revived and promoted by the various socialistic revolutionary movements of the times. These could

---

1. Larry Azar, "Biologists, Help!" *Bioscience,* Vol. 28, November, 1978, p. 714.

make little headway, however, as long as the scientists were predominantly creationists. Evolution obviously required aeons of geologic time and the scientific community, including the great Isaac Newton himself, was committed to the Ussher chronology, with its recent special creation and worldwide Flood.

Therefore, it was necessary, first of all, that the Flood be displaced as the framework of geologic interpretation, so that earth history could once again, as in the days of the ancient Greek and Oriental philosophers, be expanded into great reaches and cycles of time over endless ages. Geologic *catastrophism* must be, at all costs replaced by *uniformitarianism,* which would emphasize the slow uniform processes of the present as a sufficient explanation for all earth structures and past history. This was accomplished in two stages: first, the single cataclysm of the Flood was replaced by the multiple catastrophes and new creations of Cuvier and Buckland, each separated from the next by a long period of uniform processes; second, these periodic catastrophes were gradually de-emphasized and the uniformitarian intervals enlarged until the latter finally incorporated the entire history.

It is significant that this uniformitarian revolution was led, not by professional scientific geologists, but by amateurs, men such as Buckland (a theologian), Cuvier (an anatomist), Buffon (a lawyer), Hutton (an agriculturalist), Smith (a surveyor), Chambers (a journalist), Lyell (a lawyer), and others of similar variegated backgrounds. The acceptance of Lyell's uniformitarianism laid the foundation for the sudden success of Darwinism in the decade following the publication of Darwin's *Origin of Species* in 1859. Darwin frequently acknowledged his debt to Lyell, who he said gave him the necessary time required for natural selection to produce meaningful evolutionary results.

Nevertheless, the actual facts of geology still favored catastrophism, and Flood geology never died completely. Although the uniformitarian philosophers could point to certain difficulties in the Biblical geology of their predecessors, there were still greater difficulties in uniformitarianism. Once uniformitarianism had served its purpose—namely, that of selling the scientific community and the general public on the great age of the earth—then geologists could again use local catastrophic processes whenever required for specific geologic interpretations. Stephen Gould has expressed it this way:

> Methodological uniformitarianism was useful only

when science was debating the status of the supernatural in its realm.[1]

Heylmun goes even further:

The fact is, the doctrine of uniformitarianism is no
more "proved" than some of the early ideas of
worldwide cataclysms have been disproved.[2]

With adequate time apparently available, assisted by man's
natural inclination to escape from God if possible, Darwin's
theory of evolution by chance variation and natural selection
was eagerly accepted by the learned world. Pockets of scientific
resistance in the religious community were quickly neutralized
by key clerical endorsements of the "day-age theory," which
seemingly permitted Christians to hang on to Genesis while at
the same time riding the popular wave of long ages and evolutionary progress. For those fundamentalists who insisted that
the creation week required a literal interpretation, the "gap
theory" ostensibly permitted them to do so merely by inserting
the geologic ages in an imaginary gap between Genesis 1:1 and
1:2, thus ignoring their evolutionary implications.

The Biblical Deluge was similarly shorn of scientific significance by reinterpreting it in terms of a "Local Flood" or,
for those few people who insisted that the Genesis narrative
required a universal inundation, a "Tranquil Flood." Lyell
himself proposed a worldwide tranquil flood that left no geological traces. In any case, the field of earth history was taken
over almost completely by evolutionists.

In return, this capitulation of the scientists to evolution was
an enormous boon to the social revolutionaries, who could now
proclaim widely that their theories of social change were
grounded in natural science. For example, Karl Marx and the
Communists quickly aligned themselves with evolutionary geology and biology, Marx even asking to dedicate his *Das
Kapital* to Charles Darwin.

However harshly a philosopher may judge this
characterization of Marx's theory (i.e., that Marxism
unites science and revolution intrinsically and insep-
arably) an historian can hardly fail to agree that
Marx's claim to give scientific guidance to those who

---

1. Stephen Jay Gould: "Is Uniformitarianism Necessary?", *American Journal
   of Science*, Vol. 263, (March, 1965), p. 227.
2. Edgar B. Heylmun: "Should We Teach Uniformitarianism?", *Journal of
   Geological Education*, Vol. 19, January, 1971, p. 35.

would transform society has been one of the chief reasons for his doctrine's enormous influence.[1]

The "science" referred to in the above is, in context, nothing but naturalistic evolution based on uniformitarian geology. Similarly, Nietzschean racism, Freudian amoralism, and military imperialism all had their roots in the same soil and grew in the same climate.

Yet all the while the foundation was nothing but sand. Uniformitarian geology was contrary to both the Bible and to observable science. Now, a hundred years later, the humanistic and naturalistic culture erected upon that foundation is beginning to crumble, and men are beginning again to look critically at the foundation.

The two Biblical compromise positions are now widely recognized as unacceptable, either theologically or scientifically. A brief discussion of the fallacies of the "day-age" and "gap" theories, as well as "theistic evolution" and "progressive creation" has already been given in an earlier chapter.

The local-flood theory is even less defensible. The entire Biblical account of the Flood is absurd if read in a local-flood context. For example, there was obviously no need for any kind of an ark if the flood were only a local flood. Yet the Bible describes it as a huge vessel with a volumetric capacity which can be shown to be equal to that of over 500 standard railroad stock cars! According to the account, the ark floated freely over all the high mountains and finally came to rest, five months later, on the mountains of Ararat. The highest of these mountains today is 17,000 feet in elevation, and a flood which could cover such a mountain six months or more was no local flood!

Furthermore, God's promise never to send such a flood again, sealed with the continuing testimony of the rainbow, has been broken again and again if the Flood was only a local flood.

A list of 100 reasons why the Flood must be understood as worldwide is given in one of the writer's books.[2]

The tranquil-flood theory is even more ridiculous. It is difficult to believe anyone could take it seriously, and yet a number

---

1. David Jorafsky, *Soviet Marxism and Natural Science* (New York, Columbia University Press, 1961), p. 12.
2. Henry M. Morris, *The Genesis Record* (Grand Rapids, Baker Book House, 1976) pp. 683-686.

of modern evangelical geologists do believe in this idea (especially Davis Young, in his book *Creation and the Flood,* discussed earlier). Even local floods are violent phenomena and uniformitarian geologists today believe they are responsible for most of the geologic deposits of the earth's crust. A universal Flood that could come and go softly, leaving no geologic evidence of its passage, would require an extensive complex of miracles for its accomplishment. Anyone with the slightest understanding of the hydraulics of moving water and the hydrodynamics forces associated with it would know that a worldwide "tranquil" flood is about as reasonable a concept as a worldwide tranquil explosion!

The Flood Model of Geology

As far as science is concerned, it should be remembered that events of the past are not reproducible, and are, therefore, inaccessible to the scientific method. Neither uniformitarianism nor catastrophism can actually be *proved* scientifically. Nevertheless, the Flood model fits all the geologic facts more directly and simply, with a smaller number of qualifications and secondary assumptions, than does the uniformitarian model.

An obvious indication of global water activity is the very existence of sedimentary rocks all over the world which, by definition, were formed by the erosion, transportation, and deposition of sediments by moving water, with the sediments gradually converted into stone after they had been deposited.

Similarly, an obvious indicator of catastrophism is the existence of fossils in the sedimentary rocks. The depositional processes must have been rapid, or fossils could not have been preserved in them.

> To become fossilized, a plant or animal must
> usually have hard parts, such as bone, shell, or wood.
> It must be buried quickly to prevent decay and must
> be undisturbed throughout the long process.[1]

The importance of this fact is obvious when one realizes that the identification of the geologic "age" of any given sedimentary rock depends solely upon the assemblage of fossils which it contains. The age does not depend on radiometric dating, as is obvious from the fact that the geologic age system had been completely worked out and most major formations dated

---

1. F.H.T. Rhodes, H.S. Zimm, and P.R. Shaffer, *Fossils* (New York, Golden Press, 1962), p. 10.

before radioactivity was even discovered. Neither does the age
depend upon the mineralogic or petrologic character of a rock,
as is obvious from the fact that rocks of all types of composition, structure, and degree of hardness can be found in any
"age." It does not depend upon vertical position in the local
geologic strata, since rocks of any "age" may and do rest hori-
zontally and conformably on rocks of any other age. No, a
rock is dated *solely* by its fossils.

> The only chronometric scale applicable in geologic
> history for the stratigraphic classification of rocks
> and for dating geologic events exactly is furnished
> by the fossils. Owing to the irreversibility of evolu-
> tion, they offer an unambiguous time-scale for rela-
> tive age determinations and for worldwide correla-
> tions of rocks.[1]

Thus, the existence and identification of distinctive geologic
ages is based on fossils in the sedimentary rocks. On the other
hand, the very existence of fossils in sedimentary rocks is
prima facie evidence that each such fossiliferous rock was
formed by aquaeous catastrophism. The one question, therefore, is whether the rocks were formed by a great multiplicity
of local catastrophes scattered through many ages, or by a great
complex of local catastrophes all conjoined contemporaneously
in one single age, terminated by the cataclysm.

The latter is the most likely. Each distinctive stratum was laid
down quickly, since it obviously represents a uniform set of
water flow conditions, and such uniformity never persists very
long. Each set of strata in a given formation must also have
been deposited in rapid succession, or there would be evidence
of unconformities—that is, periods of uplift and erosion—at
the various interfaces.

Where unconformities do exist, say at the top of a formation,
there may well have been an interval of uplift or tilting, at that
location, followed by either sub-aerial or sub-marine erosion for
a time. However, since such formations invariably grade later-
ally into other formations (no unconformity is worldwide),
sooner or later one will come to a location where there is a
conformable relationship between this formation and the one
above it. Thus, each formation is succeeded somewhere by
another one which was deposited rapidly after the first one . . .

1. O.H. Schindewolf, "Comments on Some Stratigraphic Terms" *American Journal of Science,* Vol. 255, June, 1957, p. 394.

and so on, throughout the entire geologic column.

Thus, there is no room anywhere for long ages. Each formation must have been produced rapidly, as evidenced by both its fossils and its depositional characteristics, and each formation must have been followed rapidly by another one, which was also formed rapidly! The whole sequence, therefore, must have been formed rapidly, exactly as the Flood model postulates.

But, then, what about the geologic ages? Remember that the only means of identifying these ages is by fossils, and fossils speak of rapid formation. Even assuming a very slow formation of these beds, however, how can fossils tell the age of a rock?

Obviously, fossils could be distinctive time-markers only if the various kinds each had lived in different ages. But how can we know which fossils lived in which ages? No scientists were there to observe them, and true *science* requires *observation*. Furthermore, by analogy with the present (and uniformitarianism is supposed to be able to decipher the past in terms of the present), many different kinds of plants and animals are living in the present world, including even the "primitive" one-celled organisms with which evolution is supposed to have begun. Why, therefore, isn't it better to assume that all major kinds also lived together in past ages as well? Some kinds, such as the dinosaurs, have become extinct, but practically all present-day kinds of organisms are also found in the fossil world.

The only reason for thinking that different fossils should represent different ages is the assumption of evolution. If evolution is really true, then of course fossils should provide an excellent means for identifying the various ages, an "unambiguous time-scale", as Schindewolf put it. Hedberg says:

> Fossils have furnished, through their record of the
> evolution of life on this planet, an amazingly effective
> key to the relative positioning of strata in widely-
> separated regions.[1]

The use of fossils as time-markers thus depends completely on "their record of evolution". But, then, how do we know that evolution is true? Why, because of the fossil record!

> Fossils provide the only historical, documentary
> evidence that life has evolved from simpler to more
> and more complex forms.[2]

1. H.D. Hedberg, "The Stratigraphic Panorama", *Bulletin of the Geological Society of America,* Vol. 72, April, 1961, pp. 499-518.
2. C.O. Dunbar; *Historical Geology* (New York, Wiley, 1960), p. 47.

So, the only proof of evolution is based on the assumption of evolution! The system of evolution arranges the fossils, the fossils date the rocks, and the resulting system of fossil-dated rocks proves evolution. Around and around we go.

How much more simple and direct it would be to explain the fossil-bearing rocks as the record in stone of the destruction of the antediluvian world by the great Flood. The various fossil assemblages represent, not evolutionary stages developing over many ages, but rather ecological habitats in various parts of the world in one age. Fossils of simple marine invertebrate animals are normally found at the lowest elevations in the geologic strata for the simple reason that they live at the lowest elevations. Fossils of birds and mammals are found only at the higher elevations because they live at higher elevations, and also because they are more mobile and could escape burial longer. Human fossils are extremely rare because men would only very rarely be trapped and buried in flood sediments at all, because of their high mobility. The sediments of the "ice-age" at the highest levels are explained in terms of the drastically changed climates caused by the Flood.

The flood theory of geology,[1] which was so obvious and persuasive to the founders of geology, is thus once again beginning to be recognized as the only theory which is fully consistent with the actual *facts* of geology, as well as with the testimony of Scripture.

Circular Reasoning in Geology

As suggested above, creationists have long insisted that the main evidence for evolution—the fossil record—involves a serious case of circular reasoning. That is, the fossil evidence that life has evolved from simple to complex forms over the geological ages depends on the geological ages of the specific rocks in which these fossils are found. The rocks, however, are assigned geologic ages based on the fossil assemblages which they contain. The fossils, in turn, are arranged on the basis of their assumed evolutionary relationships. Thus the main evidence for evolution is based on the assumption of evolution.

A significant development of recent years has been the fact

---

1. See *The Genesis Flood,* by John C. Whitcomb and Henry M. Morris (Nutley, N.J., Presbyterian and Reformed, 1961), for a much more extensive treatment.

that many evolutionary geologists are now also recognizing this problem. They no longer ignore it or pass it off with a sarcastic denial, but admit that it is a real problem which deserves a serious answer.

The use of "index fossils" to determine the geologic age of a formation, for example, is discussed in an interesting way in an important recent paper by J.E. O'Rourke.

> These principles have been applied in *Feinstrati-graphie,* which starts from a chronology of index fossils, and imposes them on the rocks. Each taxon represents a definite time unit and so provides an accurate, even "infallible" date. If you doubt it, bring in a suite of good index fossils, and the specialist without asking where or in what order they were collected, will lay them out on the table in chronological order.[1]

That is, since evolution always proceeds in the same way all over the world at the same time, index fossils representing a given stage of evolution are assumed to constitute infallible indicators of the geologic age in which they are found. This makes good sense and would obviously be the best way to determine relative geologic age—if, that is, we knew infallibly that evolution were true!

But how do we know that? There is such a vast time scale involved that no one can actually observe evolution taking place.

> That a known fossil or recent species, or higher taxonomic group, however primitive it might appear, is an actual ancestor of some other species or group, is an assumption scientifically unjustifiable, for science never can simply assume that which it has the responsibility to demonstrate . . . . It is the burden of each of us to demonstrate the reasonableness of any hypothesis we might care to erect about ancestral conditions, keeping in mind that we have no ancestors alive today, that in all probability such ancestors have been dead for many tens of millions of years, and that even in the fossil record they are not accessible to us.[2]

---

1. J.E. O'Rourke, "Pragmatism versus Materialism in Stratigraphy," *American Journal of Science,* Vol. 276, January, 1976, p. 51.
2. Gareth V. Nelson, "Origin and Diversification of Teleostean Fishes," *Annals, New York Academy of Sciences,* 1971, p. 27.

There is, therefore, really no way of proving scientifically any assumed evolutionary phylogeny, as far as the fossil record is concerned.

> Likewise, paleontologists do their best to make sense out of the fossil record and sketch in evolutionary sequences or unfossilized morphologies without realistic hope of obtaining specific verification within the foreseeable future.[1]

It would help if the fossil record would yield somewhere at least a few transitional sequences demonstrating the evolution of some kind of organism into some other more complex kind. So far, however, it has been uncooperative.

> The abrupt appearance of higher taxa in the fossil record has been a perennial puzzle . . . . If we read the record rather literally, it implies that organisms of new grades of complexity arose and radiated relatively rapidly.[2]

Transitions are well documented, of course, at the *same* levels of complexity—within the "kinds," that is—but never into "new grades of complexity." *Horizontal* changes, however, are not really relevant to the measure of geologic time, since such changes occur too rapidly (e.g., the development of numerous varieties of dogs within human history) to be meaningful on the geologic time scale, and are reversible (e.g., the shift in the population numbers of the peppered-moth of England from light-colored to dark-colored and back again).

Thus *vertical* evolutionary changes in fossils are essential to real geologic dating, but they are impossible to prove. They must simply be assumed.

The dating of the rocks depends on the evolutionary sequence of the fossils, but the evolutionary interpretation of the fossils depends on the dating of the rocks. No wonder the evolutionary system, to outsiders, implies circular reasoning.

> Are the authorities maintaining, on the one hand, that evolution is documented by geology and, on the other hand, that geology is documented by evolution?

---

1. Donald R. Griffin, "A Possible Window on the Minds of Animals," *American Scientist,* Vol. 64, September-October, 1976, p. 534.
2. James W. Valentine and Cathryn A. Campbell, "Genetic Regulation and the Fossil Record," *American Scientist,* Vol. 63, November-December, 1975, p. 673.

Isn't this a circular argument?[1]

The intelligent layman has long suspected circular reasoning in the use of rocks to date fossils and fossils to date rocks. The geologist has never bothered to think of a good reply, feeling the explanations are not worth the trouble as long as the work brings results. This is supposed to be hard-headed pragmatism.[2]

The main "result" of this system, however, is merely the widespread acceptance of evolution. It is extremely inefficient in locating oil or other economically useful deposits. Perhaps, however, geologists feel that, since biologists had already proved evolution, they are justified in assuming it in their own work. But biologists in turn have simply assumed evolution to be true.

But the danger of circularity is still present. For most biologists the strongest reason for accepting the evolutionary hypothesis is their acceptance of some theory that entails it. There is another difficulty. The temporal ordering of biological events beyond the local section may critically involve paleontological correlation, which necessarily presupposed the non-repeatability of organic events in geologic history. There are various justifications for this assumption but for almost all contemporary paleontologists it rests upon the acceptance of the evolutionary hypothesis.[3]

And, as far as "ordering of biological events beyond the local section is concerned," O'Rourke reminds us again that:

Index fossils . . . are regarded as the features most reliable for accurate, long-distance correlations.[4]

As mentioned earlier, more and more modern geologists are now recognizing the existence of circular reasoning in their geological methodologies. Among these, in addition to those already cited, is Dr. Derek Ager, former president of the British Geological Association.

It is a problem not easily solved by the classic methods of stratigraphical paleontology, as obviously

---

1. Larry Azar, "Biologists, Help!", *Bioscience,* Vol. 28, November, 1978, p. 714.
2. J.E. O'Rourke, *op cit,* p. 48.
3. David B. Kitts, "Paleontology and Evolutionary Theory," *Evolution,* Vol. 28, September, 1974, p. 466.
4. J.E. O'Rourke, *op cit,* p. 48.

we will land ourselves immediately in an impossible
circular argument if we say, firstly that a particular
lithology is synchronous on the evidence of its fossils,
and secondly that the fossils are synchronous on the
evidence of the lithology.[1]

In another article, Dr. Ager, who is also Head of the Geology
Department at Swansea University, notes the problem involved
in trying to use minor differences in organisms (that is, what
creationists would call horizontal changes, or variations) as
time markers.

We all know that many apparent evolutionary
bursts are nothing more than brainstorms on the
part of particular paleontologists. One splitter in a
library can do far more than millions of years of
genetic mutation.[2]

It would seem that this would lead to great uncertainty in
the use of extinct marine organisms (about whose intra-specific
variability while they were living we know nothing whatever) as
index fossils.

Another geologist who has recognized the circulatory problem
is Dr. Ronald West, at Kansas State University.

Contrary to what most scientists write, the fossil
record does not support the Darwinian theory of
evolution because it is this theory (there are several)
which we use to interpret the fossil record. By doing
so, we are guilty of circular reasoning if we then say
the fossil record supports this theory.[3]

Still another comment on the circular reasoning process
involved in developing paleontological sequences appears in an
important symposium paper.

The prime difficulty with the use of presumed
ancestral-descendant sequences to express phylogeny
is that biostratigraphic data are often used in con-
junction with morphology in the initial evaluation of

1. Derek V. Ager, *The Nature of the Stratigraphic Record* (New York, John Wiley & Sons, 1973) p. 62.
2. Derek V. Ager, "The Nature of the Fossil Record," *Proceedings of the Geological Association,* Vol. 87, No. 2, 1976, p. 132.
3. Ronald R. West, "Paleontology and Uniformitarianism," *Compass,* Vol. 45, May, 1968, p. 216.

relationships, which leads to obvious circularity.[1]

In view of such admissions from many leading evolutionists, it is clear that there neither is, nor can be, any *proof* of evolution. The evidence for evolution is merely the assumption of evolution.

The most extensive recent discussion of the circular reasoning problem in evolutionary geology is the paper by O'Rourke.[2] Although he attempts to explain and justify the process as being based on induction from observed field data, he does admit many important problems in this connection. With respect to the geologic column and its development, he says:

> Material bodies are finite, and no rock unit is global in extent, yet stratigraphy aims at a global classification. The particulars have to be stretched into universals somehow. Here ordinary materialism leaves off building up a system of units recognized by physical properties, to follow dialectical materialism, which starts with time units and regards the material bodies as their incomplete representatives. This is where the suspicion of circular reasoning crept in, because it seemed to the layman that the time units were abstracted from the geological column, which has been put together from rock units.[3]

The fiction that the geological column was actually represented by real rock units in the field has long been abandoned, of course.

> By mid-nineteenth century, the notion of "universal" rock units had been dropped, but some stratigraphers still imagine a kind of global biozone as "time units" that are supposed to be ubiquitous.[4]

Behind all such assumed time units must be the doctrinaire assumption of evolution, which is the basic component of materialism.

> The theory of dialectic materialism postulates matter as the ultimate reality, not to be questioned . . . .
> Evolution is more than a useful biologic concept: it

---

1. B. Schaeffer, M.K. Hecht, and N. Eldredge, "Phylogeny and Paleontology," Ch. 2 in *Evolutionary Biology,* Vol. 6 (edited by Th. Dobzhansky, M.K. Hecht, and W.C. Steere; New York, Appleton-Century-Crofts, 1972), p. 39.
2. J.E. O'Rourke, *op cit,* pp. 47-55.
3. *Ibid,* p. 49.
4. *Ibid,* p. 50.

is a natural law controlling the history of all phenomena.[1]

And if physical data in the field seem in any case to contradict this assumed evolutionary development, then the field
data can easily be reinterpreted to correspond to evolution!
This is always possible in circular reasoning.

> Structure, metamorphism, sedimentary reworking,
> and other complications have to be considered.
> Radiometric dating would not have been feasible if
> the geologic column had not been erected first . . . .
> The axiom that no process can measure itself means
> that there is no absolute time, but this relic of the
> traditional mechanics persists in the common distinc-
> tion between "relative" and "absolute" age.[2]

In this exposition, O'Rourke thus decries the common
reliance on an implicit circular argument which he attributes
to the assumption of dialectic materialism, and urges his
colleagues to deal pragmatically with the actual stratigraphic
rock units as they occur in the field, in confidence that this
will eventually correlate with the global column built up gradually by similar procedures used by their predecessors.

He does recognize, however, that if the actual physical
geological column is going to be used as a time scale, it is
impossible to avoid circular reasoning.

> The rocks do date the fossils, but the fossils date
> the rocks more accurately. Stratigraphy cannot
> avoid this kind of reasoning if it insists on using only
> temporal concepts, because circularity is inherent in
> the derivation of time scales.[3]

Order in the Fossils

Since there is no way to tell the geologic age of rocks except
on the assumption of evolution, there is no way to be sure that
any one "age" is different from any other. Thus, they could
all well be the same age, exactly as the Biblical Flood model
requires. The rocks and fossil beds were all formed catastrophically, and by the same catastrophe at that.

An obvious question, however, involves the general order of
the strata in the geologic column. Even though the entire

---

1. *Ibid*, p. 51.
2. *Ibid*, p. 54.
3. *Ibid*, p. 53.

geologic column may have been deposited in the cataclysm of the great Flood, why are the fossils arranged in a vertical order that at least *looks* like evolution? Why are there different forms of life found as fossils in the different rock systems that evolutionists have attributed to different ages?

The answer is twofold. In the first place, the supposed order is to a considerable extent artificial, since each local geological column varies from every other and since each local column never constitutes more than a very small fraction of the total column. In the second place, such order as does exist is mainly an order of ecological zonation and is exactly what a great Flood would cause.

It is significant that every one of the great phyla and most of the classes of the animal kingdom appear in the Cambrian rocks, supposed by evolutionists to be the oldest of the fossil-producing geological ages. All the animals preserved in these rocks are marine animals, reflecting the marine fauna that lived in the pre-Flood oceans—and therefore normally were buried most deeply in the Flood sediments. They comprise the same phyla and classes that live in the present oceans, except for some that have apparently become extinct, and often are animals practically identical with living types (sponges, star-fish, jellyfish, etc.).

Evolutionists used to claim that the vertebrates did not evolve until sixty million years or so after the Cambrian period. Now, however, even vertebrates (specifically fishes) have been found in Cambrian rocks.

> . . . until recently, vertebrates have been known from rocks no older than the Middle Ordovician (about 450 million years ago). In 1976 and 1977 the known range of the vertebrates was extended about 20 million years by discoveries of fish fossils in rocks of latest Early Ordovician and earliest Middle Ordovician age in Spitzbergen and Australia. This report of fish material from Upper Cambrian rocks further extends the record of the vertebrates by approximately another 40 million years.[1]

If practically all the animal classes and phyla are found in all the geologic "ages," or more accurately, the rock systems of the geologic column, there is very little left of even a superficial

---

1. John E. Rapetski, "A Fish from the Upper Cambrian of North America," *Science,* Vol. 200, May 5, 1978, p. 529.

appearance of evolution.

Furthermore, ecological zonation accounts for what may still appear to be a semblance of evolutionary development in the column. That is, the vertical order in the rocks is usually from marine invertebrates at the lowest elevations to marine vertebrates, then amphibians (at the interface between land and sea in the antediluvian world), then reptiles, mammals, birds, and men. This is an order of increasing elevation of habitat and, therefore, of depositional elevation in the geological column. It does not represent evolution at all, though it has long been so interpreted. Some evolutionists are now recognizing the validity of this concept.

> It is worth mentioning that continuous "evolution-
> ary" series derived from the fossil record can in most
> cases be simulated by chronoclines—successions of
> a geographical cline population imposed by the
> changes of some environmental gradients.[1]

Whether or not we are able yet to sort out all the details of every local geological column in the context of the Flood model, however, the important point is that the entire geological column really bears witness to continuous catastrophism.

Return to Catastrophism

One of the surprising developments of the past decade has been the resurgence of catastrophism in geological interpretation. Although the great men who were the real founders of geology (Steno, Woodward, et al) were not only catastrophists, but believed in the Noahic Flood as the most important geologic event in earth history, the principle of uniformitarianism has dominated geological thinking for the past 150 years. The Scottish agriculturalist, James Hutton, and then the British lawyer, Charles Lyell, persuaded their contemporaries to reject the Biblical chronology and its cataclysmic deluge in favor of very slow processes acting through aeons of time. In his widely used textbook, Zumberge stated:

> Opposed to this line of thinking was Sir Charles
> Lyell (1979-1875), a contemporary of Cuvier, who
> held that earth changes were gradual, taking place at
> the same uniform slowness that they are today. Lyell
> is thus credited with the propagation of the premise

---

1. V. Krassilov, "Causal Biostratigraphy," *Lethaia,* Vol. 7, No. 3, 1974, p. 174.

that more or less has guided geological thought ever
since, namely, that the present is the key to the past.
In essence, Lyell's doctrine of uniformitarianism
stated that past geological processes operated in the
same manner and at the same rate they do today.[1]

Nevertheless, the evidence for catastrophism was there in the
rocks and it could not be ignored indefinitely. Uniformitarianism was proving sterile—present processes operating at present
rates simply could **not** explain the great geological formations
and structures in the earth's crust, not to mention its vast fossil
graveyards. Zumberge noted:

From a purely scientific point of view, it is unwise
to accept uniformitarianism as unalterable dogma
. . . . (One) should never close his mind to the possibility that conditions in past geological time were
different than today . . . . [2]

A few geologists (Krynine, Bretz, Dachile, *et al)* had even
earlier begun to call attention to certain strong geologic evidences of more than normal catastrophism in the geologic
column. Even Lyell, of course, had recognized the significance
of local floods, volcanic eruptions, and other such events, but
had included these in his overall uniformitarian framework.
Such phenomena as the "scabland" areas of Washington and
the earth's many meteoritic scars, however, had begun to convince some geologists that even "ordinary" catastrophes were
not the whole story.

The real revival of catastrophism among orthodox geologists,
however, seems to have been associated with a number of
brilliant papers by Stephen Jay Gould, a geologist and historian
of science with impeccable credentials. Gould first stressed the
necessity to distinguish between uniformity of natural laws and
uniformity of process rates.

Uniformitarianism is a dual concept. Substantive
uniformitarianism (a testable theory of geologic
change postulating uniformity of rates of material

1. James H. Zumberge, *Elements of Geology* (New York, 2nd ed., John
Wiley and Sons, 1963), p. 200. Zumberge and the writer were graduate
students together at the University of Minnesota, in the period 1946-50, in
its Department of Geology. He was more favorably inclined toward Biblical
catastrophism than were others in the Geology Department and we had a
number of good discussions and seemed to have much in common at that
time.
2. *Ibid,* p. 201.

conditions) is false and stifling to hypothesis formation. Methodological uniformitarianism (a procedur-
al principle asserting spatial and temporal invariance
of natural laws) belongs to the definition of science
and is not unique to geology.[1]

It is interesting to note that writers on Biblical catastrophism
have always stressed that they are only rejecting the concept of
uniform **rates**, not that of uniformity in natural laws. Gould
was merely repeating what catastrophists had long emphasized.

More recently, Gould has recognized this fact, while also
calling attention to the devious methods by which Lyell and
others in the 19th century had persuaded their contemporaries
to reject Biblical catastrophism in favor of uniformitarianism:

Charles Lyell was a lawyer by profession, and his
book is one of the most brilliant briefs ever published by an advocate . . . . Lyell relied upon true
bits of cunning to establish his uniformitarian views
as the only true geology. First, he set up a straw
man to demolish . . . . In fact, the catastrophists
were much more empirically minded than Lyell. The
geologic record does seem to require catastrophes:
rocks are fractured and contorted; whole faunas are
wiped out. To circumvent this literal appearance,
Lyell imposed his imagination upon the evidence.
The geologic record, he argued, is extremely imperfect and we must interpolate into it what we can
reasonably infer but cannot see. The catastrophists
were the hard-nosed empiricists of their day, not the
blinded theological apologists.[2]

Lest anyone misunderstand, it should be emphasized that
Gould is neither a creationist nor a Biblical catastrophist. In
fact he and other modern geological quasicatastrophists are confident that their battle with the Bible has been won and that
they can now safely and openly revert to catastrophism in their
geological interpretations without the danger of appearing to

---

1. Stephen Jay Gould, "Is Uniformitarianism Necessary?", *American Journal
   of Science,* Vol. 263, March, 1965, p. 223. This same point had been
   stressed earlier by the writer *(The Twilight of Evolution,* Philadelphia,
   Presbyterian and Reformed Publ. Co., 1963, pp. 59-64). Gould has been
   on the geology faculty at Columbia University and is currently Professor
   of Geology at Harvard.
2. Stephen Jay Gould, "Catastrophes and Steady-State Earth," *Natural
   History,* February, 1975, pp. 16-17.

support Biblical supernaturalism. Gould had said, for example:

> As a special term, methodological uniformitarian-
> ism was useful only when science was debating the
> status of the supernatural in its realm; for if God
> intervenes, then laws are not invariant and induction
> becomes invalid . . . . The term today is an anach-
> ronism . . . . [1]

Similarly, another modern writer criticizing uniformitarianism explains why the principle is nevertheless useful in argumentation.

> Frequently the doctrine of uniformitarianism is
> used fruitfully to explain the anti-catastrophist view-
> point of history . . . . [2]

The author of a recent book promoting geological catastrophism feels it necessary to hedge his conclusions with the following caution:

> It is both easy and tempting . . . to adopt a neo-
> catastrophist attitude to the fossil record . . . . This
> is a heady wine and has intoxicated paleontologists
> since the day when they could blame it all on Noah's
> flood. In fact, books are still being published by the
> lunatic fringe with the same explanation. In case this
> book should be read by some fundamentalist search-
> ing for straws to prop up his prejudice, let me state
> categorically that all my experience (such as it is) has
> led me to an unqualified acceptance of evolution by
> natural selection as a sufficient explanation for what
> I have seen in the fossil record. I find divine
> creation, or several such creations, a completely
> unnecessary hypothesis. Nevertheless this is not to
> deny that there are some very curious features about
> the fossil record. [3]

Another recent book[4] documents that the modern approach to geomorphology (which stresses erosion by hydraulic process-

1. Stephen Jay Gould, "Is Uniformitarianism Necessary?" p. 227.
2. James W. Valentine, "The Present is the Key to the Present," *Journal of Geological Education,* Vol. XIV, April, 1966, p. 60.
3. Derek V. Ager, *The Nature of the Stratigraphical Record* (New York, John Wiley and Sons, 1973), p. 19. Ager is Professor and Head of the Department of Geology and Oceanography at the University College of Swansea, England.
4. Gordon L. Davies, *The Earth in Decay—A History of British Geomorphology,* 1578-1878 (New York. American Elsevier, 1970), 370 pp.

es) was originally established by Woodward and the other catastrophist founders of geology, and was believed by them to be perfectly consistent with the Biblical history of the earth under the divine Curse. This true empirical approach to geology has been retarded by Hutton and other deists with their principle of uniformitarianism and a steady-state earth. A reviewer of this book makes the following interesting comment:

> With the Mosaic chronology finally discredited and denudation again theologically respectable [that is, by Hutton's rationalizations], nineteenth century British geologists could return to the issue of fluvialism.[1]

Uniformitarian Catastrophism

Creationist writers have been saying for years[2] that uniformitarianism was inadequate to explain any of the important types of geologic formations. It is not only that uniformitarianism does not explain everything—the fact is, it explains nothing! More and more, it has become apparent that the present is *not* the key (not even *a* key) to the past, as far as process rates are concerned.

This important fact, categorically denied for so long by evolutionists and uniformitarians, is now being acknowledged more and more openly by both. Typical of this modern trend is the important book by Derek Ager, *The Nature of the Stratigraphical Record,* mentioned earlier. Although Ager insists he is an evolutionist and uniformitarian, the theme of his book is that *every* type of geologic formation and structure was formed by some kind of catastrophe. He does not believe they were all formed by the same catastrophe, of course, but by many different catastrophes, separated from each other in a typical uniformitarian framework of billions of years of time—a sort of "uniformitarian catastrophism," in other words.

Dr. Ager discusses in detail all the various types of geologic formations, even those traditionally believed to have been formed very slowly, concluding that all must

---

1. R.H. Dott, Jr., *Review of "The Earth in Decay,"* Journal of Geology, Vol. 79, September, 1971, p. 633.

2. See, for example, *The Genesis Flood,* by John C. Whitcomb and Henry M. Morris (Philadelphia, Presbyterian and Reformed, 1961), pp. 200-203, etc., as well as still earlier writings by George McCready Price, Harold W. Clark, and others.

have been formed rapidly.

> The hurricane, the flood, or the tsunami may do more in an hour or a day than the ordinary processes of nature have achieved in a thousand years.[1]

This assessment by Ager almost sounds Biblical—"one day is with a catastrophe as a thousand years!" As a matter of fact, the famous verse in II Peter 3:8, though commonly misinterpreted to teach that the "days" of creation were "thousands of years" long, really means exactly what Ager implied. God is not limited to uniformitarian rates to accomplish his work. He can do in one day what uniformitarian assumptions indicate would require a thousand years. Ager continues:

> Given all the millennia we have to play with in the stratigraphical record, we can expect our periodic catastrophes to do all the work we want of them.[2]

The conclusion of Ager's book, after examining all the evidence, is as follows:

> In other words, the history of any one part of the earth, like the life of a soldier, consists of long periods of boredom and short periods of terror.[3]

That is, everything we can actually *see* in the geologic strata is the product of catastrophism. The intervening periods, which supposedly totaled billions of years, presumably left no record in the rocks. Individual formations were deposited rapidly; the "unconformities" between formations were periods of either erosion or inactivity.

One Cataclysm or Many?

The question remaining is whether these really do represent a myriad of individual catastrophes or whether they might possibly all be parts of the same catastrophe. If it is true, as Ager and others are contending, that we cannot really see the evidences of the ages between the various catastrophes, then it is legitimate to ask how we know such ages really occurred. There is nothing remaining there to measure!

> But I maintain that a far more accurate picture of the stratigraphical record is of one long gap with only very occasional sedimentation.[4]

---

1. D.V. Ager, *op cit,* p. 49.
2. *Ibid.*
3. *Ibid,* p. 100.
4. *Ibid,* p. 34.

How long does it take to form a gap?

The only real reason for imposing a billion-year time frame on the catastrophes is the necessity to provide time for evolution. As a matter of fact, the strata themselves show evidence of being a complex of interconnected and continuous regional catastrophes combining to comprise a global cataclysm.

In the first place, the rocks of all "ages" *look* the same. That is, there are rocks of all kinds, minerals of all kinds, structures of all kinds, in rocks of all ages.

Secondly, every formation grades, somewhere, up into another formation continuously without a time break.

This follows from the fact that there is no worldwide "unconformity." An unconformity is a supposed erosional surface between two adjacent rock formations, representing a time break of unknown duration between deposition periods. It was once believed that such unconformities were, indeed, worldwide:

> In the early history of stratigraphy, unconformities were overestimated in that they were believed to represent coeval diastrophism over areas of infinitely wide extent.[1]

It is now known, however, that all such unconformities are of very limited extent, and furthermore, that they have no particular time significance.

> Many unconformity-bounded units are considered to be chrono-stratigraphic units in spite of the fact that unconformity surfaces inevitably cut across isochronous horizons and hence cannot be true chrono-stratigraphic boundaries.[2]

From these facts, a simple deductive line of reasoning can proceed as follows: (1) since every formation was produced rapidly and catastrophically; and (2) since every such formation somewhere grades into another above it without an interruption in the deposition process; and (3) since the whole (of the geologic column) is the sum of its parts; therefore (4) the entire geologic column was formed continuously and rapidly, in a worldwide interconnected complex of catastrophes.

The above discussion is very abbreviated and inadequate, but it does point up the dilemma confronting modern geologists.

---

1. K. Hong Chang, "Unconformity-Bounded Stratigraphic Units," *Bulletin, Geological Society of America,* Vol. 86, November, 1975, p. 1545.

2. *Ibid,* p. 1544.

Having rejected the Biblical record of creation and the flood as the true key to earth history, geologists for a hundred years relied on uniformitarianism as their rule of interpretation. This system has proved utterly sterile, so that they are now being forced to rely increasingly on neo-catastrophism in their current thinking.

However, if all the geologic formations must be explained by catastrophic phenomena which are inaccessible to observation or measurement, and which are incommensurate with present processes, then historical geology is not science, but speculation.

> Of late there has been a serious rejuvenation of catastrophism in geologic thought. This defies logic; there is no science of singularities. If catastrophe is not a uniform process, there is no rational basis for understanding the past. For those who would return us to our Babylonian heritage of "science" by revelation and possibility, we must insist that the only justifiable key to the past is probability and the orderliness of natural process; if uniformity is not the key, there is no key in the rational sense, and we should pack up our boots and go home.[1]

This lament would, in fact, be realistic if we were limited to naturalistic and speculative catastrophism for our interpretations of earth history, for that would be even worse than uniformitarianism! There would remain no possibility at all of acquiring real knowledge about the origin and early history of the world.

But when all else fails, *read the instructions!* The rocks do bear witness everywhere to a worldwide hydraulic cataclysm. The causes, nature, duration, and effects of that cataclysm are recorded accurately, by infallible divine inspiration, in the Holy Scriptures, and all the actual facts of geology can be correlated perfectly with that record. The founders of the science of geology believed that, and it is time for their latter-day intellectual children to return to the faith of their fathers.

HUMAN LANGUAGE AND THE TOWER OF BABEL

The first eleven chapters of Genesis deal with the primeval period of human history prior to the call of Abraham and the

---

1. B.W. Brown, "Induction, Deduction, and Irrationality in Geologic Reasoning," *Geology,* Vol. 2, September, 1974, p. 456.

establishment of the nation Israel. From Genesis 12 onward, dealing primarily with the events in the history of Israel, the Biblical records have been both illuminated and confirmed by archaeology. Thus, from about 2000 B.C. to the completion of the New Testament, there is no longer any substantial question concerning at least the general historical accuracy of the Bible.

Genesis 1-11, however, constitutes the main battleground between believer and unbeliever, between creationist and evolutionist, theist and humanist. All theological "liberals," as well as all materialists, reject the historicity of these chapters, regarding them as allegorical, at best, or, for the most part, pure mythology. It is these chapters, of course, that deal with the primeval events applicable to *all* nations, not only those events bearing directly on the Jewish Nation, and it is these that are widely rejected by the scientific world as both unscientific and nonhistorical.

Two of the great events described in these chapters—the Creation of all things and the worldwide Flood—have been discussed at some length in this book, especially in this chapter, and shown to be compatible with the true data of science. In fact, scientific Biblical creationism and catastrophism form a much better scientific model within which to organize all such facts than does the evolutionary uniformitarian model that has been accepted as the primary article of materialistic faith for the past century.

But there is another great event of worldwide proportions described in these chapters, the miraculous confusion of tongues at the Tower of Babel. This event did not have much direct effect on the inorganic world or on the world of plants and animals, but it did have profound effect on the world of mankind. It not only led to the development of the many different languages of the human race, but also to the development of the different tribes and nations and the so-called "races." It produced the great migrations and generated the development of different cultures and civilizations.

It is the astronomer, the biologist, the geologist, and others in the natural sciences who study the effects of Creation and the Flood. On the other hand, the phenomena resulting from Babel are the domain of the archaeologist, the ethnologist, the anthropologist, the linguist, and others in the social sciences. These events all have affected humanity in the most direct way and so are of particular concern. If we are ever really to understand history and the human factors that have shaped the great events of the entire course of history—even to the present day—we must start with their beginnings at Babel.

The Uniqueness of Human Speech

Probably the most important physical ability distinguishing man from apes and other animals is his remarkable capacity for language. The ability to communicate with others of his own kind in abstract, symbolic speech is unique to man, and the evolutionist has never been able to bridge the tremendous gulf between this ability and the grunts and barks and chatterings of animals.

Some researchers have, of course, made extravagant claims as to the potentiality of teaching chimpanzees to speak, for example, or have developed highly imaginative speculations as to how animal noises may have evolved into human languages. Such notions are, however, not based on real scientific observation or evidence.

Man's brain is quite different from that of chimpanzees, especially in that portion which controls speech; Isaac Asimov notes this:

> Once speech is possible, human beings can communicate thoughts and receive them; they can consult, teach, pool information . . . . Once speech was developed, then the evolution of intelligence proceeded rapidly. The chimpanzee lacks Broca's convolution, but it may have the germs of communication, which could develop rapidly if it ever evolved that part of the brain.[1]

Unfortunately, one does not acquire a brain capable of abstract thought and intelligent speech (even if "Broca's convolution" is really all the brain needs to do this) merely by allowing "evolution" to create one because it might be helpful. Two top authorities on supposed human evolution, David Pilbeam and Stephen Gould, anthropologist at Yale and geologist at Harvard, respectively, have pointed out that man's brain shape is not a mere scaled-up replica of the ape's, but is qualitatively distinct in critical ways.

> *Homo sapiens* provides the outstanding exception to this trend among primates, for we have evolved a relatively large brain and small face, in opposition to

---

1. Isaac Asimov, "Chimps Tell Us About Evolution," *Science Digest,* November, 1974, p. 89.

functional expectations at our size . . . . *Australo-pithecus africanus* has a rounded braincase because it is a relatively small animal; *Homo sapiens* displays this feature because we have evolved a large brain and circumvented the expectations of negative allometry. The resemblance is fortuitous; it offers no evidence of genetic similarity.[1]

Though creationists do not share the credulous faith of the evolutionists that man's unique brain has simply "evolved," they do concur with the inference that this uniqueness has placed an unbridgeable gap between man and any of the lower animals.

Evolutionist George Gaylord Simpson has admitted that there is little possibility of tracing an evolutionary connection between animals and men, as far as language is concerned.

Human language is absolutely distinct from any system of communication in other animals . . . . It is still possible, but it is unlikely, that we will ever know just when and how our ancestors began to speak.[2]

Since Simpson is a biologist and paleontologist, rather than a linguistics scientist, certain of the younger speculative linguists may feel that he was speaking out of his field and that it may yet be possible to trace such an evolutionary origin of human language. However, most modern linguistic specialists today acknowledge Dr. Noam Chomsky, Professor of Linguistics at Massachusetts Institute of Technology, to be the "world's foremost linguist" (a term applied to him by Dr. John Oller, Chairman of the University of New Mexico Department of Linguistics, while discussing this subject with the writer), and Dr. Chomsky says:

Human language appears to be a unique phenomenon, without significant analogue in the animal world.[3]

As to whether the gap between animal noises and human language was ever bridged by evolution, Dr. Chomsky states:

There is no reason to suppose that the "gaps"

1. David Pilbeam and Stephen Jay Gould, "Size and Scaling in Human Evolution," *Science,* Vol. 186, December 6, 1974, pp. 899, 900.
2. George Gaylord Simpson, "The Biological Nature of Man," *Science,* Vol. 152, April 22, 1966, pp. 476 477.
3. Gunther S. Stent, "Limits to the Scientific Understanding of Man," *Science,* Vol. 187, March 21, 1975, p. 1054.

are bridgeable. There is no more of a basis for assuming an evolutionary development of "higher" from "lower" stages, in this case, than there is for assuming an evolutionary development from breathing to walking.[1]

In other words there is no comparison at all!

The Underlying Unity of Human Language

Chomsky and many other modern linguists have found, not only that there is no connection between animal sounds and human speech, but also that there is a deep commonality between the basic thought patterns of all men, regardless of how diverse their individual languages may be. That is, there is a fundamental connection between all human languages, but no connection at all between human language and animal "language."

Dr. Gunther S. Stent (Professor of Molecular Biology at the University of California in Berkeley), has drawn the further inference from Chomsky's studies that man has a certain fundamental being which is incapable of being reached by scientific analysis.

> Chomsky holds that the grammar of a language is a system of transformational rules that determines a certain pairing of sound and meaning. It consists of a syntactic component, a semantic component, and a phonological component. The surface structure contains the information relevant to the phonological component, whereas the deep structure contains the information relevant to the semantic component, and the syntactic component pairs surface and deep structures.[2]

Chomsky and his associates have developed what they call *structural linguistics,* with its concepts of the "deep" structure and the "surface" structure. The latter involves the ordinary phenomena of different languages and their translation one into the other. The mere fact that people are able to learn other languages is itself evidence of the uniqueness and fundamental unity of the human race. No such possibility exists between man and animals.

---

1. *Ibid,* p. 68.
2. Noam Chomsky, *Language and Mind,* Harcourt, Brace, Jovanovich, Inc., New York, 1972, p. 67.

The "deep structure" is the basic self-conscious thought structure of the man himself, and his intuitive formulation of discrete thoughts and chains of reasoning. The vocal sounds which he uses to transmit his thoughts to others may vary widely from tribe to tribe, but the fundamental thought-system is there and is universal among mankind.

> The semantic component has remained invariant and is, therefore, the "universal" aspect of the universal grammar, which all natural languages embody. And this presumed constancy through time of the universal grammar cannot be attributable to any cause other than an innate, hereditary aspect of the mind. Hence, the general aim of structural linguistics is to discover this universal grammar.[1]

Presumably, if this "universal grammar" could ever be ascertained, it would supply the key to man's original language—perhaps even its phonology and syntactical structure, as well as its semantic content.

The Unique Origin of Man

Evolutionists, as well as creationists, have in recent years come to believe in the monophyletic origin of all the tribes and races of mankind. Most of the earlier evolutionists, however, believed in man's polyphyletic origin, thinking that each of the major "races" had evolved independently from a different hominid line. This idea, of course, easily leads to racism, the belief that one race is innately superior to another race. That is, if each race has a long, independent evolutionary history, slowly developing its distinctive character by the lengthy process of random mutation and natural selection, then it is all but certain that there has been a differential rate of evolution as between the different races, with some evolving to higher levels than others. That such racist beliefs were held by all nineteenth-century evolutionist scientists (Darwin and Huxley included) has been thoroughly documented.[1]

Modern evolutionists, however, repudiate racism, which has become sociologically unpopular in the twentieth century. They now agree (with the Bible) that "God hath made of one blood all nations of men for to dwell on all the face of the earth" (Acts 17:26). Although they are now in practically complete

---

1. *Ibid*, p. 68.
2. John S. Haller, Jr., *Outcasts from Evolution*, University of Illinois Press, Urbana, 1971, 280 pp.

agreement that all present groups of men came originally from one single population of ancestral men, they are currently in complete disarray as to exactly what that lineage may have been. The Australopithecines are no longer considered man's progenitors, since fossils of true man have been found which are dated earlier than any of those.

> Theorists of human evolution, who may not yet have fully assessed the impact of Leakey's 1972 discovery, now face an even knottier problem. If members of the human genus flourished as long as four million years ago, then the time when the genus first branched from its ancestral primate stem would necessarily be even earlier. As Taieb and Johanson assert, "All previous theories of the origin of the lineage which leads to modern man must now be totally revised."[1]

Maurice Tieg, of the French National Center for Scientific Research, and D. Carl Johanson, of Case Western Reserve University, have thus demonstrated that man is "older" than his supposed "ancestors." Creationists do not accept the date of four million years, of course, but merely note that the "relative stratigraphic date has to be "older" than the stratigraphic date of Zinjanthropus, Australopithecus, etc., as accepted by evolutionists.

Not only do these discoveries indicate that man's unique body structure has (so far as actual fossil evidence goes) always been distinct from that of apes, but also that he has always had his unique capacity of communication.

> There is even the possibility, Johanson says, that he had "some kind of social cooperation and some sort of communication system."[2]

Back to the very beginning of human existence, therefore, in so far as it can be elucidated by archaeological excavation and anthropological analysis, man has always been man, culturally and linguistically, as well as physically and mentally.

The Origin of the Different Languages

Consider this ancestral human population, whenever and however it first appeared—whether several million years ago,

---

1. *Scientific American*, Volume 231, December, 1974, p. 64. (news items).
2. "Ethiopia Yields Oldest Human Fossils," *Science News*, Vol. 106, November 2, 1974, p. 276.

newly arrived by an unknown evolutionary process from unknown evolutionary ancestors, or else several thousand years ago, representing the descendants of the handful of survivors of the great Flood. In either case, they must have constituted an originally coherent body of true men, all with the same language and culture.

The question then is, how did the different languages ever develop? If the "semantic component" of language, as Chomsky puts it, is still the same for all men, how did the "phonologic component" ever become so diverse and variegated? Gradual changes are understandable (as in the gradual accretion of Latin words, Greek words, Germanic words, etc. to produce the modern English language), but how could such vastly different linguistic systems as the Indo-European languages, the agglutinative languages of the Africans, and the tonal languages of the Mongols ever develop from a single ancestral language?

Furthermore, the more ancient languages seem to be the more complex languages, as do the languages of the more apparently "primitive" tribes living today.

> Even the peoples with least complex cultures have highly sophisticated languages, with complex grammar and large vocabularies, capable of naming and discussing anything that occurs in the sphere occupied by their speakers. The oldest language that can reasonably be reconstructed is already modern, sophisticated, complete from an evolutionary point of view.[1]

Not only so, but the history of any given language, rather than representing an increasingly complex structure as the structure of its users supposedly evolved into higher levels of complexity, seems instead to record an inevitable decline in complexity.

> The evolution of language, at least within the historical period, is a story of progressive simplification.[2]

It seems necessary to assume either of two alternatives in order to explain these strange linguistic phenomena:

---

1. George Gaylord Simpson, "The Biological Nature of Man," *Science,* Vol. 152, April 22, 1966, p. 477.
2. Albert C. Baugh, *A History of the English Language,* Appleton-Century-Crafts, Inc., New York, 1957, p. 10.

1. An original population of men, at least 100,000 years ago and possibly up to four million years ago, with a highly complex language and culture. This original population (its origin completely unknown and apparently inexplicable on evolutionary grounds) somehow broke up into a number of separate populations, each then developing independently of the others for such a very long time that its extreme peculiarities of linguistic phonology and syntax could emerge as a deteriorative remnant of the ancestral language.

2. An original population of men several thousand years ago (as dated not only by the Bible but also from the known beginnings of civilization in Sumeria, Egypt, and other ancient nations). This population once used the postulated complex common ancestral language, but somehow broke up into the assumed smaller populations. However, this break-up was not a slow evolutionary process over hundreds of thousands of years, but rather was accomplished in some kind of traumatic separation, accomplished essentially instantaneously by a sudden transmutation of the one phonology into a number of distinctively and uniquely different phonologies.

The Dilemma of the Evolutionary Linguist

Note that neither of these alternatives is amenable to an evolutionary interpretation, since neither accounts for the original ancestral complex language and since both involve a subsequent deterioration (rather than evolution) of language complexity. The former, however, is favored by evolutionists because the great time spans involved seem more suitable to a uniformitarian philosophy, and because the latter clearly involves catastrophic, even supernaturalistic, intervention in human history.

The long time span interpretation, however, necessarily involves the evolution model once again in its racist connotations. For how are populations going to be separated long enough to develop such drastically different languages without also developing drastically different physical features and mental abilities? As long as they were together, or even closely enough associated to be in communication with each other (and such association would surely be to their mutual advantage), they would retain an essentially common language, would intermarry, and thus retain common physical and mental characteristics as well.

Yet the languages and cultures and physical features are, indeed, quite different, and have been since the dawn of recorded history! A genetics professor at Stanford says:

> When we look at the main divisions of mankind, we find many differences that are visible to the unaided eye . . . . It is highly likely that all these differences are determined genetically, but they are not determined in any simple way. For example, where skin color is concerned there are at least four gene differences that contribute to variations in pigmentation.[1]

If such an apparently simple and obvious difference as skin color is determined in such a complex fashion, and if all such gene factors have developed originally by mutation (as evolutionists believe), then a very long period of racial segregation must have been necessary.

> The simplest interpretation of these conclusions today would envision a relatively small group starting to spread not long after modern man appeared. With the spreading, groups became separated and isolated. Racial differentiation followed. Fifty thousand years or so is a short time in evolutionary terms, and this may help to explain why, genetically speaking, human races show relatively small differences.[2]

Furthermore, if obvious differences such as skin color and facial morphology can arise by mutation and selection in 50,000 years, then surely subtle differences in mental abilities could also arise in such a time, and these would have considerably more selection value for survival than would skin pigmentation. The inferences for racism are again very obvious.

As a matter of fact, as creationists have repeatedly pointed out, there is no empirical evidence of mutations that confer any kind of "beneficial" effect in the natural environment upon either the individuals or populations that experience them. The various physical changes (skin color, etc.) can be much more easily explained as *created* genetic factors that were latent in the human genetic system ever since the creation but which could become openly expressed only in a small population being forced to reproduce by inbreeding after segregation from

---

1. L.L. Cavalli-Sforza, "The Genetics of Human Populations," *Scientific American,* Vol. 231, September, 1974, p. 85.

2. *Ibid,* p. 89. From what has been noted, however, it is obvious that even the author's 50,000 year estimate is much too small in the evolutionary framework. Even this, however, would surely involve significant racist connotations.

its ancestral population.

If the initial population were somehow forced to break up into small reproductively isolated populations, only a relatively small number of generations would be required to allow distinctive physical characteristics (all representing created genetic factors already present, though latent, in the larger population) to become manifest and fixed in different combinations in the different tribal clans. The enforced segregation would most expeditiously be arranged by the postulated sudden transmutation of the ancestral phonology (spoken language) into a number of uniquely different phonologies. No other traumatic changes would be necessary, as the physical changes would easily and quickly develop genetically from the linguistic segregation.

Furthermore, no basic change in human nature would be involved. All would still "think" in the same way and would still be, distinctively, men. The "deep structure" of human consciousness and communicative ability would be unaffected even by a traumatic change in the "surface structure." Dr. Stent makes a fascinating comment in this connection.

> Hence it is merely the phonological component that has become greatly differentiated during the course of human history, *or at least since the construction of the Tower of Babel.*[1]

The Creationist Answer

Whether or not Dr. Stent believes in the confusion of tongues at Babel as a real event of history, it is at least symbolic to him of the fact that there must have at one time been some such division, and that no normal evolutionary development could accomplish it. To the creationist, of course, Babel is not only symbolic, but actual. The supernatural confusion of phonologies, with its resultant tribal dispersions throughout the world and its logical genetic consequences in the rapid emergence of distinctive tribal (not "racial"—the Bible knows nothing of the racial categories of evolutionary biology) characteristics, fits all the known facts of philology, ethnology, and archaeology beautifully.

Furthermore, man's universal semantic consciousness is at once an attestation of his uniqueness in the living world and of the inability of naturalistic science to comprehend this deep

---

1. Gunther S. Stent, "Limits to the Scientific Understanding of Man," *Science,* Vol. 187, March 21, 1975, p. 1054.

inner nature of man. Dr. Stent himself has recognized this:

> No matter how deeply we probe into the visual
> pathway, in the end we need to posit an "inner
> man" who transforms the visual image into a pre-
> cept. And as far as linguistics is concerned, the
> analysis of language appears to be heading for the
> same conceptual impasse as does the analysis of
> vision.[1]

Chomsky and the other structural linguists have found it
necessary to postulate a "deep structure" of self-consciousness,
but they do not know where this comes from nor how it
functions. Materialistic science can explain much with its
chemical and physical equations, but it founders when it reaches
the domain of "soul" and "spirit." Stent continues in this
vein:

> That is to say, for man the concept of "meaning"
> can be fathomed only in relation to the self, which is
> both ultimate source and ultimate destination of
> semantic signals. But the concept of the self . . .
> cannot be given an explicit definition. Instead, the
> meaning of "self" is intuitively obvious. It is another
> Kantian transcendental concept, one which we bring
> a priori to man just as we bring the concepts of
> space, time, and causality to nature.[2]

The concept of "self" may be intuitively obvious, but its
cause is not so obvious, at least to an evolutionist. Its reality
is found to be necessary, even by naturalistic science, but as
an "effect," it requires an adequate "cause," and no naturalistic cause is available to explain it. A supernatural Creator is
required!

All of which leads to the conclusion that the *ultimate* purpose
of language is not merely for communication between man and
man, but even more for communication between man and
his Maker. God speaks to man through His Word and man
responds in praise and prayer to God.

SUMMARY

In this chapter, the most up-to-date data of the key sciences
of thermodynamics, statistics, biochemistry, geology, paleontology, biology, and linguistics have been applied to the study

1. Gunther S. Stent, "Limits to the Scientific Understanding of Man,"
   Science, Vol. 187, March 21, 1975, p. 1054.
2. *Ibid*, p. 1057.

of origins. These *facts* of science, as distinct from the speculations of scientists, are in full agreement with the Genesis record.

Thus, even though the world's leaders have set themselves up in opposition to creation and its great King (see Psalm 2:1-3), the actual facts accessible to the true scientific study of the world all agree with His revelation of creation. True science is not in rebellion against creation, as is the man-made world system, but is in strong alliance with its King. The age-long conflict could realistically be denominated as: *"Scripture and true science versus the nontheistic philosophical faith of evolutionary uniformitarianism."*

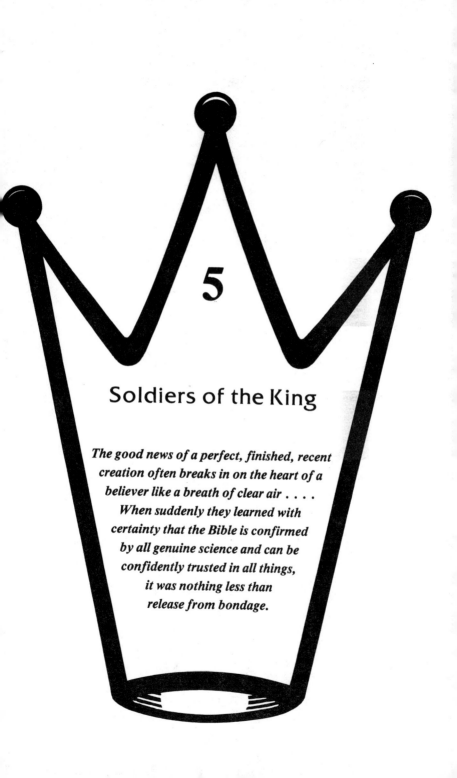

5

Soldiers of the King

The good news of a perfect, finished, recent creation often breaks in on the heart of a believer like a breath of clear air . . . . When suddenly they learned with certainty that the Bible is confirmed by all genuine science and can be confidently trusted in all things, it was nothing less than release from bondage.

Soldiers of the King

CREATION AND TRUE EVANGELISM

The Liberating Gospel of Creation

The good news of a perfect, finished, recent creation often breaks in on the heart of a believer like a breath of clean air. We hear this testimony over and over again from Christians who once were uncertain in their spiritual convictions and vacillating in their testimonies, not quite sure whether they could really believe what God has said. When suddenly they learned with certainty that the Bible is confirmed by all genuine science and can be confidently trusted in all things, it was nothing less than release from bondage.

To them, God is no longer a God of the long-ago and far-away, but a God who is near, a very-present help, not far from every one of us. The world is no longer a decadent remnant of vast aeons of grinding struggle and chance mutation, but is a beautiful, friendly world—everywhere bearing witness to the One who "did good, and gave us rain from heaven, and fruitful seasons, filling our hearts with food and gladness" (Acts 14:17).

It may be true, of course, that one who believes in a real creation will encounter a measure of opposition and ridicule, but that is nothing—not when compared with the wonderful freedom of knowing that God's Word and God's World are both true and are good for time and eternity. God is really *there!* And He *created* us—for Himself!

Even the sorrows of the world become understandable, and therefore bearable. God indeed has cursed the ground, but even that was "for man's sake" (Genesis 3:17). God so loved the world that He could not leave man to wander unhindered forever, and so He uses (not *causes*) the discipline of suffering and the fear of death to show man his need of salvation.

And then—to realize that the same powerful God who created him is the gracious Savior who loved him and died for him—to really realize *that* is immediately to bow in humble adoration and there proclaim: "My God, how great thou art!"

Only the one who knows the Lord Jesus Christ as Creator and Sustainer of all things (Colossians 1:16, 17), can begin to comprehend the majesty and magnitude of the peace He made "with the blood of His cross, by Him to reconcile all things unto Himself'' (Colossians 1:20). Sensing His eternal purpose and His continued providential care for His wounded creation, we can thus know Him with real thanksgiving as Savior and Lord.

This is high freedom—freedom not merely from the guilt of sin, but also freedom to enjoy God's world, freedom from the need to compromise with man's errant philosophies, freedom from lingering doubts as to the reality of those things we profess to believe, freedom from fear lest God is unable to perform what He has promised. "If the Son therefore shall make you free, ye shall be free indeed" (John 8:36).

Creation and the Apostolic Witness

At the beginning of the book of Acts, the Lord Jesus Christ gave His great command to His disciples: "Ye shall be witnesses unto me . . . unto the uttermost parts of the earth" (Acts 1:8). The remainder of the book of Acts tells how the first-century believers attempted to obey His command, witnessing first in Jerusalem, then in all Judea, then in Samaria, and on throughout the world as far as they were able to go. Generation after generation of Christian witnesses has continued to try to fulfill His command, but it must be admitted that no generation has ever been so effective in doing this as was that first generation.

Many reasons could be given for the remarkable spread of the gospel in the first century. One that has not been adequately considered by most modern-day witnesses, however, is the specific procedure followed by the early Christian evangelists and missionaries when they first encountered a new audience. That is, they always started preaching or witnessing at the level of faith and knowledge already shared by their listeners, and then went on from there to direct their minds and hearts eventually to Christ, building on the specific foundation corresponding to the particular background of the audience.

The initial ministry was, of course, to the Jews, and these people already believed in God and in the inspiration and authority of the entire Old Testament. Therefore, Peter and the others always began by referring to the Scriptures, showing that Christ was indeed the fulfillment of the Messianic prophetic promises (note Acts 2:16-21, 25-31, 34-36; 3:20-26; 4:10-12; 7:48-51; 8:30-36; 10:43; etc.). Continually using two powerful Christian evidences—namely, the fulfillment of Old Testament prophecy and the bodily resurrection of Christ—they were able to win great multitudes of their Jewish countrymen to faith in Christ.

Even when they began to go to the Gentiles, they would almost always begin at the local synagogue. There were colonies of Jews in almost every city and, since these also believed the Old Testament, Paul and the other missionaries always began as they had back in Jerusalem, by reasoning out of the Scriptures (note Acts 13:5, 14-15, 32-40; 14:1; 17:2-3, 10-11; 18:4, 28; 19:8, etc.).

There are two recorded instances, however, where Paul found himself confronted by a crowd composed exclusively of pagan Gentiles. These people neither knew nor believed the Old Testament Scriptures, and it would have been futile to preach to them on the basis of a common acceptance of Biblical revelation. Therefore, Paul began by referring to the evidence of creation, which they could see and appreciate entirely apart from Scripture.

In the first case he was at Lystra, in Asia Minor, speaking to pagan worshippers of the Roman gods. To turn them away from these idols, he urged their attention to the evidence of the true God in the creation. "We . . . preach unto you that ye should turn from these vanities unto the living God, which made heaven, and earth, and the sea, and all things that are therein: Who in times past suffered all nations to walk in their own ways. Nevertheless, He left not Himself without witness, in that He did good, and gave us rain from heaven, and fruitful seasons, filling our hearts with food and gladness " (Acts 14:15-17).

The other occasion was at Athens, in the midst of the Epicureans, the Stoics, and other evolutionary philosophers at Mars Hill. To them he preached: "God that made the world and all things therein, seeing that he is Lord of heaven and earth, dwelleth not in temples made with hands: Neither is worshipped with men's hands, as though He needed anything, seeing he giveth to all life, and breath, and all things; And hath made of one blood all nations of men for to dwell on all the face of the earth . . . that they should seek the Lord, if haply they might feel after him, and find Him, though He be not far from every one of us" (Acts 17:24-27).

In neither case, of course, was the preaching of God as Creator sufficient to bring salvation. The message must not stop there, but it often must begin there. Only when God is acknowledged as Creator and Sovereign is one able to understand his need of a Savior.

The twentieth century in North America is far removed in space and time from first century Jerusalem. Except for a fundamentalist minority, modern skepticism concerning the Scriptures is exceeded only by modern ignorance of the Scriptures. Especially among young people, years of indoctrination in evolutionary humanism have made them almost impossible to reach simply by exposition of the Scriptures. Like the pagans at Lystra and the philosophers at Athens, they first must be made to see the majesty and love of the God of creation, and then perhaps they will listen to His Word and believe His promise of forgiveness and salvation.

The Urgency of Real Gospel Preaching

On the flyleaf of the study Bible used by the writer has been affixed for many years the famous statement attributed to Martin Luther:

> If I profess with the loudest voice and clearest expression every portion of the truth of God except precisely that little point which the world and the devil are at that moment attacking, I am not confessing Christ, however boldly I may be professing Christ. Where the battle rages, there the loyalty of the soldier is proved, and to be steady on all the battlefield besides, is mere flight and disgrace if he flinches at that point.

Luther perhaps spoke even better than he knew, and his challenge has served the writer as a reminder and encouragement in times of opposition and discouragement again and again. Whether or not we like it, we *are* in a battle for the minds of men, especially the minds of our young people, and the enemy is brilliant in persuasion and mighty in influence. Souls by the millions hang in the balance and "the god of this world hath blinded the minds of them which believe not, lest the light of the glorious gospel of Christ, who is the image of God, should shine unto them" (II Corinthians 4:4).

Unless they believe the glorious gospel, they are lost forever. "If our gospel be hid, it is hid to them that are lost" (II Corinthians 4:3). "With the heart man believeth unto righteousness" (Romans 10:10), but how can the heart believe when the mind is blind? Saving faith is not an emotional subjective credulity, but a confident conviction, based on facts and objective truth, a faith based on knowledge. "I *know* whom I have believed," asserted the Apostle Paul, "and am *persuaded* that He is able to keep that which I have committed unto Him against that day" (II Timothy 1:12).

Satan, the age-long enemy of our King of Creation, is the one "which deceiveth the whole world" (Revelation 12:9) and who, at the very end of the age, will still be able "to deceive the nations—and to gather them together to battle: the number of whom is as the sand of the sea" (Revelation 20:8). Yet, clever and powerful as Satan may be in his campaign to deceive and blind the minds of men, "greater is He that is in you, than he that is in the world" (I John 4:4).

Satanic deception can only be overcome by divine truth, and the powers of darkness by the light, so the followers of Christ must know the truth and see the light—then preach the truth and send the light. "Thy word is truth," and "the entrance of thy words giveth light" (John 17:17; Psalm 119:130).

It is the gospel which Satan has hid, because it is the gospel which is "the power of God unto salvation to everyone that believeth" (Romans 1:16). It is, therefore, the gospel which must be preached "to every creature" (Mark 16:15).

But the gospel which is preached must be the true gospel, not "another gospel" (Galations 1:6). It must be the complete gospel "according to the Scriptures" (I Corinthians 15:1, 3, 4), not a one-third gospel or two-thirds gospel. As already demonstrated (pages 64-66), the true and whole gospel is founded on creation, empowered at the cross, and centered on the coming Kingdom, embracing the past, present, and future work of the Lord Jesus Christ, the great King of Creation.

And since the preaching of this saving gospel is bitterly resisted by the devil, it involves a real battle. Those who would preach the gospel are, therefore, soldiers of the King. And since creationism is the foundation of the gospel, its preaching must become the "cutting edge" of "the sword of the Spirit, which is the word of God" (Ephesians 6:17). Those who especially wield this weapon as they proclaim the great truth of Christ as Creator are, so to speak, in the front ranks of those who would "endure hardness, as a good soldier of Jesus Christ" (II Timothy 2:3).

Such a role in the battle is no place for those who are "at ease in Zion" (Amos 6:1), those who love "the praise of men more than the praise of God" (John 12:43). But they are the ones who follow their King into the forefront of the battle, and "they that are with Him are called, and chosen, and faithful'' (Revelation 17:14).

CREATION AND THE CHURCHES

The Command To Preach Creationism

In view of all the foregoing considerations, surely true Christian pastors and teachers in churches everywhere should preach and teach frequently the doctrine of creation—not merely by incidental references in messages on other topics, but systematically and fully expounding this great truth, as revealed both in Scripture and in God's world. There are many reasons for emphasizing creation, but there are three especially urgent commands of Scripture to this effect.

1. *Guard the Faith!*

These are days in which many in Christendom, even professing Christians, are departing from the Christian faith, which was "once for all delivered unto the saints" (Jude 3). Some have departed in the direction of cultism and occultism (I Timothy 4:1), others in the direction of liberalism, humanism, and general ungodliness (II Timothy 3:1-7). These trends will eventually become so widespread that the Lord Jesus asked the rhetorical question—"When the Son of Man cometh, shall He find the faith on the earth?" (Luke 18:8).

Now if one studies carefully the history of such apostasies, in all ages, he will find they always begin with the undermining of this doctrine of special creation. There is always an evolutionary cosmogony of some sort opposing the true Genesis record of the Creator and His creation of course, attractively presented by the currently dominant philosophies in the name of "science." (This was as true with the ancient pagan philosophies as with the modern Darwinian philosophies. The Genesis record is the *only* cosmogony which begins with the transcendent God creating the very universe itself). This recurring tension between revelation and philosophy is inevitably followed by those men in the Christian world who seek to compromise. Compromise on special creation, however, is soon followed by a compromise on special incarnation, and so on; *eventually this road of compromise ends in a precipice!*

It is urgent, therefore, that each generation of pastors and teachers carefully transmit the full Christian faith to the next generation (II Timothy 2:2), especially its foundational doctrine of creation. The apostle Paul commanded, "Keep (literally *guard)* that which is committed to thy trust, avoiding profane and vain babblings (that is, ungodly and empty philosophies) and oppositions of science falsely so called" (I Timothy 6:20). The command to *avoid* such things does not mean to hide from them, but rather to keep the Christian faith utterly free from their contaminating influence! This can best be done by an informed and regular emphasis on Biblical creationism from both pulpit and classroom.

2. *Give the Answer!*

In our day and age, when practically everyone has been indoctrinated in evolutionary philosophy most of his life, the Christian worker quickly finds that some application or other of this philosophy is the greatest obstacle to winning educated people to an intelligent and lasting conversion to Biblical Christianity. Most people realize that, if the first chapter of the Bible is unreliable or vague, there is no reason to take the rest of the Bible very seriously.

The command of the Apostle Peter is clear. "Be ready always to give an answer (literally, an *apologetic*—a systematic, logical, scientific defense) to every man that asketh you, a reason of the hope that is in you" (I Peter 3:15). Whatever problem an unbeliever may have with respect to the Christian faith, there *is* an answer! The Christian has not been asked to follow cunningly-devised fables. He must be saved by faith, of course, but that faith is a *reasonable* faith, founded on facts. It is not a credulous faith, like that of the evolutionist.

The Christian witness will *not* be ready always to give the answer, of course, unless he or she *knows* the answers. And they won't know them unless someone either teaches them or sees that they get them. This is the Scriptural function of the pastor and teacher (Ephesians 4:11-14).

3. *Preach the Gospel!*

This command is the Great Commission, given by Christ to the church and to every believer. The Commission incorporates also the obligation to teach *all* things (Matthew 28:20) that Christ had taught (which obviously includes special creation), but it is even more important to realize that the Gospel itself must include the doctrine of creation.

The word "gospel" means *good news,* and it refers specifically in the New Testament to the glad tidings of all that Jesus Christ has done for mankind. This necessarily includes the entire scope of His work—past, present, and future, from the creation of all things (Colossians 1:16) to the reconciliation of all things (Colossians 1:20).

It is significant that the final reference to the Gospel in the Bible is found in Revelation 14:6, 7, in a context just prior to His glorious Second Coming. There it is called the "everlasting gospel" (thus stressing that it will be the same then as it is now), and the essential injunction is that men should "worship Him that made heaven, and earth, and the sea, and the fountains of waters." The everlasting gospel thus always stresses recognition of God as Creator, as well as Savior (the reference to "the fountains of waters" is probably a reference even to His sovereign judgment on sin during the great Flood—note Genesis 7:10, 11).

The command to "preach the gospel to every creature" (Mark 16:15) therefore includes not only the substitutionary atonement and bodily resurrection of Christ (I Corinthians 15:1-4), but also—as a necessary foundational preparation (especially in the last days when there would be widespread denial of creation)—the great truth that God in Christ is the supernatural and omnipotent Creator of all things.

Ecumenical Creationism

One of the most significant aspects of the study of creation, in fact, is that men from every type of denominational background recognize its vital importance and are concerned about its relevance to their own denominational doctrines. For example, the writer has been invited at one time or another to speak on this subject in the churches and schools of over 65 different religious denominations. This has nothing to do with the popularity of the speaker, but it does provide a striking testimony to the importance of the subject.

There are multitudes of people and churches in practically every denomination that have been harmfully affected by evolution. At the same time, there are some in each denomination who are vitally concerned about the problem and are doing what they can to restore or to retain special creation as a basic doctrine in their system. Furthermore, although there are still large numbers in each group who are indifferent, it is encouraging that more and more people are getting involved all the time.

This common concern about creationism is drawing together from all these backgrounds people who have heretofore been kept apart by other theological differences. Special creationists, of course, no matter what their denomination, generally share certain other basic beliefs, such as belief in the God of the Bible and belief in the divine inspiration and authority of the Bible. Evolutionists in all denominations, on the other hand, also tend to share certain beliefs among themselves, including a rather loose concept of Biblical inspiration and even of the nature of God.

Lest anyone misunderstand, creationists are not advocating ecumenicalism or church union as the concept is usually promoted today. The church union movement is unrealistic when it proposes that Christians of strong Bible-based convictions give them up for the sake of a superficial unity. Each church is to teach "the whole counsel of God" to its members, as it understands that counsel, and it must not reject that responsibility.

However, although there is no doctrine that is *not* important, surely there are some that are *more* important, and special creation is the most basic of all, except perhaps the doctrine of God Himself. It is amazing that so many churches, schools, and other institutions have very detailed and explicit "statements of faith," comprising what they believe to be their fundamental doctrines, but almost none of these include a specific statement regarding the special creation of all things in the beginning. This tragic oversight has directly resulted in the defection of great numbers of such institutions to the evolutionary world-view, and then inevitably later to liberalism and finally to humanism.

Church unification on any basis short of spiritual unity on *all* the essential doctrines and practices taught in the Bible is probably impossible to attain before the Lord returns. In the meantime, however, it is quite practical to enjoy a genuine fellowship among believers in such truly *basic* doctrines as the fact of God, special creation of all things by God, the reality of Satanic and human rebellion against God, the necessity of salvation provided through God, the future consummation of all things in God, and authoritative Biblical revelation from God. In each case, of course, Christians understand by "God" we mean the personal, omnipotent God of the Bible, manifest fully in Jesus Christ (Colossians 2:9).

At the practical level, all such believers can work effectively together in public movements and institutions to revive recognition of God as Creator, the doctrine which is the foundation of all other truth. All believers ultimately are in a warfare not *against* each other, but *with* each other, against Satan and his purposes (Ephesians 6:12). The creation-evolution issue is at the very center of this warfare. Is God really the sovereign Creator of this universe, or is He somehow limited by eternal matter or by other beings in the universe? Is His Word true and clear or is it tentative and vague, subject to man's shifting opinions? These are the ultimate issues, and genuine believers ought to be united on them.

Unfortunately man is an inconsistent creature, often governed by emotion and temporal things rather than by sound reasoning and eternal truths. Not all evolutionists are "bad guys," some are highly moral and spiritual in their personal relations. By the same token, not all creationists are "good guys"; some are opinionated cranks and some even self-seeking charlatans.

Such inconsistencies in human belief and behavior, however, do not invalidate the consistency of the immutable God and His infallible Word. The character of God demands the doctrine of special creation and the word of God clearly reveals it. These fundamental truths constitute the only sound foundation for the development of all other doctrines. Unity in these is, therefore, prerequisite to any true unity in other doctrines. It is just such unity which is excitingly developing today among godly creationist Christians in all denominations.

"Thou art worthy, O Lord, to receive glory and honor and power: for thou hast created all things, and for thy pleasure they are and were created" (Revelation 4:11).

THE AFFAIRS OF THIS LIFE

One of the classic New Testament passages dealing with the military aspect of the life of each true Christian is II Timothy 2:3, 4: "Thou therefore endure hardness as a good soldier of Jesus Christ. No man that warreth entangleth himself with the affairs of this life; that he may please Him who hath chosen him to be a soldier."

It is easy to become so involved with our personal affairs that we forget our Great Commission. We have been commissioned individually as soldiers of the great King, and His command is to proclaim His gospel and to transmit all His instructions to those who receive it. Our time belongs to Him, and we must use it most effectively, as unto Him.

An effective soldier must spend much time in both preparation and practice. Especially is this true in that aspect of the gospel involving creationism. This is the front line, and neither the poorly prepared recruit nor the ease-loving laggard will see many victories. May our desire, therefore, be to "love not the world" (I John 2:15), to "study to shew ourselves approved unto God" (II Timothy 2:15), and to be "steadfast, unmoveable, always abounding in the work of the Lord" (I Corinthians 15:58). It is worth it all when we know we have pleased Him who chose us to be His soldiers.

Attendance to Reading

One of the Apostle Paul's insistent commands to his young disciple, Timothy, was to "give attendance to reading" (I Timothy 4:13). If this admonition was important for Christians in the first century, it is surely much more so now. This is the age of the information explosion, and the annual publication growth rate today is nearly five times the population growth rate. The world population is increasing at a rate of 2% each year, but publications at over 9%!

People of influence in any field are always those who are informed people. Furthermore, if information is to be understood and retained, there is no substitute for reading. One may be stirred at the hearing of a sermon or a lecture, or by a drama he witnesses on stage or television, but the details and fine points are almost invariably quickly forgotten unless they are written down and reviewed again later. To prove this to yourself, merely try to recall in full the sermon you heard two or three weeks ago: you'll probably do well even to remember the subject!

A book can be read and re-read—as often as necessary to master its contents. It is available for reference and review whenever needed. It is significant that the Apostle Paul, in the last chapter of his last epistle, written from his dungeon on Rome's "death row" shortly before his martyrdom, still felt it important to keep on reading! "The cloak that I left at Troas with Carpus, when thou comest, bring with thee, and the books, especially the parchments," he wrote to Timothy (II Timothy 4:13).

One cannot read every book and every journal, of course. In the field of science, for example, approximately 10,000,000 scientific articles are published in 100,000 scientific journals every year!

Therefore, a conscientious Christian must be selective in his reading, spending as much time in reading and study as necessary to be the most effective person he can be in the work and ministry to which God has ordained him, yet not wasting precious time on the useless or harmful literature which is so abundantly available today.

His first responsibility, of course, is to know the Holy Scriptures, which are profitable in every part for every Christian (II Timothy 3:15; 4:2). Paul's admonition to "give attendance to reading" applied first of all to the Scriptures, both to their private study and their public reading. (In earlier days, before the printing press, most people had no direct access to the Scriptures, so it was vital for their pastor to read them aloud in the assembly.)

His responsibility for reading goes much beyond this, however. He is commanded: "Be ready always to give an answer (literally, an 'apologetic') to every man that asketh you a reason of the hope that is in you, with meekness and fear" (I Peter 3:15).

In these days of global skepticism concerning God's Word and ignorance of His divine purpose for man, one can only be an effective Christian "answerer," one whose witness will be taken seriously and whose "fruit will remain" (John 15:16), if he is both an informed witness and a gracious witness. One can only *give* an answer if he *knows* the answer, and the answer will only be effective if given in "meekness and fear." God uses neither ignorance nor arrogance, and the truth must be spoken in love.

All of which is possible only if the Christian spends adequate time in diligently studying both the Scriptures and other books which confirm and apply the Scriptures in the modern world.

Most especially it is important that he or she become familiar with the Biblical doctrine of special creation and with the data of science and history relevant to the issue of origins which support creation and refute evolution. Many Christians are reluctant to do any reading in this field, feeling that they don't have an adequate background in science. Nevertheless, they owe it both to themselves and to those whom they might influence to make a serious effort to do so. Most likely, they will be pleasantly surprised when they see how easily understood are the basic facts and arguments for defending and promoting creationism. A science background is not necessary at all, nor is any other specific course of study.

This book itself will provide a good introduction and survey of the broad fields of scientific and Biblical creationism, but the reader should follow it up with others, especially a sound creationist commentary on Genesis, a book covering systematically the major scientific evidences for creationism, and a book dealing with the impact of the evolution/creation issue in other fields than science.[1]

In addition, it is important for every Christian to be well grounded in general Christian evidences, able to defend the Christian faith and answer the questions of inquirers and the objections of adversaries. There is no substitute for diligence and no excuse for indolence. "Study to shew thyself approved unto God, a workman that needeth not to be ashamed, rightly dividing the word of truth" (II Timothy 2:15).

The Christian Creationist in The Classroom

The creationist student in a public school or state university is in a real battleground. He or she is certainly one "soldier of the King" who is in the very thick of the fight and, thus, in special need of the "whole armor of God" (Ephesians 6:11).

How should such a student, as a Christian and a creationist, behave in a class taught by a teacher who is a strong and opinionated evolutionist? This is one of the most common and urgent questions asked by creationist students and their parents. If the student is silent about his convictions and pretends to go along with the classroom teachings, is this a hypocritical compromise for the sake of expediency? On the other hand, if he challenges the teacher, arguing and taking an open stand against the evolutionary philosophy, will this not result in a failing grade in the course, ridicule by the teacher and other students, and possibly even shut the door to the career he has chosen?

This is a very real problem, with no easy answer. Essentially the same question is asked even by graduate students working on their Ph.D. degrees. The writer has known students who have failed courses and some who have been denied admission to graduate school, or otherwise hindered from obtaining their degrees, largely for this very reason. When the writer was on the faculty at Virginia Tech, a professor who was on the graduate faculty there in the Biology Department told him that he would never approve a Ph.D. degree for any student known to be a creationist in his department, even if that student

---

1. The Institute for Creation Research will send a descriptive list of relevant books on request, as well as a complimentary subscription to a very helpful monthly publication, *Acts and Facts*. Send request to I.C.R., 2716 Madison Ave., San Diego, California 92116.

made straight A's in all his courses, turned in an outstanding research dissertation for his Ph.D., and was thoroughly familiar with all the evidences and arguments for evolution.

On the other hand, there are many other students who have received excellent grades even while taking a strong stand against evolution, as well as many who have earned graduate degrees, in spite of being known as Christians with solid creationist convictions.

What makes the difference? There is certainly no simplistic solution which is applicable always and everywhere. Individual teachers are different, schools are different, and students are different, and these differences all make a difference! However, there are certain general principles that should always be at least considered:

1. Wherever possible, one should bypass the problem by enrolling in a Christian school, or at least in a class with a Christian teacher. Whenever such vital questions as origins or basic meanings are to be discussed in courses or textbooks, the happiest situation is for both student and teacher to have the same ultimate motives and goals. Unfortunately, this solution is often impossible or impracticable.

2. As long as a student is enrolled in a given class or program, he is under the authority of the teacher and is supposed to be there for the primary purpose of learning, rather than witnessing. He should, therefore, at all times be respectful and appreciative, doing his best to learn the material presented, whether he agrees with the teacher's personal philosophy or not. This is the Biblical admonition (Titus 2:9, 10; Colossians 3:22-24; Ephesians 6:5-8) concerning masters and servants, and this would apply, in principle at least, to the relationship between (school)-masters and those in their charge. Also, especially in the case of minor children, the teacher is *en loco parentis*, and the obedience of children as to parents is commanded (Galatians 4:1, 2). If this situation becomes intolerable, due to gross irresponsibility or abuse of authority on the teacher's part, then probably the proper course is to withdraw from the class, giving a careful and objective explanation, in writing and with documentation, of the reasons for withdrawal, to both the teacher and administrator concerned.

3. Differences in attitudes and beliefs between teachers and students can often be resolved, or at least ameliorated, by a sincere attempt to maintain an attitude of objectiveness and

good humor relative to their differences. Emotional arguments, especially when defensively oriented around religious or anti-religious convictions, will alienate, rather than attract (Proverbs 15:1, 25:11; Colossians 4:6).

4. The student should be well-informed on both sides of the evolution-creation question, so that such objections as he may have opportunity to raise (whether in class, on term papers, informal debates, or by other means) will be based on sound evidence, not on hearsay or misunderstanding. Most teachers (not all, unfortunately, but most) will respond with interest and fairness to a well-prepared and soundly reasoned argument for creationism, especially if presented objectively and scientifically, in an attitude of respect and good will (II Timothy 2:15; I Peter 3:15).

5. Other things being equal, a person should be able to do a better job in any course or at any task if he is a Christian than he could have before becoming a Christian, since he now has greater resources and higher motives than before. The subject matter of any course has value to him as a Christian witness, even if for nothing else than to make him better informed concerning what others believe. Therefore, he should study diligently and do the best job of which he is capable (I Corinthians 10:31; Colossians 3:23). Any teacher is more likely to respond favorably to the suggestions of a good student than of a poor, lazy, belligerent student.

6. There is no substitute for a consistent and winsome Christian walk in public and a life based on prayer and the study of Scripture in private—in meeting this particular problem as well as other problems involving similar tensions and confrontations in life (Proverbs 16:7).

The student, though he is at the battlefront, so to speak, is thus not yet fully involved as a regular soldier. In effect, he is a soldier in training and thus must deal with the battle situation in this perspective, somewhat as an observer, recognizing that he is preparing for a more active and more effective role in the conflict later on. He must survive the present skirmish in order later to become a leader in the Christian warfare.

Creation and the Public

Another good means of promoting creationism in the whole community is the public opinion poll. This can prove effective not only in terms of opportunities for personal witness, but as a means of informing entire communities about the creation/

evolution question and its importance. Furthermore, the data so accumulated will almost always strengthen creationist awareness and influence in the community.

One of the characteristics of these latter days has been the emergence of such public opinion polls as a strong policy-making tool. Television programming is largely dependent on the famous "Nielsen ratings" and politicians seem to base their campaigns and programs almost entirely on a wide assortment of popularity polls conducted, supposedly, by scientific statistical techniques of opinion sampling.

So far as we know, neither the Gallup poll nor the Harris poll nor any other "official" sampling agency has conducted a survey of public opinion on the issue of creation or evolution. Nevertheless, evidence is accumulating that such a poll would show that a large majority of American citizens would say—if they had the chance—that they favor including creation as an alternative scientific model of origins in the nation's public schools and colleges, rather than the present practice of teaching only evolution.

For example, in a semi-rural northern California school district, the Del Norte County District, the Citizens Committee for Scientific Creationism conducted a survey of 1346 homes in the county, showing that 89% favored the teaching of creation (see *Acts and Facts,* April, 1974). A few months later, a similar survey was carried out in the more cosmopolitan Cupertino school district, the largest in the state. This survey reached 2000 homes, and found that 84% favored teaching creation along with evolution. Both polls were conducted on a scientific statistical sampling basis (see *Acts and Facts,* July, 1974).

Members of the ICR Midwest Center, headquartered in Wheaton, Illinois, under its president, Paul MacKinney, have for several years been conducting a random telephone survey on this question, asking people whether they favor the teaching of: (1) Creation and evolution both, as scientific models; (2) Creation only; (3) Evolution only. So far, from samples in many midwestern states, the survey has obtained the following results: favoring the teaching of both creation and evolution, 68%; wanting only creation taught, 15%; wanted only evolution taught, 6%; no opinion, 11%. Thus, it is reasonable to conclude that at least 83% of the citizens in the midwest want creation taught in the schools, at least as a valid alternative to evolution.

It is interesting that one subsample of the above group was a random telephone survey of 56 dormitory students (mostly male) at the University of Illinois. This group showed 84% favoring the impartial teaching of both evolution and creation, 4% wanting only creation taught and 12% wanting only evolution taught. Even university students, exposed as they have been to nothing but evolutionary teaching, thus turned out to show 88% preferring to have creation added to their curriculum on at least an equal basis with evolution.

A similar random survey was conducted among dormitory students at the University of Kansas at Lawrence. Of the 173 students polled, 87% thought creation should be taught at least equally with evolution, while only 13% thought the present practice of teaching only evolution should be retained. Very similar results have been obtained at many other places.

Thus, whenever and wherever public opinion polls have been taken on this issue, it has been found that a large majority of people of all ages and backgrounds agree that the present system is wrong, and that scientific creationism should be taught in all public schools and colleges on at least an equal basis with evolution. This conclusion is the more remarkable because most of these people—like everyone else—had probably been themselves indoctrinated solely in evolutionary thinking by their own schools.

School administrators, textbook publishers, and others in a position to do something about this matter should take note of these facts. They should themselves assume the lead in re-introducing creationism into our public educational systems, rather than waiting until they are pressured to do so by concerned parents and citizens everywhere.

Readers of this book are encouraged to organize similar public opinion polls in their own communities. Even if others cannot be enlisted in such an effort, any individual can easily make his own random telephone survey. He should phrase the question somewhat as follows:

I am helping conduct a random telephone survey. We are attempting to determine community opinion about how our public school system should handle the subject of origins. Please tell us which of the following three choices represents your opinion: (1) only the evolution model should be taught as the explanation of how things began; (2) only the creation model should be taught; (3) both the evolution model and the creation model should be taught as alternative explanations of origins.

Any person or group making such a survey should also send the results to ICR where the results are tallied and analyzed on a nationwide basis. Such data should be helpful to any local group seeking to encourage their own school boards to pass creation-evolution equal time resolutions.

Other good means of influencing public opinion, and thereby opening doors for the gospel of creation, include "letters-to-the-editor," call-in radio and television programs, sponsoring and advertising meetings with creationist speakers, and similar undertakings. Such activities require real concern on the part of someone, as well as time and money, but this is all significant in the over-all campaign for creation, and God will lead and bless them if carried out graciously and wisely, for His Name's sake.

THE SPIRITUAL VICTORIES OF CREATIONISM

"The heavens declare the glory of God" (Psalm 19:1). "For the invisible things of Him from the creation of the world are clearly seen, being understood by the things that are made, even His eternal power and Godhead, so that they are without excuse" (Romans 1:20). " . . . the living God, which made heaven, and earth, and the sea, and all things that are therein . . . left not Himself without witness, in that He did good, and gave us rain from heaven, and fruitful seasons, filling our hearts with food and gladness" (Acts 14:15-17).

These and many other Scriptures unite in testimony to the spiritual impact of creationism. That is, the structure and processes of the created cosmos, properly understood and explained, bear irrefutable witness to the glory and power of God, as well as His grace and goodness—even His very nature, His Godhead. This is as it should be, of course. There can be no conflict between the Creator and His creation, and the proper study of the natural world must direct men to the true God.

Unfortunately, the wrong study of nature—"science falsely so called" (I Timothy 6:20)—has generated a serious dichotomy between cosmology and theology ("the study of the cosmos" and "the study of God"). The educational and scientific establishments today believe there are irreconcilable conflicts between science and Scripture, between God's world and God's Word. Unfortunately the same attitude prevails in the religious establishment. Consequently, even many who theoretically believe in the verbal inspiration and scientific accuracy of Scripture often tend to downgrade doctrine and objective truth—especially topics related to science and history—in favor of subjective evangelism and an introspective emphasis on the spiritual life.

The Great Commission, however, enjoins Christians not only to "preach the Gospel," but also to teach "all things whatsoever I have commanded you" (Matthew 28:20). In fact, the very emphasis of the "everlasting Gospel" is on the Creator of all things (Revelation 14:6, 7). It is vital to preach the necessity of saving faith in Christ, who died for our sins, but it is essential to preach Christ as He is, not a Christ of one's subjective experience. The Lord Jesus Christ was Creator and Sustainer of the universe (Colossians 1:16, 17) before He became its Redeemer (Colossians 1:20, 21), and He must be presented in His fullness. A religious experience based only on an emotional decision without roots in objective truth will "wither away" when "persecution ariseth because of the word" (Matthew 13:6, 20, 21).

Because of the widespread belief that "science" has disproved Scripture, especially its accounts of Creation, the Flood, and other great events of history, many Christians feel they should avoid such "controversial" questions in their witnessing. This tactic, of course, is tacit admission to the unbeliever that the Scriptures indeed are mistaken on these matters, and therefore not really reliable at all.

But this is all wrong. The Biblical records are completely true, and there is no need for compromise or equivocation. Furthermore, instead of hindering the presentation of Christ to an unsaved person, or the spiritual growth of the Christian, the great truths of creationism, rightly expounded from both science and Scripture, will be found an invaluable foundation for true Christian faith and life.

The ICR Survey

In an attempt to evaluate this issue quantitatively, in 1976 the Institute for Creation Research conducted a mail survey among the readers of its monthly publication *Acts and Facts,* asking them to respond to a brief questionnaire, "Spiritual Values in ICR Ministry." They were asked to indicate whether the science-Bible ministries of ICR (lectures, debates, books, radio broadcasts, literature, etc.) had been of definite spiritual help to them in any of the following ways: (1) "Instrumental in leading us to Christ;" (2) "Helpful in our personal spiritual growth as Christians;" (3) "Effective in helping us win others to Christ;"

(4) "Other." Comments also were invited.

The readers of *Acts and Facts* come from a large range of denominational backgrounds. Most are either college graduates or college students, so that the educational level is probably somewhat higher than among people in general. A large number are pastors or Christian leaders of one sort or another. Therefore, the results of the survey should be more meaningful than a typical man-in-the-street poll.

Over 3,000 questionnaires were filled out and returned, an extremely high response. Almost half were accompanied by comments, some by long letters. The evangelistic effectiveness of the ICR ministry was clearly indicated by the fact that well over 100 people[1] indicated it had been instrumental in leading them to Christ, while 900 or more said it had been effective in helping them win others to Christ.

As far as personal Christian life is concerned, almost 2,000 replies stated the ICR ministry had been helpful in their own spiritual growth. There were 350 who indicated it had helped them in various "Other" ways. Since normally only one questionnaire was returned for each family, all the above figures should be increased by some factor.

Perhaps of more interest than the numerical statistics are the comments. These were far too numerous to reproduce here, but typical comments appear below:

> *Genesis Flood* instrumental in leading me to Christ. Conference at Bibletown in 1974 was a great blessing.
>
> Although I am a Catholic, I commend you highly for the admirable defense of the Scriptures.
>
> Instrumental in our seeing the possibility of God and rethinking our naturalistic presuppositions.
>
> I was a hard-core skeptic.
>
> As a scientist I would not have understood the reality of God and Christ if it weren't for ICR.
>
> Your materials have helped me to gain assurance in

---

1. Some might think that 100 is not a very impressive total of converts, but it should be remembered that practically all readers of *Acts and Facts* were already Christians when they first requested the publication. *(Acts and Facts* is only sent to people requesting it.) A more significant result is the fact that almost a third of the readers had themselves become more fruitful soul-winners through use of the I.C.R. materials.

the Word of God as authority for living a practical Christian life.

The ICR ministry has helped increase my faith more than any other work.

As a science teacher, I am very grateful for the information, which has opened my eyes.

Your ministry had a lot to do with winning my wife to Christ.

Really exciting. Praise the Lord for your work.

Before your information shattered my evolutionary beliefs, my chances of becoming a Christian were virtually nil.

The search for Noah's Ark played a part in my conversion from atheism to Christ.

Belief in evolution is the main factor that prevents many persons from becoming Christians.

Apologetics is a very vital part of evangelism, and a must for building up Christians in the Lord.

I was saved in a church I was visiting through the speaker's message on the Noahic flood.

I passed your materials on to my (unsaved) husband, who was first outraged by your "biased" opinions—now he loves you!

The Genesis Flood broke the barrier (veil)!

Your message is clear—a Christ-centered life means salvation! Your work in creationism is wonderful.

This literature has helped some of my students to accept creation and to believe in Christ!

To a Christian biologist—ICR is as vital as any other Gospel area, including Moody, Wycliffe, Billy Graham, etc.

I saw one science teacher come to Christ through this.

As a biological scientist (Ph.D.), I had almost overwhelming conflict with evolutionary "law" as taught in our universities. ICR has helped resolve this conflict.

I had been brainwashed by evolution while pursuing my biology degree, but have just finished reading *Scientific Creationism* and it was a real eye opener.

As a Director for Child Evangelism Fellowship, I have found many opportunities to use the knowledge with young people personally, as well as with teachers.

People are generally astounded when they find there is scientific evidence supporting creationism. They are quicker to find a personal Savior who has suddenly become tangible.

I enjoyed the Santa Ana seminar immensely and use the scientific knowledge of creation I acquired in my witnessing regularly.

Tremendous witnessing tool, especially to the college student.

Especially helpful in the academic community in witnessing to other professional educators.

I regard your ministry, along with the Christian school movement, as the most valuable spiritual ministry today!

The issue of origins is an exceptional tool in apologetics and evangelism. A very vital ministry.

A debate with Morris and Gish—was the most refreshing thing which ever happened in my scientific study. It helped me to worship God through what He has made.

My opportunities to witness for Christ in a public classroom setting have increased from practically nothing to a common occurrence.

Started out totally brainwashed in evolution . . . now use the material in my own teaching . . . virtually all in my classes have become creationists.

This has helped me to realize the truth of God's Word. I am soon to enter a Russian Orthodox monastery.

I doubted the Bible as being true until ICR. One year later I was born again!

One student was led to Christ by Morris' *Bible and Modern Science.*

Dennis was a boy in our youth group to whom my husband made available several of his ICR books and Impact Series. As a result of this . . . we have watched Dennis grow into an enlightened and bold witness . . . He has led friends to Christ.

I am a science teacher and find everything you write helpful to me personally.

As an airline pilot, it has been used tremendously.

Dr. Morris' book *The Bible and Modern Science* was very instrumental in my conversion.

Accepted Christ as a result of your weekend seminar in Philadelphia.

Dr. Gish's book *Evolution the Fossils Say No* helped give a confused young man faith to trust Scripture.

His reading of Dr. Morris' books led him, occupied by geology, to Christ.

A friend of mine committed his life to Christ as a result of Dr. Morris' book *Scientific Creationism.*

The ICR is an answer to prayer.

I as a science teacher have seen that students must see Christ as Creator before they will ever see Him as a "Purpose Giver."

I was turned away from the Scriptures as a high school freshman when I was taught evolution.

The work of ICR is so essential that it would be a great loss if it would ever be curtailed.

Have seen many young believers greatly strengthened by use of your materials. One young man decided to go into the ministry.

Helped me to accept the Bible as the Word of God.

Words do not express the worth of *Acts and Facts* to our spiritual encouragement.

You are doing what organized religions have failed to do.

I have just completed a 13-week course using Dr. Morris' tapes, and it was a pleasure to see the growth in the lives of those participating.

I am 63 years of age. Thank God and you, I've had the privilege to live to see this *great, important* ministry, finally. (From a foreign missionary.)

This has given me a much stronger testimony to the saving power of Jesus Christ.

ICR—one of the all-time great events of Christian Bible history.

The Genesis Flood is the most exciting book (next to the Bible) I have ever read.

I have found that, after they digest scientific creationism, they are very open to witnessing.

My wife and I work with Campus Crusade for Christ, and are so grateful for your dedication to this ministry.

Reading the ICR publications has had a great deal to do with my being a convinced follower of Christ. I have found it very helpful in my preaching and teaching ministry in the church.

This material has been invaluable in my teaching and preaching ministry.

Four years ago Dr. Gish and Dr. Morris were on the campus at Oklahoma University. I attended on a lark and was amazed . . . . God used that debate and subsequent material to change the direction and course of my entire life and ministry. (From a Methodist pastor.)

I personally have had my own Christian life deepened and strengthened through the various ministries of ICR.

Acts and Facts has enriched my life this year and added to my love for God's Word.

I really appreciate your weekly radio broadcast. I just wish it were longer.

I was a trained evolutionist, and I went to hear

> Dr. Morris fall on his face. He didn't—instead I fell
> to my knees.

The above comments are only a very small sampling of all the encouraging testimonies received. There can no longer be any doubt that a creationist ministry does have an exceedingly significant spiritual impact on the lives of thousands.

In contrast, there were 25 replies that were negative or critical in one way or another. Most of these were from non-Christians whose names were on the mailing list inadvertently. (ICR only adds names to its mailing list by request, but occasionally people will sign requests for friends to whom they wish to send *Acts and Facts* without obtaining their friends' consent.)

Some might feel that the poll was biased in that the questionnaire only went to people already interested in creationism. As a matter of fact, this makes it all the more significant. That is, these are the people best qualified, in terms of knowledge and experience, to make an intelligent appraisal of the spiritual impact of creationism. Those who have not "tried it" are hardly able to evaluate it!

Conclusions

It is now evident, both from Scripture and from experience, that scientific Biblical creationism can and should play a vital role in evangelism and in Christian faith and life, as well as in true science and education. It is especially important when dealing with those who have been educated in public schools and colleges in recent decades.

In no way does this conclusion minimize the importance of prayer and the Bible in witnessing, or of the need of faith and the work of the Holy Spirit in regeneration. It is not "either-or," but "both-and." It is a matter of being ready to "give an answer to every man" (I Peter 3:15), as need and opportunity arise and as God has commanded.

THE WEAPONS OF OUR WARFARE

> For though we walk in the flesh, we do not war
> after the flesh: (For the weapons of our warfare are
> not carnal, but mighty through God to the pulling
> down of strong holds:) Casting down imaginations,
> and every high thing that exalteth itself against the
> knowledge of God, and bringing into captivity every

thought to the obedience of Christ (II Corinthians 10:3-5).

Christians are, indeed, involved in warfare and the objectives in the conflict are the minds and hearts of men. Conflict, of course, is difficult, and sometimes the tension and weariness of the battle may influence the judgment. Often we are tempted to "fight fire with fire," using the same weapons and tactics as the enemy, but this is a dangerous mistake. Perhaps even more often we are tempted by the great forces that seem arrayed against us to retreat, or to compromise, or even to surrender, and this is a *fatal* mistake! In the face of the first temptation, we always need to remember that the *weapons of our warfare are not carnal* and, in the face of the second, that they are *mighty through God to the pulling down of strong holds.*

As already emphasized, the Christian warfare involves all aspects of the preaching and implementation of the gospel, in all of its aspects throughout the world. The "cutting edge" of the "everlasting gospel" (Revelation 14:6, 7) is the great truth of special creation, with the exhortation to worship the Creator of all things. The creationist witness is thus in the very forefront of the battle. It is he who is most directly subject to these temptations and who, therefore, needs especially to keep these admonitions of the Apostle constantly before him.

The Law, The Schools, and the Christian

The weapons of our warfare are *not* carnal weapons! We must, therefore, never even consider attempting to use the police power of the state (with its apparatus of fines, imprisonments, and, ultimately, even military might and the power of life and death) in enforcement of either the gospel in general or creationism in particular. Some "Christian" governments have attempted this sort of thing in the past, and the results have always been destructive of *both* church and state. The Biblical teaching is that education is to be controlled only by the home and the church. It is tragic when Christians have allowed governments to usurp control over education at all, but it is doubly tragic whenever Christians have tried to *use* the state to control education.

The Biblical purpose of nations and governments is essentially to protect the lives and liberties and properties of their people, particularly to maintain conditions that will enable their citizens to freely seek God and worship Him (Acts 17:24-27; I Timothy

2:1-4). As *citizens,* we have the right and obligation to do all we can to establish and maintain governmental structures that accomplish these divinely-ordained functions of government. As Christians, however, we also have the obligation—through our homes and churches, not through government—to provide a sound, creation-based education for our young people. This latter obligation involves the establishment and support of true Bible-centered Christian schools and colleges, and rejection of all attempts by governmental or other secular organizations to influence their curricula.

But what about tax supported schools and other secular educational institutions and organizations? These obviously constitute a very important component of modern society, influencing the minds and destinies of millions of young people, even though—Biblically speaking—they are not really *true* schools at all. They are all structured within the false framework of evolutionary humanism rather than the true framework of theistic creationism. Since they have been established under government control, and since this was not the intention of God when He established the institution of human government in the first place, it is not surprising that such schools have departed so far away from God's truth in their teachings.

As far as the Christian creationist is concerned, therefore, the modern secular school or college is, like every other organization of human invention, essentially only a community of people who need the gospel. It is, like every other part of God's world, a mission field, and its inhabitants should be permitted and encouraged by their government to "seek the Lord, if haply they might feel after Him, and find Him" (Acts 17:27). In no way does this suggest an *establishment* of religion, however, but only *freedom* of religion. This, of course, is exactly the purpose intended by the "founding fathers" of our own government when they framed the constitution. Unfortunately, that high purpose has been, in recent years, largely subverted and distorted by ill-advised legislation, devious judicial construction, and authoritarian administrative interpretation and regulation. Thus the school has become not only a mission field, but also a battlefield.

And how do we fight the battle? Well, certainly not with the carnal weapons of legislation, judicial decision, or administrative regulation! To *require* that the gospel be taught in public schools (even biblical creationism, which is the cutting edge of the gospel) is to call on the police power of the state to do something that God did not establish the state to do. How can God bless and prosper that which contravenes His will?

It is not surprising, therefore, that the many attempts in recent years by Christian creationists to get the teaching of creationism mandated by legislation or jurisprudence have all been notably unsuccessful. Well-meaning Christians, with high motives and seemingly persuasive logic, have filed lawsuits in many places and gotten legislation introduced in many assemblies, to no avail. Furthermore, each new courtroom defeat or legislative rebuff sets another precedent which makes it all the more difficult to get creation back into the schools anywhere.

But supposing such an attempt *were* successful, how could it be enforced? Would every teacher be compelled to teach the gospel, (remember, biblical creationism *is* a part of the gospel!) even when he did not believe it, on penalty of losing his job, or worse? If he did teach it under these conditions, wouldn't his teaching likely (perhaps even unintentionally) be a caricature of true creationism, thereby doing more harm than good? Or, to prevent this happening, would there not have to be a continual monitoring process, manned by multitudes of parents or other concerned citizens? And wouldn't this turn the educational system into chaos?

This is why the Institute for Creation Research, from its very beginning, has discouraged attempts by well-meaning creationists to *force* the teaching of scientific creationism in the public schools, even though a large part of I.C.R.'s efforts have been directed toward the *promotion* of creationist teaching in the schools. Whenever Christians have gone ahead with such attempts, anyhow, we have tried (when requested) to help in any way feasible (we would certainly rather see the case won than lost), but so far the efforts have failed.

Some have suggested that a well-planned lawsuit should be carried all the way to the United States Supreme Court, to get a ruling once and for all that would get creationism back in our schools and textbooks. The present situation, whereby students all over the land are indoctrinated exclusively in the religion of evolutionary humanism, is clearly wrong, illegal, and unconstitutional, and should be so declared by our highest court.

Or at least that is how *we* see it. But suppose the Court renders a negative decision, declaring creationism to be "religious" and evolution "scientific"—what then? We would be far worse off than at present, and a constitutional amendment would be the only forlorn hope still remaining of ever getting creation taught in the schools.

But surely the Supreme Court justices would not rule against us, especially if the case were carefully planned and argued by the nation's best Christian attorneys—*would they?* Well, all the other courts so far have ruled *that* way. Remember, the "law of the land" is not what the Congress says or the constitution says, or common law judicial precedent says, but what *five men* say! And what they, as a majority of the Court, say may well depend as much on their political and religious philosophies (or even how they are feeling that day) as on the constitutionality of the case.

At the very least, such a procedure would involve great risk that the case would finally be lost and the cause of creationism thus almost irrevocably blocked in the public schools. Furthermore, whether won or lost, the preparation and prosecution of the case from court to court would cost many hundreds or thousands of dollars which, even if it could be raised, would necessarily divert funds from other urgently needed uses which might well be more fruitful. Finally, even if the case were won, its implementation and enforcement would be practically impossible.

The Real Weapons of the Believer

With all these considerations in view, it seems highly doubtful that we should try to use such carnal weapons as these to *mandate* the teaching of creationism. On the other hand, it is not only feasible, but fully consistent with God's purposes, to do all we can to *encourage* the teaching of creationism.

The real weapons of the Christian warfare are spiritual weapons, not carnal. The armor of the Christian, for example (see Ephesians 6:13-17), consists of truth, righteousness, peace, faith, and salvation, with the word of God (Ephesians 6:17) as his offensive weapon. These weapons are to be used to "preach the gospel" (Mark 16:15) and in "teaching them to observe all things whatsoever I have commanded you" (Matthew 28:19).

Now, since the public school is essentially a mission field in which the gospel needs to be preached, and since scientific creationism can well be regarded as the cutting edge of the sword of the Spirit with which we are to preach the gospel, and since God's purpose for human governments primarily involves maintenance of an environmental climate in which the true Creator God can be found and known, we are well within God's will when we do what we can to persuade the government to *allow* and *encourage* the teaching of creationism in all its institutions, even though it is wrong to try to *force* the government to *require* it.

There is only one example in the New Testament of a Christian using the existing political and judicial systems in an effort to accomplish his purposes, and he was the defendant, not the plaintiff, in the case. In fact, Christians are specifically instructed *not* to go to the law for redress against fellow Christians. "Now therefore there is utterly a fault among you, because ye go to law one with another. Why do ye not rather take wrong? why do ye not rather suffer yourselves to be defrauded?" (I Corinthians 6:7). Although this passage is not directly applicable to the situation at hand (dealing as it does only with personal disputes between fellow Christians), the very silence of the New Testament on other types of political activity, especially any actions designed to compel the state either to allow or compel the teaching of the gospel, is eloquent.

The one example of a Christian going to law is the case when the Apostle Paul exercised his special rights as a Roman citizen not to be "examined" by scourging (Acts 22:24-29) and then, later, to appeal to be tried by the Roman emperor instead of by the Jews (Acts 25:7-12; 26:32). This was obviously a defensive situation, and could not in any way justify a Christian legal action to force the teaching of creationism. However, it could well justify defensive legal action in situations where the state has acted to interfere (contrarily to the implications in God's primeval mandate to the nations) with either the proper education of children from God-fearing homes in private schools or with the non-sectarian and non-enforced teaching of theism and the gospel (particularly in its foundational aspect of scientific creationism) in public schools.

It is significant, however, that there is nothing in the United States constitution or in our present federal laws that would *forbid* the teaching of scientific creationism in the public schools or state universities or national museums or any other public institutions. If such proscriptive legislation or court decisions *were* on the books, then we would be justified as citizens in trying by lawsuit or lobbying or other means to get the situation remedied. As a matter of fact, however, no such restrictions exist. It is already perfectly legal and constitutional for any teacher in any school to teach scientific creationism. If he isn't doing this, it is not because of legal restraints, but because he either doesn't want to or, perhaps, because his department chairman or other school administrator doesn't want him to.

The remedy for this situation is not compulsion, but persuasion—education, not legislation! And this, of course, is exactly the command of the Scriptures to every believer: "preach—teach—answer—persuade—reason." And beyond all this is the greatest spiritual weapon of all—"pray!"

Christian creationists should do all they can to inform, encourage, and persuade school boards, school administrators, and teachers to teach scientific creationism. The same is true of college administrators and faculty members, of museum curators, of communications media editors, and others who influence what students and the general public learn. This also means informing pastors and other Christians, as well as community leaders in general, concerning the importance of the issue and the scientific and sociological case for creationism.

All of this should be done, not in an attitude of belligerence or compulsion, but of gracious persuasion, remembering that the battle is spiritual, not political. "And the servant of the Lord must not strive; but be gentle unto all men, apt to teach, patient, in meekness instructing those that oppose themselves; if God peradventure will give them repentance to the acknowledging of the truth; And that they may recover themselves out of the snare of the devil, who are taken captive by him at his will" (II Timothy 2:24-26). Furthermore, all should be done in the assurance that the efforts have been preceded and accompanied by prayer for God's leading and enablement. "Beloved, if our heart condemn us not, then have we confidence toward God. And whatsoever we ask, we receive of Him, because we keep His commandments, and do those things that are pleasing in His sight" (I John 3:21, 22).

As the old hymn reminds us: "Stand up, stand up for Jesus: stand in His strength alone. The arm of flesh will fail you; ye dare not trust your own." The weapons of *our* warfare are not carnal weapons; we do *not* war after the flesh!

Mighty Through God

We tend to become impatient, wanting victory *now*. This desire often tempts us to resort to the methods which seem to produce results quickly for the unspiritual causes of worldly organizations. We engage in high-pressure advertising and fund-raising; we use emotionalism to try to generate large, enthusiastic crowds; we commit our limited resources to techniques with visibility and quick audience appeal; we preach an easy, diluted "gospel" in hope of seeking many "decisions." Perhaps, worst of all, we try to engage the police power of the state to *compel* the teaching of the gospel to its citizens.

But all these are carnal (that is, "fleshly") weapons, and can only accomplish carnal results. If we wish to win real victories in a spiritual battle, we must use our spiritual weapons, and we must be willing to allow God to work in His own time. "So then neither is he that planteth any thing, neither he that watereth; but God that giveth the increase," (I Corinthians 3:7). "Cast not away therefore your confidence, which hath great recompence of reward. For ye have need of patience, that, after ye have done the will of God, ye might receive the promise" (Hebrews 10:35, 36).

And God *does* give the increase! Although our weapons are not carnal, they are "mighty through God, to the pulling down of strong holds" (II Corinthians 10:4).

From the writer's perspective, having been actively engaged in this "battle for creation" for almost 40 years, it already seems that great and mighty victories have been won—and they have all been won without the use of the carnal weapons noted above.

The writer first became concerned about creationism soon after graduating from Rice University in 1939, especially after returning there to teach in 1942. At that time there were no other creationists that could be discovered on the Rice faculty, and practically none on other secular college and university faculties. Perhaps there were a few at Christian institutions, but if so, they were all very reserved about it. Almost the only books advocating recent special creation and flood geology were the books of George McCready Price and other Seventh-Day-Adventist writers, and these were generally held in low esteem by the "evangelical" world. The most popular writer on Bible-science topics was Harry Rimmer, a Presbyterian minister and evangelist with no degree in science, who advocated the gap theory and the local flood theory as the means of harmonizing creation and geology. There were a few valuable older books, including books by Byron Nelson (Lutheran), George Barry O'Toole (Catholic), and Theodore Graebner (Lutheran), but these men also were theologians rather than scientists. Practically everyone (except the Adventists) promoted either the gap theory or the day-age theory, both of which logically must be accompanied by either the local flood theory or the tranquil flood theory.

So far as known, the writer's first book, *That You Might Believe* (1946) was also the first book ever written by a scientist on a secular college faculty who accepted the recent special creation of all things and advocated flood geology. Since its author only had a B.S. degree at the time and the book had only 156 pages and was published by an unknown publisher, this was not a very auspicious breakthrough. Actually the manuscript was rejected by two leading evangelical publishers, the ones that should have been the most interested in this type of book. It was finally published by a gospel tract publishing company, on condition that the author buy enough copies himself to underwrite the cost of the first printing. It was the first book ever published by that company. The money for underwriting it was donated by a friend in the Gideons, with the books so purchased to be given away to interested students.

In spite of the unimpressive outward aspects of this venture, there was much prayer behind it, along with the desire to honor God's Word above all else, presenting positive Christian evidences which had been found, through considerable witnessing experience, to answer the questions posed by thinking people of open mind and heart. God did bless the book abundantly, and many were brought to Christ through it and its later editions, including some who would later play key roles in the modern creationist revival. The book had little advertising promotion, although it did receive a number of good reviews, and it was generally rejected by the evangelical "establishment." Bernard Ramm, for example, listed it in his bibliography of "Fundamentalist Works of Limited Worth," when he later published his widely-used *Christian View of Science and Scripture,* a book which became practically the final word on "science" for neo-evangelicals.

When *The Genesis Flood* was written (published 15 years after *That You Might Believe*) it was also rejected by the leading Christian publishing companies, practically all dominated by neo-evangelicals. A virtually unknown company (Presbyterian and Reformed), finally published it. Again there was no advertising, and the reaction of the evangelical leadership was quite hostile (not to mention the reaction of the scientific and educational leaders who were aware of the book). The book was based on many further years of training and study, all undertaken with the primary goal of a complete reorientation of scientific interpretation, bringing all relevant scientific data into correlation with Biblical revealed truth, especially literal creation and the worldwide deluge. The project was many years in preparation and was saturated with much prayer and concern.

The Lord blessed it far beyond human expectations, in spite of intense opposition from the "neo-evangelicals," and large numbers were converted to sound creationism (many also were won to Christ, although the book was not written primarily as an evangelistic work).

One outgrowth was the Creation Research Society, which now has over 650 full members (with post-graduate degrees in one or more fields of natural science) and approximately 2000 other members. The Society also had a small beginning, with ten initial members, including the writer. It has never held conventions, or other public meetings, and is firmly opposed to promoting creationism through political means, but has had a tremendous impact since its founding in 1963, two years after *The Genesis Flood* was published.

Similarly Christian Heritage College and its wide-ranging research publications division, (known since 1972 as the Institute for Creation Research) had a notably inauspicious beginning, founded in 1970, under the sponsorship of a single church and the planning leadership of just three men (the pastor and associate pastor of the church, plus the writer—who was the only one with any experience in either science or education). The College enrolled initially only seven full-time students, and the I.C.R., as Dr. Tim LaHaye, the pastor, likes to say, was nothing but a file drawer.

But, as the Scripture says: "Who hath despised the day of small things?" (Zechariah 4:10). The growth of neither I.C.R. nor the College has been spectacular, but it has been solid, in the nine years (as of the present, 1979) since their founding. The college now has about 500 students, plus over 350 graduates who have already received B.A. or B.S. degrees in many critical fields in the work of the Kingdom. The I.C.R. has produced over 40 books, and its scientists have lectured thousands of times on scientific Biblical creationism in churches, on campuses, and in other places all over the world. It is not too much to say that the entire educational, scientific, and religious establishments are now keenly aware of the growing strength and viability of the creationist movement, and there is little doubt that I.C.R. is more responsible for this, under God, than any other single organization or group of associated individuals.

All of this has been accomplished with only a very "soft" approach in fund-raising, with practically no advertising, and with no lawsuits or legislation. There are now many thousands of scientists who are creationists, many public schools and state colleges where students at least have access to creationist teaching, many other creationist organizations and movements, and innumerable other evidences of the Lord's great blessing.

If God can accomplish all this, through just a handful of people who prayed and believed His Word, from such insignificant beginnings, in only one generation, think what could be accomplished in one *more* generation with the base we *now* have! If carnal weapons were not needed *then,* they are surely not needed *now.*

The real weapons of the believing, diligent, praying creationist Christian are far more potent than the legislature and the judiciary, than Madison Avenue and the media, or even than swords or guns. They are, indeed, "mighty through God to the pulling down of strong holds." There is no need for discouragement or impatience.

Those who oppose God and His truth may prosper for a time, but His truth will eventually prevail. "Commit thy way unto the Lord; trust also in Him; and He shall bring it to pass . . . . Cease from anger, and forsake wrath: fret not thyself in any wise to do evil . . . For yet a little while, and the wicked shall not be . . . But the meek shall inherit the earth; and shall delight themselves in the abundance of peace" (Psalm 37:5-11). "These shall make war with the Lamb, and the Lamb shall overcome them: for He is Lord of lords, and King of Kings: and they that are with Him are called, and chosen, and faithful" (Revelation 17:14).

Outcome of the Battle

The King James Translation puts it this way: "Casting down imaginations, and every high thing that exalteth itself against the knowledge of God, and bringing into captivity every thought to the obedience of Christ" (II Corinthians 10:5). These are the "strong holds" which the weapons of our warfare are "pulling down."

The word "imaginations" means "reasonings," and "thought" is the same word as "mind" in the Greek. It is, therefore, legitimate to paraphrase this promise somewhat as follows: "The genuine spiritual weapons which you use (that is, as stressed in Ephesians 6:13-17, the weapons of truth and righteousness, faith and peace, salvation and the Word of God) will certainly defeat the intellectual reasonings and proud scientism that would oppose the knowledge of the true Creator-God, finally bringing the mind of every man into willing submission to Christ."

Therefore, we are on the winning side in the battle for the mind, as surely as the world exists! Satan has "blinded" many minds (II Corinthians 4:4) for a little while, but one day "the devil that deceived them" will be "cast into the lake of fire" (Revelation 20:10). In confidence of God's truth and in assurance of that day, we even now are active in the battle, proclaiming the complete and wonderful true gospel of creation and redemption and the eternal Kingship of Jesus Christ, seeking to win the mind of every person to obedient faith in Him.

There is one final word of caution and clarification, however. This book has been addressed primarily to Christian people, seeking to enlist them as active participants in the great battle for creation. This doctrine is foundational and should be taught systematically in every Christian home, church, and school.

However, as far as *public* schools are concerned, it is only *scientific* creationism (not Biblical creationism) that we seek to encourage in the classroom and in the textbooks. The facts of science are perfectly consistent with the Biblical record of creation, of course, but they do not teach Biblical doctrine. That is, for example, scientific data point to the fact of special creation, but they do not identify Jesus Christ as the Creator. Similarly, science recognizes a universal principle of decay in the world, but it cannot show this to be the result of divine judgment on human sin. The same applies to the geological evidence for a universal flood.

It is fully constitutional and legal to teach scientific creationism in the schools, as well as pedagogically sound and scientifically effective to employ such a "two-model" approach to the teaching of origins. This is all that Christians (as well as other creationists and believers in true civil rights, academic freedom, and scientific objectivity) are asking for in our tax-supported institutions. In our churches, homes, and Christian institutions, of course, we must seek to implement and defend the full Biblical doctrine of creation and divine authority in every realm of life and thought.

I ndexes

INDEX OF SUBJECTS

A

Adam
Creation of body, 20, 42
Fall, basic to Christianity 97-98
Genetic descent, 17
Humanity, true, 21-22, 24
Age-dating
See Geologic age; Young earth
American Humanist Association, 71, 76, 82, 97
American Scientific Affiliation, 49
Angels
Creation of, 5
Relation to stars, 13
Apologetics, important in witnessing, 191, 196-197
Archaeopteryx, supposed transitional fossil, 144-145
Artificial Insemination, supposed explanation of virgin birth, 19

Astrology, pagan origin, 13, 29
Atheism
Based on evolutionism, 82, 85-86
Opposed to creationism 96-99
Australopithecus, supposed ancestor of man, 138-142, 172, 175

B

Babel, Tower of, 170, 179
Battle for the Mind
See Warfare, Christian
Bible
Creation teaching, 42-44, 47, 88-90
Inerrancy, 41-46
Interpretation, 41-42
Big-Bang Theory
Cosmos, supposed origin, 8, 10-11
Future destruction of earth, 36
Body of Christ

All believers, 22-23
Physical body, 21-25
Resurrection body, 38

C

Cain and Abel, offering on Sabbath, 57
Canopy Theory, 27
Catastrophism
    Empirical evidence, 99-100
    Evolutionary, 99
    Flood, evidence of single global cataclysm, 168-169
    Regional, 103, 166-167
    Rejection by evolutionary geologists, 147-149
    Revival among modern geologists, 163-166
    See also Flood; Uniformitarianism
Christ
    Body specially created 18, 20-25
    Creator of all things, 48-49, 185
    Curse borne by, 31
    Glorified body, 38
    Humanity, true, 23-26
    Incarnation, 16-18, 52-53
    Redemptive work, 16, 18, 94-95, 185
    Resurrection, 32
    Sabbath, doctrine of, 54, 59-60
    Sinless nature, 18, 24
    Teaching concerning creation, 53-55
    Virgin birth, 2, 18-20
Christian Heritage College 218

Christmas, 52
Church
    Creation of, 23
    Creation teaching in, 190-194
Circular Reasoning, in geology, 154-160
Communism
    Evolutionism, basis of 85-86, 149-150
    Scientists promoting, 105-107
Complex Systems
    Improbability, by statistical theory, 127-136
    Languages, 176
    Living organisms, 118-120
    Man, 13, 20-21
Conservation of Energy
    See First law of thermodynamics
Continental Drift, supposed time required, 91-92
Cooling of Rocks, argument for old earth, 90-91
Cosmology
    Evolutionary religion, 72-73
    Two models of origins, 7-13
Creation
    Adam, body of, 20, 42
    Biblical doctrine, 42-44
    Body of Christ, 20-23
    Christ, teaching of, 53-55
    Church, 23
    Complete and perfect, 31
    Fiat, 9-10, 22
    Genesis accounts, 53-54
    Inerrancy, relation to, 46
    Praise, 49-52
    Purpose, 11-13, 180
    Recent critique of, 90-93

Creation
  Rejection, arbitrary, 113
  Universe, 9-11, 34
  Week, 26-32
  Witnessing, importance in,
    185-188
Creation Research Society,
  76, 90, 96, 218
Creationism
  American Scientific Affili-
    ation, rejection by, 49
  Christian indifference,
    44-46, 48-49
  Churches, emphasis in,
    190-194
  Founding fathers, belief
    of, 81
  Gospel, foundation of,
    64-66
  Importance, preeminent,
    46-49
  Promotion, methods of,
    199-202
  Revival in recent years,
    47-48, 84, 87
Crucifixion, day of week,
  26, 32
Crystallization, apparent in-
  crease in order, 115-116,
  124-126
Cultural Evolution, 105-106,
  138-143, 149-150
Curse
  Borne by Christ, 31
  Earth affected, 36
  Mankind, 24, 185
  To be removed, 37
  See also Second law of
    thermodynamics

D

Darwinism
  See Evolution, Natural
  selection

Dating, geologic
  See Geologic age; Radio-
    metric dating
Day-Age Theory, fallacies,
  88-90
Deluge
  See Flood, Biblical
Dissipative Structures, sup-
  posedly producing order,
  103, 104, 116, 121-123
D N A, 21
Doppler Effect, 9

E

Earth
  Creation, 26-32
  Destruction, 35-36
  Permanence, 34-35
  Renewal, 36-38
Ecological Zonation, expla-
  nation of fossil order, 160-
  162
Ecumenical Creationism,
  192-194
Eden, garden of, 28
Education
  See Schools; Evolution;
    Students
Embryonic Growth, 20-21, 24
Energy
  God as King, 4
  Sun, supposedly support-
    ing evolution, 114, 125-
    126
  Universe, 27
  See also First law of ther-
    modynamics; Second
    law of thermodyna-
    mics
Entropy
  Creation, testimony to, 117
  Increasing, law of, 33, 111-
    112

Open system, significance,
103, 113-117
See also Second law of
thermodynamics
Evangelism
  Apologetics, importance
  of, 191, 196-197
  Creation, importance of,
  185-188
  Early Christians, example
  of, 186-187
  Results of creation empha-
  sis, 202-209
Events, possible maximum
number, 130-131
Evidences of Christianity,
191, 196-197
Evolution
  Circular reasoning, 154-
  160
  Contrary to teachings of
  Christ, 53-55
  Entropy principle opposed,
  111-113
  God, contrary to nature of,
  83-85
  Gospel, opposed to, 66
  Human origins, evidences
  confused, 138-143
  Scripture, contradicted by,
  44-46
  Theistic, 83-88, 93
  Unscientific, 76-78, 111-
  113
Evolutionism
  Atheism and amoralism,
  82, 85-86
  Chance and naturalism,
  69-70
  Communism, 85-86, 149-
  150
  Cosmology, 72-73
  Education, 79-83

Eschatology, 75
Ethics, 48, 74-75
Humanism, 71-72
Paganism, 5-6
Racism, 106
Religion of, 69-75, 79
Revolutionary, 99-107
Societal effects, 105-106,
149-150
Soteriology, 73
Expanding Universe, 9
Extraterrestrial Life
  Angels, 13-14
  Creationist rejection, 14-16
  No scientific evidence, 12-
  13

F

First Law of Thermodyna-
mics
  Cosmology, 11
  Permanence of universe,
  35-36
  See also Energy; Matter;
  Second law of thermo-
  dynamics
Flood, Biblical
  Fossil sequences, best ex-
  planation, 154, 160
  Geologic catastrophism,
  evidence for, 147, 151-
  153
  Local flood theory, 149-
  150
  Tranquil flood theory, 149,
  150-151
  Worldwide flood, evidence
  for, 149, 169
  See also Catastrophism
Fluctuations, order through
  See Dissipative structures

Fossils
  Catastrophism, required to
    explain, 151
  Dating, use in, 153-154
  Destruction in coming
    cataclysm, 36
  Hominid forms, 138-143
  Horse series, 143-144
  Order in sequences, 160-
    162
  Random distribution, 102
  Transitional, universal ab-
    sence, 99, 101, 143-146,
    156
Founding Fathers, U.S.A.,
  believers in creation, 81
Fourth "Law" of Thermo-
  dynamics, and evolution,
  124, 125
Fuller Seminary, 45

G

Gap Theory, fallacies, 47
Genesis, book of
  Creation, two accounts,
    53-54
  Day-age theory, 88-90
  Doctrine of creation, 42-
    44
  Gap theory, 47
Genetics
  Defective genes, 18-20, 24
  Human differences, 178
  Inheritance, 17
  Mutations, 70, 128-130
Geologic Age of Rocks
  Based on evolution, 152-
    153
  Circular reasoning, 154-
    160
  Determined solely by fos-
    sils, 151-154, 156
  Rocks all of same age, 163

God
  Attributes of, 3-6
  Creative work, 26-32, 42-
    44, 53-54, 94
  King of creation, 4-6
  Redemptive work, 94-95,
    185-186
Gospel
  Foundation in creation, 65-
    66, 185-186
  Necessity of preaching in
    full, 188-189, 191-192,
    203
  Use of word in New Testa-
    ment, 64-65, 192
Grace, first mentioned at
  time of Noah, 62
Gradualism, 105
  See also Uniformitarianism

H

Hermeneutics, used to change
  Bible teachings, 41-43
Holiness, of God, 17
Homo Erectus, supposed
  early form of man, 138,
  142
Homo Habilis, supposed
  human ancestor, 138,
  142
Hopeful Monsters, device for
  explaining evolution, 145-
  147
Horse, supposed evolution,
  143-144
Humanism
  Biblical anticipation, 72
  Evolutionary basis, 71-72
  Motivations, 75-76
Humanist Association, 71,
  76, 82, 97

I

Incarnation of Christ, 16-18, 52-53
Index Fossils, for dating rocks, 155, 157, 158
Inerrancy of Bible, 41-46
Information
Coded program required for ordered system, 134
See also Probability
Institute for Creation Research
Creation-evolution debates, 96
Extraterrestrial life, predictions, 15-16
Flood model, research on, 90
Humanist opposition, 96-97
Ministry of, 218-219
Schools, promotion of creation teaching in, 212-213
Survey of spiritual effects of creationism, 203-209
International Council on Biblical Inerrancy, 45-46

J

Java Man, 138
Jesus
See Christ
Judas, 29, 30

K

King, God as, 4-6

L

Language, human
Complexity of primitive, 176

Creative purpose, 180
Different languages, origin of, 176-180
Unique non-evolutionary origin, 104, 171-173
Unity of all languages, 173-174
Life
Creation of, 4, 27, 30
Extraterrestrial, 12-14, 15-16
Naturalistic origin impossible, 115-116, 118-119, 123, 125, 126-127
See also Living systems
Light
Energized in creation, 27
Spiritual, 29, 31
Stars, 29
Linguistics
See Language, human
Living Systems
Complexity, 118-120, 127-130
Impossibility of evolutionary origin, 122-123, 125
Local Flood Theory, 149, 150
Lord's Day, Christian observance, 60-62
Lucifer, 3, 4
See also Satan

M

Magmas, cooling of, 90-91
Man
Complexity, 13, 20-21
Evolution supposed fossil evidence, 138-143
Monophyletic origin, 174-175
"Self" attribute, 180
Unique to earth, 12-13, 16, 175

Mary, mother of Jesus, sinful nature, 25

Marxism
See Communism

Matter
Convertible into energy, 36-37
Eternal, in evolutionary cosmology, 73
God as Creator and King, 4

Metamorphism, supposed evidence of old earth, 91

Methodological Uniformitarianism, 164-165

Miracles
Grade A and Grade B, 25
Virgin birth, 18-20

Missouri Synod Lutherans, 45

Moon, Structure of, 12

Mountains, 28

Mutations
Basis of evolution, 70
Effect on incarnation of Christ, 18, 24
Improbability of accumulation of good mutations, 128-130
Random nature, 127

N

Nations, established by God, 5

Natural Selection
Essence of Darwinism, 69-70
Impossibility of generating life, 137
Sieve for retaining beneficial mutations, 127
Supposed "creator" of new characters, 70-79

Negentropy, 126

Noah
Example of saving faith, 62-64
Observance of weekly calendar during flood, 57-58
Type of coming of Christ, 62

O

Open Systems, supposed answer to entropy argument against evolution, 113-118, 120, 123, 126

Ordered Systems
Improbability, 135
Information required, 134

Origins
See Creation; Evolution

P

Paleontology
See Fossils

Parthenogenesis, supposed explanation of virgin birth, 19

Particles, number in universe, 130-131

Passover, 29-30

Peking Man, 138

Piltdown Man, 138, 141

Polytheism, ancient evolutionary belief, 5, 6, 29

Praise
Creation, subject of, 49-52
First mentions, 51

Probability
Increased order, 127-136
Origin of life, 115-119, 123-127
Zero probability, 130-131

Progressive Creation
Day-age theory, 88-90

God of the gaps, 86-87
Modern attacks on true
   creationism, 87-88
See also Theistic Evolution
Prophecy
   Anticipation of humanism,
      72
   Fulfilled by Christ, 31-32
Punctuated Equilibrium
   Hopeful monster concept,
      145-147
   Improbability, 129
   Related to catastrophism,
      102
   Wide acceptance, 101
Purpose, in creation, 11-13,
   180

R

Racism
   Evolutionary basis, 106,
      174
   Geographical isolation,
      177-178
Radiometric Dating, 92-93,
   151, 160
   See also Geologic age of
      rocks
Ramapithecus, supposed
   early hominid, 138, 139
Reading, importance of, 195-
   197
Recent Creation, 90-93
Redemption
   Finished work, 31-32
   God as King, 5
   Qualifications of redeemer,
      18
   Week of, 26-32
   Work on earth, 16, 94-95,
      185
Resurrection
   Believers, 37-38

Christ, 32

S

Sabbath ("rest")
   Christ, teaching of, 54, 59-
      60
   Creation, commemorative
      of, 55-62, 89
   End of creation week, 43,
      94
   Permanent validity, 61
   Rest after creation, 94
   Rest of Christ in tomb, 32
   Ten commandments, in-
      corporation in, 56, 58-59
Satan, 4, 14, 189
Schools
   Attitudes of Christian stu-
      dents, 197-199
   Legal aspects of teaching
      creationism, 210-215
Scopes Trial, 47
Second Law of Thermody-
   namics
   Cosmic decay principle, 32-
      34
   Creation model prediction,
      117
   Decay tendency, 103, 112,
      118
   Evolutionary cosmology
      contradicted, 10-11, 111-
      113, 120
   Open-system argument
      vacuous, 113-117
   Supposed statistical excep-
      tions, 113
Seven, number of complete-
   ness, 56
Southern Baptists, 45
Space
   Creation, 3, 4
   Travel, 37-38

Stars
    Inhabitants, 13-14
    Light, 29
    Number, 7, 14
    Origin, 7-8
    Purpose, 7, 12
Steady-State Theory, 8, 10
Students, problems of creationist, 197-199
Substantive Uniformitarianism, 163-164
Surveys of Creationist Opinion, 200-202

T

Ten Commandments
    Incorporation of Sabbath, 56, 58-59
    Permanent validity, 61
Testimonies
    Impact of creationism, 203-209
    Personal experiences of author, 216-219
Theistic Evolution, 83-86, 88, 93
    See also Progressive Creation
Theologians, compromising with evolution, 83-87, 149
Third Law of Thermodynamics, 124
Time
    Arrow of, 33
    Creation of, 3, 4
    Entrance of God into, 52
    Restoration, 37
Tower of Babel, 170, 179
Tranquil Flood Theory, 149, 150-151

U

Unconformities, significance in geology, 152-153, 167-168
Uniformitarianism
    Methodological, 164-165
    Modern questioning, 99
    Noah's day, 63
    Rise of, 147-149, 162-163
    Substantive, 163-164
Universe
    Expanding, 9
    Origin, 7-8, 10-11, 26
    Purpose, 11-13
    Size, 11

V

Virgin Birth of Christ, 18-20

W

Warfare
    Christian battle for the mind, 210-211
    Victories in creation battle, 216-219
    Weapons, spiritual, 213-215
Waters
    Above firmament, 27
    Flood, 149, 169
    Life, 31
Week
    Creation, 26-32
    Evidence of creation, 55, 62, 89
    No basis in astronomy, 55
    Redemption, 26-32
    Seven-day, 55-62
Witnessing
    Apologetics, value of, 191, 196-197
    Creationism, importance of, 185-188

Results of creationist emphasis, 202-209

Y

Young Earth, 90-93

Z

Zinjanthropus, varied reconstructions, 141

INDEX OF NAMES

Abelson, Philip 78
Ager, Derek 100, 102, 103, 157
        158, 165, 16 6, 167
Alfven, Hannes 11
Angrist, Stanley W. . . 119, 123
Asimov, Isaac 13, 76, 171
Ayala, Francisco J. 70,78
Azar, Larry........ 147, 157

Babloyants, Agnes. . . 115, 121
Baugh, Albert C. 176
Beecher, Henry Ward 80
Behrman, Daniel 92
Bertalanffy, Felix B. 116
Bethell, Tom 86, 106, 107
Bishop, Jerry E. 12
Borel, Emil 114, 131
Boucot, A.J.............. 99
Bozarth, G. Richard ... 97, 98
Bretz, Harlan 163
Brooks, C. 93
Brown, B.W. 169
Buckland, William....... 148
Buffon, Georges L. 148

Campbell, Cathryn A..... 156
Cavalli-Sforza, L.L. 178
Chambers, Betty 76
Chambers, Robert 148
Chang, K. Hong......... 168

Chomsky, Noam ... 104, 105,
        172, 173, 176, 178
Christian, James 15
Clark, Harold W........ 166
Cloud, Preston, ... 77, 78
Compston, W. 93
Cudmore, Lorraine 85, 86
Cuvier, Georges 148

Dachile, Frank 163
Darwin, Charles 84, 100,
        106, 107, 148, 149, 174
Davis, Gordon L........ 165
De Chardin, Pierre Teilhard
                        79, 81
De Vaucouleurs, G........ 8
Dewey, John 71, 72, 80
Dobzhansky, Theodosius . 71,
        73, 74, 79, 100, 159
Dott, R.H. 166
Dubos, Rene.......... 71, 73
Dunbar, Carl O. 153
Duncan, R.A. 93
Dyson, Freeman........ 119

Eckelman, Herman J. 87
Eddington, Arthur....... 113
Einstein, Albert 36
Eisely, Loren 76
Eldredge, Niles 101, 102,
                105, 130, 159

Engels, Friedrich 105

Fox, Sydney 136

Gish, Duane T. 96, 202,
        207, 208, 209
Golay, Marcel. 131
Goldschmidt, Richard. . . . 146
Goodfield, June 84
Gould, Stephen J. 70, 100,
    101, 105, 130, 145, 146, 149,
        163, 164, 165, 171, 172
Graebner, Theodore 216
Grasse, Pierre 100
Griffin, Donald R. 156

Haller, John S. 174
Hart, S.R. 93
Hecht, M.K. 159
Hedberg, Hollis T. 153
Hegel, G.W.F. 105
Hepler, Loren G. 119, 123
Heylmun, Edgar B. . . . 91, 149
Hoagland, Hudson 75, 76
Horowitz, Norman H. 17
Hubbard, David. 45
Hutton, James . . 148, 162, 166
Huxley, Aldous 82
Huxley, Julian . 69, 71, 73, 100
Huxley, Thomas H. . . . 82, 174

James, D.E. 93
Jefferson, Thomas. 81
Jensen, James. 144
Johanson, Carl. 142, 175
Jorafsky, David 150

Keith, Arthur 74
Kitts, David B. 157
Krassilov, V. 162
Krynine, Paul D. 163

La Haye, Tim 218
Lamont, Corliss 76
Laszlo, Ervin 105
Lawman, Geoffrey 131
Layzer, David. 112, 114
Leake, Chauncey 76
Leakey, Richard 138, 141,
        142, 143
Lepkowski, Wil 105
Lewin, Roger 143
Lewontin, Richard . . 100, 104,
        105
Lindsell, Harold. 45
Lowenstein, Jerold M. . . . 140
Luther, Martin 188
Lyell, Charles . . . 99, 100, 148,
        162, 163, 164

Mac Arthur, R.H. 102
Mac Kinney, Paul 200
Mann, Alan 139
Marx, Karl . . 85, 86, 106, 107,
        149
Matthews, L. Harrison 77
Maxwell, John C. 91
Mayr, Ernst . . . 70, 73, 84, 100
Mc Kown, Delos B. 96, 97
Mendis, Azoka 11
Molnar, Stephen 142
Mora, Peter T. 136
Morris, Henry M. 76, 88,
    89, 106, 122, 139, 150, 154,
    164, 166, 197, 206, 207, 208,
        209
Motulsky, A.G. 48, 75
Muller, H.J. 73, 74
Murdy, W.H. 74

Neilsen, Kai 81
Nelson, Byron 216
Nelson, Gareth V. 155

Nevins, Stuart E. 92
Newman, Robert C. 87
Newton, Isaac 147, 148
Nicolis, Gregoire 115, 121

O'Hair, Madalyn Murray . . 97
Oller, John 172
O'Rourke, J.E. 155, 157,
                          159, 160
Ostrander, Gilman M. . . 80, 81
O'Toole, George Barry . . . 216
Oxnard, Charles 140, 141, 142

Pauling, Linus 76
Peduccia, Alan 145
Peters, R.H. 77
Pilbeam, David . 143, 171, 172
Pippard, A.B. 113
Potter, Van Rensselaer 33
Price, George Mc Cready. 166,
                               216
Prigogine, Ilya . 103, 104, 105,
    112, 115, 116, 120, 121, 122,
                123, 124, 126

Rak, Yoel 142
Ramm, Bernard 217
Rapetski, John E. 161
Raup, David M. . 102, 136, 144
Rezanov, I.A. 92
Rhodes, F.H.T. 151
Ricklefs, Robert E. . . 101, 102
Rimmer, Harry. 216
Rogers, Carl 76
Rush, J.H. 112
Russell, Bertrand 33, 83

Sagan, Carl 15
Salet, Georges. 131
Salisbury, Frank B. 131
Schaeffer, B. 159
Schindewolf, O.H. . . 152, 153
Shaffer, P.R. 151

Simpson, George Gaylord . 76,
                   100, 172, 176
Skinner, B.F. 76
Smith, Adam 106
Smith, Charles 116
Smith, William 148
Soffcn, Gerald 15
Stebbins, G. Ledyard. 100
Steere, W.C. 159
Steno, Nicolaus 147, 162
Stent, Gunther S. . . . 172, 173,
                       179, 180
Stravropoulos, George P. 124,
                               125

Taieb, Maurice. 175
Tax, Sol. 76
Thomsen, Dietrick V. 11
Thurman, Duane 87
Tieg, Maurice 175
Turdoff, Harrison B. 145

Valentine, James W. . 156, 165
Villee, Claude A. 19

Waddington, C.H. 70
Wald, George 112, 113
Weisskopf, V.F. 118, 124,
                       125, 126
West, Ronald R. 158
Whitcomb, John C. . . 88, 154,
                               166
Wonderly, Daniel. 87
Woodward, John. . . . 147, 162

Yockey, Hubert P. . . . 115, 126,
                       127, 136
Young, Davis A. . . . 87, 89, 90,
                        91, 151

Zihlman, Adrienne L. 140
Zimm, H.S. 151
Zuckerman, Solly . . . 140, 141
Zumberge, James H. . 162, 163

INDEX OF SCRIPTURES

GENESIS

1:1	3, 26, 30, 34, 46
1:2	26
1:3	27, 46
1:4	37
1:5	37
1:9	28, 37
1:10	28, 37
1:11	28
1:12	28
1:16	9
1:21	30, 31
1:26	21, 31
1:27	4, 31, 53
1:28	16
1:28-30	28
1:30	54
1:31	26, 31, 37
2:1	9
2:1-3	32, 57, 89, 94
2:2	89, 94
2:3	89
2:5	63
2:7	20, 21
2:12	63
2:15	28
2:21	52
2:24	54
3:5	4
3:6	26
3:15	20
3:17	24, 26, 36, 185
4:3	57
4:4	57
6:4	62
6:8	62
6:9	62
6:11	62
6:22	63
7:1	63
7:4	57
7:5	63
7:10	57, 192
7:11	57, 58, 192
8:3	57, 58
8:4	57, 58
8:5	57
8:6	57
8:7	57
8:8	57
8:10	58
8:12	58
8:14	58
12:1	170
22:17	7
29:27	58
29:28	58
29:35	51
49:10	51
50:10	58

EXODUS

13:15	58
13:16	58
16:4	58
16:5	58
16:25-30	58
17:6	31
20:8-11	43, 59, 89
20:11	9, 59, 94
31:13	57
31:15-18	43
31:17	89, 95
31:18	59

LEVITICUS

17:11	30

JOSHUA

10:13	60
10:14	60

I CHRONICLES

16:25	50
16:26	50

II CHRONICLES

6:18	4

NEHEMIAH

9:6	4

JOB

14:1	18
14:4	18
38:7	13

PSALMS

2:1	6
2:1-3	181
19:1	12, 46, 202
22:15	31
24:10	4
29:10	4
33:1	50
33:6	10, 50
33:9	10
37:5-11	219
47:7	4
51:5	18
74:12	4
90:9	52
95:1	50
95:3	6
95:5	50
95:6	50
100:3	6, 50
100:4	50
102:25	33
102:26	33
103:20	13
104:5	35
115:16	12, 16
119:130	189
136:3-7	50
139:14	20, 50
139:15	20, 21
139:16	20, 21
139:17	22
147:7	50
147:8	50
148:3-6	35
148:5	50

PROVERBS

15:1	199
16:7	199
25:11	199

ECCLESIASTES

1:4	35
3:14	35

ISAIAH

9:6	53
14:13	3
14:14	3
40:15-17	22
40:28	57
51:6	33
52:14	31
55:9	7
57:15	52
65:17	36
66:22	37, 61

JEREMIAH

2:26	6
2:27	6
10:7	5
10:10	4
33:22	6

EZEKIEL

28:15	3
28:17	3
46:3	61

DANIEL

4:37	4
7:25	70
11:37	70
11:38	70
12:2	14
12:3	14, 35

AMOS

6:1	189

MICAH

5:2	52

ZECHARIAH

4:10	218
9:9	27
9:10	27
14:16	5

MALACHI

1:14	4

MATTHEW

1:23	17
4:23	65
5:45	54
6:26	54
7:16	54
7:18	54
8:28-32	14
12:28	59
12:40	32
13:6	203
13:20	203
13:21	203
15:36	51
15:37	51
16:21	32
19:5	54
19:6	54
21:1-9	27
21:28-32	28
21:33-43	28
22:30	14
24	28
24:21	54
24:35	33
25:	28
26:6-13	30
26:14-16	30
27:46	31
27:50	32
27:51	31
28:18	53
28:19	38, 213
28:20	38, 191, 203

MARK

1:1	65
2:27	59
2:28	54
10:6	54
11:12-14	27
11:15-19	27
11:19-24	28
12:1-11	28
13:	28

13:19	54
13:31	35
14:1	30
14:2	30
14:3-9	30
14:10-11	30
14:12-17	30
16:15	64, 189, 192, 213

LUKE

1:35	20
4:4	63
17:26	62
18:8	190
19:39	27
19:40	27
20:9-18	28
21:11	13
21:33	35
21:37	28, 29, 30
21:38	29, 30
23:31	31
23:45	31
23:54-56	32
24:30	38
24:43	38

JOHN

1:1	17, 52
1:2	17
1:3	52
1:12	23
1:13	23
1:14	16, 17, 24, 52
1:29	30
1:49	5
3:14	31
3:16	52
4:14	31

4:34	94
5:17	94
8:12	31
8:36	186
9:4	94
11:25	31
12:1-8	30
12:20-50	29
12:35	29
12:43	83, 189
12:46	29
14:6	31
15:1	31
15:16	196
17:4	60, 94
17:17	189
17:24	54
19:14	30
19:28	31
19:30	31, 60, 95
20:17	38
20:19	38
20:27	38

ACTS

1:8	186
1:9-11	38
1:11	16
2:16-21	186
2:23	31
2:25-31	186
2:34-36	186
3:20-26	186
3:21	37
4:10-12	186
7:48-51	186
8:30-36	186
10:43	186
13:5	187
13:14	187
13:15	187
13:32-40	187

14:1	187
14:15-17	46, 187, 202
14:17	185
17:2	60, 187
17:3	187
17:10	187
17:11	187
17:20	16
17:22-31	46
17:24-27	187, 210
17:25	5
17:26	174
17:27	211
18:4	187
18:28	187
19:8	187
20:7	60
22:24-29	214
25:7-12	214
26:32	214

ROMANS

1:3	20
1:16	189
1:20	6, 46, 51, 111, 202
1:21	49, 51
1:22	5, 49
1:23	5
1:25	4, 5, 70
1:28	6, 49
2:14	61
2:15	61
3:3	6
3:4	6
5:6	53
5:12	85, 95
8:3	18, 24
8:8	17
8:21	34, 36, 95
8:22	24, 31, 33, 95
10:10	188

11:36	65
13:9	61

I CORINTHIANS

3:7	216
5:7	30
6:7	214
10:31	199
12:13	22
15:1-4	64, 189, 192
15:22	17
15:41	7
15:44	37
15:47	20
15:54	31
15:58	195
16:2	60

II CORINTHIANS

4:3	188
4:4	4, 188, 220
5:17	23
5:21	22, 24
10:3-5	210
10:4	216
10:5	219

GALATIANS

1:6	189
3:13	31
4:1	198
4:2	198
4:4	21
4:5	21

EPHESIANS

2:2	4
2:4-7	38
2:10	23, 51
2:12	4
4:8-10	16
4:11-14	191

4:15	22
4:16	22
4:24	23
5:27	23
6:2	61
6:5-8	198
6:11	196
6:12	194
6:13-17	213-219
6:17	189, 213

PHILIPPIANS

2:5	53
2:6-8	95
2:7	24, 53
3:20	37
3:21	37

COLOSSIANS

1:13	5
1:14	5
1:16	5, 30, 48, 59, 95, 185, 192, 203
1:16-20	65
1:17	95, 185, 203
1:20	30, 49, 95, 186, 192, 203
1:21	203
2:9	193
3:10	23
3:22-24	198
3:23	199
4:6	199

II THESSALONIANS

2:3	70
2:4	70
2:13	32

I TIMOTHY

1:17	4

2:1-4	211
2:5	52
3:16	53
4:1	190
4:13	195
6:15	4, 5
6:16	5
6:20	191, 202

II TIMOTHY

1:12	189
2:2	190
2:3	194, 189
2:4	194
2:15	195, 197, 199
2:24-26	215
3:1-7	190
3:15	196
4:2	196
4:13	195

TITUS

2:9	198
2:10	198

HEBREWS

1:2	65
1:3	95
1:14	4, 14
2:3	32
2:17	18, 24
4:3	94
4:3-10	66
4:4	61
4:9	61
4:10	95
4:15	23
5:9	32
7:25	25
7:26	18, 25
10:5	21, 52
10:12	30, 61

10:35	216
10:36	216
11:3	22, 64, 66
11:7	63, 64
11:13	66
12:22	13
13:2	14
13:21	22

JAMES

1:13	24

I PETER

1:19	18
1:20	21
2:21	53
2:22	24
2:24	22, 26, 52
3:15	191, 196, 199 209

II PETER

1:19	34
1:21	70
3:5	6, 26
3:10	36
3:12	36
3:13	37
3:16	44

I JOHN

2:15	4, 194
3:2	38
3:5	24
3:21	215
3:22	215

4:2	17
4:3	17
4:4	189

JUDE

3	190

REVELATION

1:8	32
1:14-18	22
3:14	49
4:9	4
4:9-11	50
4:11	4, 194
12:4	13
12:9	4, 14, 189
13:6	70
13:7	70
14:6	49, 65, 66, 192, 203, 210
14:7	49, 65, 66, 192, 203, 210
15:3	5
17:14	5, 219
19:16	5, 65
20:8	189
20:10	220
20:11	35, 36
21:1	37
21:1-3	16
21:4	37
21:5	28, 36
22:2	28
22:3	26, 37
22:5	29, 37